The Clockwatcher

The Clockwatcher

Blair Farish

Dewdney Publishing
2015

Copyright © 2015 by Blair Farish

All rights reserved. This book or any portion thereof may not be reproduced or used in any manner whatsoever without the express written permission of the publisher except for the use of brief quotations in a book review or scholarly journal.

First Printing: 1988

ISBN 978-0-9693589-1-6

Dewdney Publishing

4 – 1401 30th Avenue North
Cranbrook, British Columbia V1C 0C1

www.blairfarish.com

Cover design by Ryan Lawrence.
Cover artistry by Chris Eimer and Craig McNamar.

To my sons, Ian and Craig.
Knowing you were waiting for me
made each hour more bearable.

*"...and keep us ever mindful
of the needs of others."*

As often quoted by my great friend,
the late William Gilbert Gordon.

CONTENTS

11	90:04 Split Time
16	20:02 Zulu
20	Runway 16
23	1:27, Ten Seconds in Hell
31	3½ Hours, Almost a Lifetime
43	4:56 Rescue
46	6:05 Disturbed Chef
52	10:50 Flying High
55	23:29 Saturday Night Fever
58	Glasgow Scale 0 – 15
62	2:10 The Speed of Bad News
66	Turbulence at 11:00 Hours
70	Lost Days 1 – 8
74	Gathering of the Clan
78	Unit 31 at Last, the Burn Ward
83	Noisy Time Day & Night
88	8 – 9 Hot Tub Time
97	Dressing Time 9 – 10
103	Code-4 Time of Death
109	Physio Time, 10-Minute Km
117	O.T. Time
122	12:27 Jobst Time
130	40 Pounds in 20 Days
135	Visiting Time, 2 – 8
141	Storytime 1001 Ways
145	The Big Shopping Trip
152	Phone Time

155	Prayer Time
159	Departure
165	The Homecoming
171	In Four-Wheel Drive
177	Happy Christmas
181	The Impatient Outpatient
187	Goal Setting Time
192	Kicking The Habit
195	Back in Harness
201	Jobst II
208	The Year of the Hat
212	On the Road Again Over 50
216	Fireweed Time
219	Epilogue: Looking Back
220	Blair's Retreat
224	Boy Meets Girl
227	The Practice
231	The Sporting Life
233	The Blended Family
235	Reigning Cats and Dogs
238	The Bent Propeller
241	The Bucket List

ACKNOWLEDGEMENTS AND DISCLAIMER

Some names appearing in this book are actual people, but many of those mentioned are fictitious.

Those named by first and family name are some of the many people who contributed, in greater or lesser part, in the team which helped in my rescue and ongoing care and support. Others—professionals, volunteers, friends, family, and many individuals previously unknown to me also helped. Many have not been directly named in this book, either at their request or because the list is too long to include each, or because I never became aware of their name.

Those described in the book by first name only are fictitious. This has been the protocol decided upon to protect their identity in some cases and to avoid missing out others deserving of mention, but purposely left unnamed.

SPECIAL THANKS

I have special gratitude and indebtedness to Diana D. Cavers for her patient typing, editing, retyping, and her constant cheerful support during the writing of the original 1988 manuscript.

The revised edition is the result of a magnificent contribution by two very special people in my life.

The horrendous task of deciphering my scribbled text and converting it to typed print was performed brilliantly, despite my constant interruptions and changes, by the love of my life, my wife Maureen.

Keeping it in the family, I'm also deeply indebted to Maureen's son Ryan Lawrence for his skill and dedication in converting the whole finished work to re-print and e-book readiness.

He inserted my new pencil sketches in each chapter and created the new revised edition graphic front cover. He also improved on many elements of my questionably archaic Scots' vocabulary and grammar deficits.

All other members of my extended family, including my ten grandchildren have encouraged me in this endeavour.

They all deserve huge hugs.

Blair Farish
October 15, 2015

CHAPTER 1
90:04 Split Time

"90:04 split time – I believe we can do it."

This was the excited but puffing voice of my running partner, Bruce Williams. It was a great moment of achievement, marked by crossing the halfway line of the 26 mile, 385 yard Calgary Marathon, 28th May 1983. For Bruce and me it was the culmination of years of running and recent months of arduous training leading up to this special event. Our true hope, on that pleasantly cool spring morning, was to complete the race in 3 hours 10 minutes and thus qualify to run in the following year's Boston Marathon. A 90-minute first half augured well for that goal.

Running had become a big part of both our lives. For each of us the miles from where it had all started were countless, but each mile had provided its own special mixture of pleasure and pain, yet failed to quench the thirst for more. My miles had started 40 years earlier running the mile from the one-room country school to my home in rural southern Scotland. Even those early runs, unknown to me at the time, developed the legs, the lungs, the heart to drive me further, and the persistence to prevail despite the adversities of the elements and terrain. Simultaneously, stride by stride, a tenacious mental streak had been developing, stubbornness some called it, which was to help me face the inevitable ups and downs of life.

Unlike the twisting narrow Scottish roads, Calgary's straight flat streets seemed purposely designed to create havoc with the runners' minds as they watched the faster runners ahead being swallowed up into the vanishing point on the far distant prairie horizon.

We had chosen Calgary as the venue for our first marathon, the ultimate, we gauged, of distance running. It was only 250 miles from our East Kootenay valley home in Cranbrook which, although located on the opposite side of the Rocky Mountains, was easily accessible in a five-hour car journey. As part of a six man team from our local running club, the Kootenay Big Foot Association, we had all completed the required training in our rugged home terrain and were buoyed up with the prospect of a less hilly race in Calgary. Historically, the Maclin Marathon, held annually in late May, had proven a well organized, popular and yet uncrowded marathon with a meagre four or five hundred runners competing. This was a far cry from the thousands who set off in some of the truly big runs. Another feature that made this late May schedule attractive for us was the probability of moderate temperatures at that time of year in that location, avoiding either the extreme cold likely to occur earlier in the year or the disturbing heat of the southern prairies in mid-summer.

Our own expectations on achievable goals had already undergone insidious increases from 6-mile runs through 10-mile runs, half marathons, 15-milers, 20-milers, and now finally the big one – the Marathon. We had rationalized to our own satisfaction that this was a sane, achievable objective.

As the final seconds ticked off to the moment of truth of the start of the race, a high state of nervousness pervaded the thronging crowd of runners edging forward inch by inch. We had all been reasonably accepting of the race steward's advisory dictating our starting positions. Those presuming to run the distance in under 2 hours, 20 minutes, were located in the first two rows along the starting line. There was usually a mix of sporting spirit, honesty, and downright cheating in this. We all positioned ourselves according to our most optimistic finishing time.

An expectant hush descended, every dominant hand nervously poised to synchronize the owner's timepiece with the sound of the gun. Every runner became a clockwatcher for the duration of the race.

Like projectiles from the starter's gun, the front runners bolted forward, dragging their tardy followers in their wake. The herd instinct pushed each faster than his preplanned first mile time. Bruce and I had planned to try for a 90-minute first half, which required a sub-seven-minute mile average in those first 13 miles. To our dismay, despite keeping our early pace purposely slow, the caller giving the times at one mile shocked us with a six-minute report. There is an oft used cliche in the running world that states, "You can't bank time." The penalty for a fast early surge beyond one's true ability, is paid for heavily by slower than expected miles later in the race.

As relative strangers to this city, the changing scenery was an ongoing stimulus for us as we sweated it out on the well-marked route. Pouring through the tree-lined Calgary streets, then along the perimeter of the Calgary zoo, we heard the alien voices of foreign animals and fowls. As my mind drifted, different runners took on animal resemblances. A lithe long-limbed speedster appeared as an antelope, while a petite, graceful, soft-treading girl ran as smoothly as a gazelle. A chunky overweight fellow rolled and wobbled past us, though deceptively and disconcertingly fast, with all the finesse of a lumbering rhinoceros.

In contrast to the zoo's cacophony of sound, for runners speech and speed are incompatible. Easy jogging may well tolerate conversation, but the talk-test is the dividing line. This is the point where physical exertion and the subsequent heavy demands of breathing preclude ongoing verbal communication. Silence is the mark of a serious runner.

On a course buckling back on itself numerous times, there was the anguish and joy of meeting other runners. The leaders, yards and eventually miles ahead of our slower pace, sped towards us bringing envy in their stride. However, there was some compensating satisfaction in meeting the sloths who were similar distances behind our place in the race.

Meeting a group of gabbling stragglers, Bruce and I exchanged knowing looks which silently said of them "All talk and no traction." Runners can be cynics, too.

Our running pace and stride, developed over many practice miles together, was a mutually encouraging, steadying, and yet challenging one. Our training miles gave us the confidence to know that our 90-minute first-half goal and subsequent three hour marathon were a realistic aim. Crossing the halfway mark at 90:04 gave us a surge of confidence. With a leeway of ten extra minutes for the second half, nothing barring tragedy could stop the eventual success of our mission. Pride always comes before the fall. Just as ups so frequently precede the downs in life's cyclical wave forms, so on that day it went from the high of achievement to the depths of despair.

The taste of achievement sparked up our pace and brought us up behind a group of six or seven runners taking up most of the width of the one-lane designated raceway.

"Let's pass this bunch," I said, and moved over to the narrow gap at the left while Bruce breezed past on a wider margin at the right.

Error compounded error. As the gap at my side narrowed, I had to slow up, fearful of committing that unforgivable sin of treading on the heels of one of the other runners. By that time Bruce had cleared the group and was some five yards ahead. Anxious not to slow his pace, yet fearful of being left behind, I changed my tactics and moved across behind the group and sprinted past them on the right.

The demands of that surge on muscles that had become accustomed to a steady, predictable, seven minutes per mile pace, proved to be the last straw for my left hamstring. Like an arrow striking into the flesh, a searing flash of pain engulfed the back of my thigh causing me to stumble. Persistent, untimely, and unwarranted stubbornness drove me on.

In what seemed a lifetime, but was perhaps a second or two, my pace slowed to a struggling, ungainly gait while the herd I had so recently cantered past overtook me effortlessly. Having seen the unmistakable signs of my grief, they gave sportsmanlike utterances of "tough luck, mate," "hang in there, pal," "run through it," and other questionable guidance. Further up ahead, Bruce, now a hundred yards away, turned to see what had happened.

I could imagine his dilemma. Should he wait for me or must he push on? Distant as he was, I could sense his relief and acknowledgement as I waved him away on his quest for a three-hour finish.

Torn hamstrings, although new to me personally, were injuries I had seen and treated many times in my professional capacity as a physiotherapist. Purportedly knowledgeable on matters of sports medicine, even a modicum of common sense should have told me to drop out of the race. I was, however, determined to continue the run.

A day that had started so full of promise, so full of joy, satisfaction, and success, turned from pleasantly cool to sickeningly parched and hot. My pace dropped from its earlier flowing, seven-minute glide to an abysmal nine-minute mile struggle. Previously slower runners passing me one by one and in groups poured grains of salt in my wounds.

Miles that had ticked past with exciting regularity for the first 90 minutes dragged endlessly. The erstwhile faithful chronometer surged maddeningly ahead while my leaden legs dragged.

The course took a tantalizing five-mile stretch west and buckled back on itself to provide greater anguish for the slower runners. Passing the seventeenth mile I met the race leader as he surged back along the course entering his last mile. Only a hundred yards behind the leader the second-placed runner had a look of even greater determination as he calculated when to make his kick, the final big push to overtake the leader. As they played their game of chess, with surges and counter moves, I was crestfallen by the awareness of another nine miles ahead at my stumbling pace. Ten minutes later I met Bruce as he pressed on toward the finish line. His time of 3:02 was his passport to a triumphant finish in the Boston the following year. His cheery wave and friendly words helped push me on, despite the pain.

A mile north of our pathway along the scenic Bow River, like a sentinel on the hill stood Foothills Hospital, towering 12 stories high. A weary momentary glance in its direction caused me to think of ways to lessen the miseries of suffering that I was inflicting upon myself in that run. Surely there, in that haven of wonders of modern medical skill, was respite from the traumas that afflicted my body and mind.

Little did I know that the persistence and stamina exerted during my day of anguish on that marathon would be so influential in the successful outcome of time to be spent in that hospital in the days ahead.

Three months later, a glimmer of a smile indicating a gleam of hope would brighten the habitually self-controlled face of the Trauma Unit specialist. This instant of optimism overcame his earlier fears for the safety of his failing patient and was inspired by the newly-gained information that his patient had recently run the Calgary marathon in 3 hours and 29 minutes.

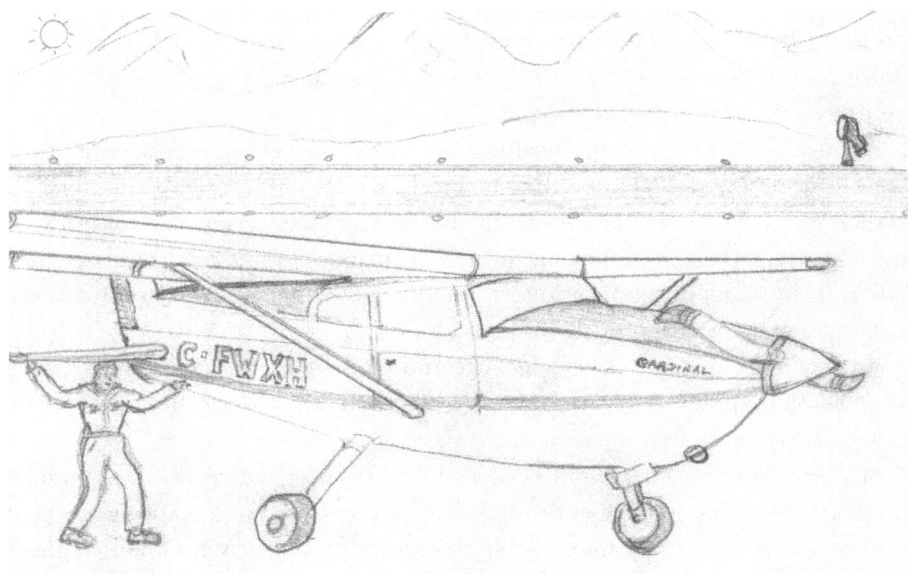

CHAPTER 2
20:02 Zulu

Walk-around is a pilot's systematic inspection of the aircraft prior to flight. First of all, it involves standing off and observing the general overall appearance of the airplane. Then, proceeding in a set sequence, the flyer carefully walks around the craft checking wings, flaps, hinges, landing gear, fuel tank, propellers, and many other vital details to ensure that all is well.

In many aspects, walk-around is as vital and exciting as the pre-race checklist of a long distance runner. The runner needs to be confident that all is well about his fuselage, salubrious lubrication where indicated to minimize undesirable friction, laces secured, fuel adequate and preloaded. He must also have current knowledge of the route to be followed including hills, winds, estimated time required for his race, and frequency and location of refuelling stops.

My tour guide on my first walk-around was Kelly Daziuk, an instructor at Cranbrook Horizon Air Flying School. I had progressed through the required segments of ground school, the book-work part of learning to fly, and was confident that some of my new fund of knowledge would at last be put to the test. I had learned many pertinent details, some peculiar to aviation. Port was left and starboard consequently, or by process of elimination, must then be right. This piece of information had not come easily until Kelly had astutely observed that left and port both had four letters. My walk-around was the end result of a long, often frustrated interest in flying. My earliest recollections of machines in the air were on nights in the early 1940's hearing the frightening drone of German bombers as they passed at low altitudes across the Scottish moors en route to wreaking devastation on the ship building centres of Clydebank near Glasgow.

I was both intrigued and mystified by many facets of that sad historical period. Occasionally, one of the elders in the family would lead me through the darkened porch that was a light trap in the compulsory blackout of wartime night in Britain. Only the fascination of these great machines in the air overcame my terror of the dark. What kept them in the air? How did they know where they were going? How could they miss the mountains and where would they get more "petrol" if they ran out of fuel?

I didn't realize I'd have to wait another forty years for the answers and that Kelly would be the man to tell me all I wanted to know about flying.

I'd had another earlier chance to learn more about flying at age sixteen when I flew from Scotland to Canada to attend the 8th World Scout Jamboree at Niagara-on-the-Lake in 1955. Just before takeoff, the inner port engine had an outburst of fire. Although the flames were quickly quenched with fire extinguishers, my desire to pursue a flying career was considerably diminished.

Despite that early fright, subsequent flights to Singapore, Australia, and numerous transatlantic trips restored my faith in man's ability to fly. The final decider was a trip from Cranbrook to Phoenix, Arizona, with two friends in a small Cessna 172XP. This allayed all fears and persuaded me that I must take up this exciting pursuit.

The early hours of actual flight training following that first walk-around were the most exhilarating experiences of my entire life. Each lesson proved more challenging and yet rewarding than that before it. The memory of these many firsts stayed with me in utmost clarity, never diminished by the newfound skills of later triumphs. There was the first weaving along the providentially empty taxi-way, as a result of the novice's heavy footed over-reaction on alternate rudder pedals. The day my instructor relinquished his captaincy of our two-man Cessna 152 with the words, "You have control," was a memorable occasion.

The use of the aircraft radio offered unexpected hilarity. As has happened to many a Scot, times of tension accentuated the brogue in my speech and raised its pitch to an embarrassing prepubertal squeak. It wasn't long before I was the laughingstock of all ears listening in on the mandatory ground frequency at Cranbrook airport. Blair's shrill burr was easily recognized.

First takeoff was unforgettable. Keeping the anxious little craft pointing straight down the centre line of the 200 foot wide, 8,000 foot long runway seemed impossible. This was then followed by careening and porpoising my way aloft, zigzagging with over-correction and only haphazard attention to required direction. Flight instructors have nerves of steel and a gift of tolerance beyond description. Only the occasional comment, "Gee – I wish this was a rental plane," gave me any indication of Kelly's true thoughts about my doubtful flying skills.

Next came the circuits. Circuit training is another term common to runners and flyers. Just as the purposely varied distance repetitions challenge the athlete, so too these set patterns for takeoff and landing practice hone the skills of the airman. "Take off into the wind, keep directly over the centre line of the runway after lift-off." "Turn onto the crosswind leg of the circuit only when at 500 feet and half a mile beyond the runway." "Maintain steady climb, watch turn and bank indicator, reach circuit height 1,000 feet, turn onto downwind leg of the circuit." I can still hear these words.

It was all so fascinating. Each new lesson reviewed what had previously been learned then progressed to something new and exciting. Soft field landings, short field landings, emergency landings, overshoots, all in a day's work and each one was a vital part of the training. Each established automatic reactions to help cope with the unexpected.

Then the big day came for stalls and spins. I thought I had conquered all fear and was well in control of the aircraft until I was required to learn to recognize the point-of-stall. That is the time when an aircraft ceases to produce the necessary lift to support its own weight in the air. There are various stall-warning devices located in the cockpits of small airplanes. This warning can be a red light, a bell, or a buzzer. The sound of the stall-warning attracts one's immediate attention and initiates the ingrained recovery procedures. "Nose down, apply power, pull out."

Practising spins enables a pilot to have experience in coping with a vertical rotating plunge and trains the flyer to restore the aircraft to smooth and level flight. It was a maneuver that always brought turmoil to my every sense of self-preservation.

All these delightful, sometimes disquieting and never dull maneuvers, contribute to the fascination of flying.

Air travel communication has its peculiar vocabulary. This language is designed to minimize the risk of mistakes and lessen the likelihood of accidental misunderstanding or misinformation.

Time measurement is specified according to a worldwide clock, all times being related to the time at the Greenwich meridian or zero degrees of longitude. Designated as Zulu Time, the local time in each time zone is translated into the corresponding digit of time at the Greenwich meridian measured on a 24-hour day. Thus the seven hour difference from Mountain Standard Time at Cranbrook makes the 8 a.m. MST read as 15:00 Zulu Time.

Even with all the safeguards, special rules, careful training, and stringent policing of flight travel, accidents can still happen. Though a pilot may attend to every detail with meticulous care in preplanning a flight, there are still moments when circumstances, such as unexpected weather, dictate a rapid change in plan. Despite the hours of training and practice, things can go wrong and a plane goes down.

The need to locate and rescue downed airmen and the urgency and accuracy needed to do so, has spawned an organization dedicated to this mission. In British Columbia the organization is the Search and Rescue branch of the Provincial Emergency Programme, or PEP. Along with CARES, Civil Air Rescue Emergency Service of Alberta, each province has a local representative member on each part of the Canadian Air Search and Rescue Association, CASARA.

On Saturday, 1st October 1983, a full morning of professional instruction and training was provided by members of 442 Squadron Royal Canadian Air Force. Those Search and Rescue specialists tutored the group of 40 local flying enthusiasts, to teach them the skills needed in these missions.

After lunch the participants in the training sessions, experienced pilots, navigators, and many newly trained spotters, were grouped into teams to fly either with the R.C.A.F. leaders or in set teams in smaller aircraft. Each aircraft was given a five by ten mile section of mountainous terrain as its search area. For this practical training exercise, I was selected to occupy an airplane callsigned Canada-Foxtrot Whiskey Xray Hotel, C-FWXH. It was a single engine Cardinal with a pilot, designated navigator, and two spotters.

Pilot Bill Quilley, with skill and confidence gained from thousands of hours flying time, his pre-checks completed, held the vibrating craft momentarily at the threshold of Runway 16 preparatory to rolling down the one-and-a-half-mile runway. The time was 20:02 Zulu.

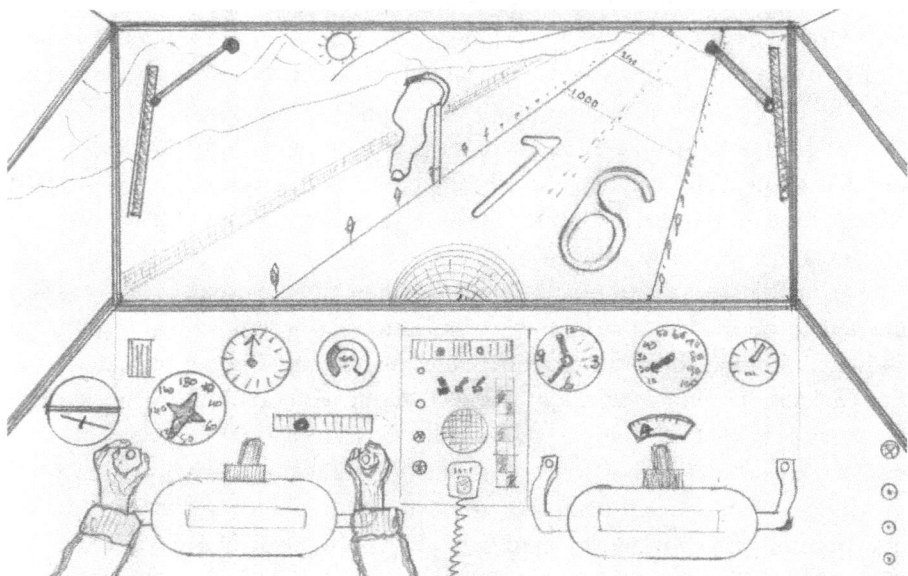

CHAPTER 3
Runway 16

The 30-foot-long numbers 1 and 6 at the north end of the Cranbrook runway had taken on a whole new meaning following my exposure to ground school and 20 hours of flight training. Previously, the numbers at the end of various runways, observed during approaches or takeoffs from airports around the world, had meant little to me. Flight training brought a vital recognition of the value of all those numbers even from thousands of feet above the airports.

The compass bearing is obtained by adding a zero to the end of the two digits, thus 1-6 indicated a bearing of 160 degrees or just 20 degrees east of directly south. A reciprocal bearing of 340 degrees provided the number 3-4 at the other end of the runway and, by contacting Ground Control, pilots arriving or taking off would be instructed to choose the "runway in use." As a rule of thumb, this is usually the pathway pointing into the wind.

Sitting there that Saturday afternoon, right at the end of the runway looking straight down the 8,000 feet of concrete, there was a mounting feeling of anticipation among us three passengers as Bill pushed the throttle forward. The little plane trembled and surged with power as it started its roll southward.

Sitting in the front right-hand seat was a new experience for me. Traditionally, student pilots occupy the left-hand seat. So many things were different. As the speed increased and we flashed past the first thousand-foot marker on the runway, Bill confidently eased the little craft off the ground with a barely perceptible change of tone. What I noticed most was the relaxed state of his hands, bronzed by the constant exposure to sunlight during his work as the golf professional at the Kimberley Golf Course. Where were the white knuckles that I had when I tried to lift the plane bodily off the runway?

As we cleared the end of the runway at 500 feet, I took a last glance at the majestic beauty of the Rockies to our left, silhouetted against an azure, cloudless sky. I gloried in a final glimpse of Mt. Fisher, the 9,300 foot pinnacle atop the ridge, the mecca for local climbers. I recalled the joy of that summer's climb with my 12-year-old son just two months earlier. Turning west, we left the circuit, climbed to a thousand feet, and crossed over the dry fields of Joseph's Prairie. This maneuver coincided with yet another revelation of Bill's experience in the confident use of the radio. Simultaneously, as if giving the perfect answer to my flight instructor's frequent questions, "Who are you? Where are you? What are you doing?" Bill skillfully informed Cranbrook Flight Service that he was Cardinal C-FWXH leaving the circuit westwards and proceeding to St. Mary's Lake.

Moments after leaving the circuit, Bill informed his inexperienced passengers of some of the important features of the practice search ahead at the designated area. Passing over the flat land, Bill pointed out that we were at one thousand feet above ground level and asked us to observe the size of the vehicles travelling north along the road to Kimberley. On the open road, although the cars were minute, they were at least easily seen, but it was their size in relation to trees and ground features that we were to try to memorize. This would be valuable when trying to spot a lost aircraft or a mock crash site in our practice search programme. We had undergone training that morning with lectures presented by the Search and Rescue specialists to teach us how to scan in a set pattern with deliberate care. This technique would provide the best chance of recognizing target features in our search area.

Bill also pointed out relative distances so that we would know the half-mile optimum distance which would be the distant edge of our search pathway while flying at that height.

Search and Rescue techniques vary considerably, depending on terrain. Where the land is relatively flat, a designated search area is usually divided up and approached in a grid fashion so that the entire area is covered by flying in a series of straight parallel lines. Depending on the height of the search, an initial visual search may well follow parallel lines two miles apart, spotters viewing from each side of the craft being able to cover one mile on their side of that line.

Our designated area of search was close to St. Mary's Lake, starting some nine miles west of the airport and covering territory ten miles long by five miles wide. This was not a region suitable for grid pattern search so, instead, the search pattern would follow selected contour lines around the mass of mountain peaks overshadowing St. Mary's Lake. The lake itself is at 3,000 feet above sea level with the surrounding peaks reaching 8,000 feet.

The first sweep of our practice search took us along the north edge of the lake following the zigzagging contours formed by the creeks that tumbled down into the lake. Anticipating that the search coordinators had placed a mock crash site somewhere in our search area, we had several false sightings which turned out to be campers enjoying the last bit of bright sunshine on a clear fall day.

This land, with little change for the next 600 miles west to the Pacific, bristles with a tree every five feet. The trees seen from a thousand feet are little bigger than match sticks and trying to locate a downed aircraft is like looking for a thumb tack in a shag carpet. The vivid flashes of fall colour, sunshine on the occasional bare rock, reflections from creeks and waterholes, dark shadowy patches, and the ever-present trees makes spotting a very demanding task. This is especially so because of the awful finality and responsibility implicit in taking on this task.

Search and rescue training is no joy-ride and falls to those with a desire to train themselves to be ready to help those unfortunate enough to be lost and probably injured. This concern for others was the driving force and the one feature that had brought the plane's four occupants together. Hitherto strangers, pilot Bill Quilley, spotters Cynthia Griffiths, John Craig, and I, melded into a team in the common goal of search and rescue.

The strain of the spotters' searching was quickly taking its toll and, recognizing their fatigue, the pilot called a halt to the duties as we completed our first path along the lake's northern edge. He then turned back over the placid waters of the lake to allow a few moments of relaxation. Tired so soon! It was only 15 minutes since we had set off from Runway 16.

CHAPTER 4
1:27, Ten Seconds in Hell

The pilot performed a couple of lazy circles in level flight high over the calm lake surface. This was the time for a relaxing smoke for those who indulged. An ardent nonsmoker, I used the time to enjoy the beauty of the sunny fall colours.

The tamarack gleamed with burnished gold, their final autumnal flourish prior to losing their needles. They are the only coniferous trees that follow the example of their deciduous cousins in defoliation each winter. Near the water's edge, stands of cottonwood had already preceded the larch in losing their leaves and stood silent, ghostlike, with blotchy dark patches on their grey-brown trunks.

On sheltered creek banks small clumps of shimmering reddish-gold indicated the last groups of trembling aspen, reluctant to give up their leaves and bare themselves for winter.

The five-minute rest period over, Bill gently turned the plane south to follow the contours along the banks of the next creek bed. At the time the name meant nothing to me other than that it designated one of the dozen or so rivulets that tumble into St. Mary's Lake. Subsequent events etched the name unforgettably on my mind. It was appropriately Scots in origin – Angus Creek.

Maintaining his height and direction to ensure that the uphill starboard spotter would have a clear unobstructed view of the steep western bank of the creek, Bill flew south along the rising incline of the creek's course towards the peaks ahead towering to some 8,000 feet.

Judging that he had entered along the creek far enough, Bill turned east and back north towards the lake when suddenly the plane was struck by a fierce unexpected downdraft. I was not aware of the impending disaster. I had shifted my focus from outside the plane to study the map on my lap, trying to locate the squiggles of contours which corresponded to the ravines and tree covered slopes below.

Suddenly, shrill with desperation yet quiet in terror, Cynthia's voice intoned, "Oh my God!" I jerked my head up, looked out the starboard window, and was amazed to see just inches away – a Christmas tree.

As if the plane had stopped, I could see the minute details of the four-foot top section of a Douglas Fir. Time stood still, fixing the vision in my memory forever. I could see the tiny bristles of that summer's new growth, a lighter green than the darker branches just below. My instinct was to photograph such a memorable sight just a hand's-breadth away.

That Christmas tree at the window meant that we were only a hundred feet above the most inhospitable territory imaginable. During the next fraction of a second actions and perceptions were rocketed by a surge of body chemistry. I scanned briefly to my left, all senses taking in the inevitable horror. There was no time for panic, no screams, no swearing, not even time to grit the teeth.

The treetop had barely swept beneath that starboard wing when straight ahead there appeared the ten-inch trunk of a tamarack. As we were travelling at between 80 and 100 miles per hour, we covered those last ten feet in 0.1 of a second – not even time to blink!

The propellor, weighing 100 pounds and turning at 2400 revolutions per minute, clipped the tree, deflecting the aircraft marginally to the right. The rushing speed tore off the left wing and whipped the plane from its nose-first attitude completely around, to continue its fatal trajectory backwards for another 90 feet and crash tail first into the base of a grove of 20-inch diameter trees.

Although the time taken between first sighting the Christmas tree and final impact with the ground was probably less than three seconds, I instinctively crouched forward in a self-preservation reflex, with my hands raised to protect my face and head.

The tail-first impact drove the two front seats fiercely back on their ratchets onto the legs of John and Cynthia in the back seat. As I was cringing forward, my landing posture drove me backwards hard into the cushioning of the seat and the combination of position, vertical and backward force was sufficient to compress my spine, causing a fracture at the third lumbar vertebra.

The force of the kinetic energy in the 1500 pound engine drove it back through the firewall and supporting chassis into the the cockpit. Its rearward movement struck and deflected off Bill's right leg, breaking the bones like matchsticks just above the ankle, simultaneously striking my left foot and dislocating the ankle joint. Other than those injuries, Bill and I surprisingly had no other immediate skeletal damage or direct trauma from the crash.

As if in a slow motion horror movie I immediately saw, felt and smelled the flames. They were everywhere – a yellow, red, growling, devouring monster. The flames made a vision so graphic and incredible that it could only be conjured up in the mind of some pyromaniac or painted by some artist hell-bent on using every red, gold, and yellow that money could buy.

In its final death throes of descent the aircraft's fuel lines had sliced and the inside of the cabin had been deluged with high octane gasoline.

Whether this volatile combustible fuel ignited before or on impact was of no consequence – death was in the air.

I instinctively closed my eyes in a protective reflex. I had to force them open again in my vain search for the handle of my starboard side door. I lunged to the right and forward through the wall of fire to where my brain told me a Cessna 152 door handle should have been easily located.

Groping frantically, I tore at that door. But this was not the familiar little trainer plane where I had practiced such unlikely needs as locating door handles and fire extinguishers till I could do it with my eyes closed. This was a different craft.

"Oh God, I'm in the wrong plane!" Finding no handle where it should have been, I battered with my bare fists at the door, at the window, although I could see neither. The flames were solid, not just a sheet, but a three dimensional inferno.

The door latch was immediately to my right, tucked in at the edge of my seat. I'd never have found it in a thousand years. For a moment there was no rush, I knew the end was near.

During my frantic search for that door handle, I had forgotten the presence and proximity of others in the plane until I heard a shout from my left, "This way!"

Being more familiar with the plane, Bill had managed to locate his door handle and wrenched the door open, diving out and calling as he went. He was some ten feet from the aircraft, trying to get away from the tongues of flame in the grass and undergrowth and the searing heat in the plane. The voice gave me a glimmer of renewed hope and strength. As the seconds ticked by I somehow knew to avoid inhaling the lethal heat. In desperation bred by finality, I lunged left through the awful gold toward the direction of the shout.

Hell still had its grasp upon me. In all my frantic measures I had failed to undo my safety belt and was trapped. Somehow, my blackened hands, their hair singed off and skin already bubbling, found the release clasp on the belt.

As if some greater being had seen my need and freshly oiled the mechanism, the belt opened quickly in response to my grasp.

In agonizingly slow motion I clawed my way left, every inch a mile through a flame-filled jungle – a tangle of enmeshing wires, broken joysticks, and molten seats.

As my head cleared the doorway, I half dived, half fell to the ground some three feet below and, as if trained a thousand times to do so, rolled over and over to try to quench the flames from my burning clothing.

Worst of all was the burning hair on my scalp. I knew it was still alight and hysterically lashed it with my bare hands, frantically calling to Bill, "Is it out yet? Is it out yet?" I think the blood and tissue fluid leaking from my baked skin finally put out the flames in my hair.

Self-preservation prevailed and I frantically hobbled up the incline away from the plane following along the track that Bill had taken. Fearful that the plane's fuel tanks might still be intact and about to explode, I tried to put greater distance between myself and its lethal load. At about 50 feet away, I finally looked down to see why I was hobbling and found that my foot was facing obliquely away to the left. Rational thought dictated that I could not step on that bent limb, so I promptly fell.

Only then did I think of the others. With horror, guilt, and shame all tangled up inside me, I quietly wept. My shame and guilt was that I was 50 feet away to safety before I ever thought of John and Cynthia still in the back seat. There in front of me was a 40-foot high pyre.

I sat silently in disbelief. Nothing else was there: no trees, no grass, no pain for me, no feelings, except that sight, and then the sounds.

It was a tumult of crackling, burning, hissing, popping, pinging explosions. Here and there spurting jets of trapped fuel spat fiery tongues out into the grass and forest. Those sounds will remain with me forever.

For a long slow time, as the height of flames gradually diminished, I thought of John and Cynthia and in that eternity of horror I searched to find some token, some fragile symbol of peace to hold onto for the years ahead. And all I found was the knowledge that they didn't suffer long.

This was a very private time, when even earth stood still for Bill and me. Each of us was now a survivor of a fatal crash, each frantically busy with his own soul-searching and disbelief at this impossible nightmare. It was a time of no pain, no fear, just deep sorrow. Gradually, with all the fuel devoured, the flames crept slowly lower until at last the mangled outline of what was left stood naked to the eye with only little flickers of flame in the surrounding grass. The smoke poured straight up through the void of blackened trees, their branches denuded of foliage by the earlier insatiable hunger of those flames. Eventually, after what seemed an eternity but was only minutes, my immediate environment started bombarding me with sensory impulses. The gradual onset of what was to be seemingly unending pain, was accompanied by an entirely new stench. My blackened charred hands stank of scorched hair and burned flesh. I turned them over. The palms were bloodied and that golden oozing of vital body fluid from every pore sent my memory back a thousand years to student days in anatomy and physiology labs. A quizzical wondering, "Where is all that stuff coming from?" brought greater despair with the knowledge that that fluid was irreplaceable in my present environment and was probably the drops of my life departing one by one.

In what was to become a cycle of emotion, of confidence and fear, of dejection and hope, I began an analysis of my body status.

Starting at the farthest end I checked things over. The good news. The right foot seemed okay. My Nike Air running shoe had blood on it but it wasn't from that foot, so all was well there.

Then the bad news. The left foot was still kinked badly to the left. Somewhere, where the joint should anatomically bend up and down at the ankle, it had become strangely misshapen. The heel seemed forward a bit compared to the other one. I judged that something was sadly amiss. There was a lot of blood all over the laces. I made a mental note that I'd have to wash these shoes in cold water to get the blood off. So the good news was I planned to run again but my next marathon might be delayed a spell. I tried moving the left ankle and to my absolute astonishment it moved reasonably well although not in the expected directions. I figured out that it was probably just dislocated and a good yank might fix it.

The jeans were definitely in bad shape. They were a beige colour – a bad choice for such a day. They, too, would need a cold water treatment or more. The right leg up to the knee was pretty good, the left was not worth describing. The left knee was badly burned, with fragments of the denim material forming a matrix for the blood to congeal around. This was a far cry from the brawny knee that had once peeked from beneath a kilt.

The thighs horrified me. They must have had a good drenching of high octane gasoline as they had just frizzled. There were gaping holes in the skin which had previously covered the contours of those soccer-player quadricep muscles.

And then the hands came into view. I could not look at them.

I had been wearing a synthetic track suit top and the sleeves were now unrecognizable but surprisingly not burned right through. A thin cotton shirt under the sleeves seemed intact. I ventured a tentative dig at the sleeves to pull them up to survey the situation. Back to the good news. The arms were okay.

Unbelievably, materials that I would have expected to burn with furor had not ignited and had, in fact, saved my arms.

"You've still got hair there, Blair," I thought, but that was about the last of my humour for the next three months.

I dared myself to look back at the hands. I had once heard of a physiotherapist who had insured his hands for a million dollars and I thought at the time, "What a great idea. I should really do that. "I cannot recall whether I had even investigated how much it would have cost to insure them but I knew at that awful moment of self-appraisal that I hadn't done so and fervently wished I had. The hands looked bad.

Keeping them up off my clothing and off the surrounding grass, I slowly turned those tortured hands over and back trying to find one surface that looked better. Neither front nor back was worth a second glance. The back was a mosaic of blisters, cracks, weeping fissures, oozing blood and golden life fluid. Surprisingly, the nails looked white but this was only in relation to the surrounding charred tissues of the fingers. Those digits still moved, but only just.

The back of the hand wasn't particularly painful. I didn't realize at the time that the nerves supplying sensation to that surface of the hand were probably all destroyed, but the palms were telling me something. Was it really good news that the nerves, or at least those exposed fibres that conducted pain, were still intact? Each movement or attempt to straighten and bend brought lancing arrows of pain and all I could think was one descriptive term, "bad." Perhaps that embodied the whole spectrum from "severe" to the unmentionable "gone," but I wouldn't allow myself to think any worse than "bad."

I continued my analytical assessment of my body's disaster areas. Elbows moved. Fine! Left shoulder didn't seem to do what I asked it but it didn't merit great concern. It had felt much worse after many a rugby game. But the spine was not in great shape.

Having spent my last ten years treating spinal disorders in about 50 percent of my patients, I imagined I could get somewhere close to a diagnosis of the problem. To get into a posture suitable for spinal analysis I tried to sit up, but this proved to be an ill-advised maneuver. Following this I gently squirmed around, twisted here and there, and came to the vague but acceptable diagnosis that something was wrong but could have been worse. I became more acutely analytical and recognized that I had no neurological disturbance to my legs and didn't seem to be particularly kinked to one side or the other but was just generally "damn sore." A quick review of my meagre knowledge of injuries sustained in aircraft crash landings led me to the assumption that I probably had a compression fracture of one of the vertebrae and took a guess at the third lumbar level as my final diagnosis.

That calmed me down a bit. The knowledge that my spinal lesion had good prognosis buoyed me somewhat to continue my self-analysis. I couldn't really see my own head, in fact I became aware that I couldn't see peripherally or very clearly even straight ahead. I made a valiant effort to open my eyes wide and realized that this effort brought on considerable pain around my face – things were not well there either. I did some tentative poking around at my face with my insensitive finger tips and had the dilemma of not knowing whether the bloody marks were from my fingers or the face. Most of the hair on the top of my scalp was burned off but I wasn't aware of that at this time. I knew there was a mess at the back of my skull. I finally found a little corner at the heel of my hand that had some sensation and dabbed at the back of the head, but found there only a pulpy mess. This was not a good ending to my review of my bodily status and plummeted me into depths of self-pity.

The thought of the sum of all these findings triggered alarm and need for action. I began to badger Bill.

I had been oblivious of his proximity some seven or eight feet away from me through all this time of self-analysis and self-pity. He was sitting quietly nursing his wounds, similar in nature and extent to mine, and going through his own personal anguish of self-recrimination.

The fire had at last stopped flaming and was by now just a trickle of smoke. The noise of the inferno had gone completely except for the occasional whoosh and pop of some exploding cell or tube that had been sheltered deep in the rubble. The ashes of the aircraft and its contents and the bodies of our two comrades were partially hidden by a floppy lopsided six-foot segment of the wing that had fallen close to the flames but had not burned.

"Hey, let's get some green foliage and throw it on the fire to make more smoke."

It seemed a great idea but proved a pretty tough assignment when we realized that neither of us could walk, and trying to break off green twigs with our charred hands was next to impossible.

"Do you think they'll have missed us yet?" I asked.

"I doubt it," replied Bill. His brevity should have forewarned me that this was hardly the time for chatting.

I squinted at my watch. The fine gold hands were only barely discernible amongst the blood and gore. The glass of my watch was gone and in a moment of nostalgia, I recalled buying the watch 25 years earlier in Kuala Lumpur. My mind drifted back to those glorious days in Malaysia. As I reminisced, everything was beautiful. Forgotten were the mosquitoes, snakes, torrential rain, prickly heat, and sunburn. Nothing but wonderful memories remained and my poor old watch was now 25 years old. I suddenly realized the watch had stopped. It must be later than it showed. They must have started looking for us.

"What's the time?" I asked Bill. This was to be the first of hundreds of askings.

"Twenty to two."

An entire lifetime had gone by in the 13 minutes since impact had crushed the watch face and stopped that clock forever at 1:27.

CHAPTER 5
3½ Hours, Almost a Lifetime

As part of their standard equipment, most small airplanes have an emergency location transmitter, an ELT. This tiny radio device is usually located in the baggage section of the airplane and accessible from both inside and outside the plane.

Its purpose is to emit a signal which could be picked up on emergency radio frequency, pinpointing the location of a downed or lost aircraft. ELTs may be triggered by the force of impact or may be manually activated. Occasionally, they are inadvertently set off by a heavy landing, to the great embarrassment of the pilot of that craft. The signal may be picked up 40 to 50 miles away provided there is not some solid obstacle to obstruct the transmission of this signal through clear air. Mountainous territory is infamous for its capacity to impede these signals.

At 1:27 the ELT on our plane was activated by either the impact on the large tree which spun us around or when we finally hit the ground. As the crash occurred in heavily treed territory in a location almost surrounded by steep slopes and mountains, the pathway of these signals was unluckily severely limited. The ELT's call was not heard by any planes flying over the area, nor did our landing coincide with the regular 40-minute passing of an earth-circling communications satellite, one of whose capabilities was to receive and relay any such signals.

In its awful hunger, the fire consumed every combustible item on the plane. Consequently, the ELT relayed its anxious message for only a few seconds, then was silent forever.

Part of the education program of the Search and Rescue training sessions being held at the Cranbrook airport that day included the manual activation of an ELT. This was to help train pilots, spotters, and those involved in the exercise as well as airport communications personnel in hearing and recognizing such a signal. This part of the exercise was to be performed at two o'clock that afternoon and forewarnings had been given to the appropriate authorities to ensure their readiness for its reception, and to obviate unnecessary initiation of a search. One pilot on "short final," the last segment of his flight prior to touchdown at Cranbrook airport, thought he heard one beep of an ELT. The final few seconds of flight preceding a landing are the most critical time of the entire flight. The pilot's full attention is on placing the craft at the right speed on the right location, and preferably with wheels down. It is not the ideal time to do an in-depth study on whether or not a quick beep was a real or practice ELT signal.

Being aware that a practice ELT activation was imminent, the pilot assumed, quite naturally, that he had just heard the tail end of this exercise alarm.

Consequently, our plane's crash had not been seen, or heard by any other people involved in the exercise. Similarly, neither our flight over the lake nor our search pattern had been worthy of more than a scant observation by local residents around the lake.

The smoke from our crash in dense undergrowth might have attracted attention, but at that time of year fall clean-up was in progress and any smoke sightings would be presumed to be intentional bonfires.

The flight plan for our practice search area indicated 2 p.m. as the estimated time of arrival for a return trip to Cranbrook Airport. There had been no time prior to our crash to send out a Mayday distress call. Bill's awareness of the likelihood of the ELT having perished in the flames gave him sound reason for reminding me again at two o'clock, that they would not yet have started a search. Our absence would not be considered suspect until 30 minutes had elapsed beyond our expected return time.

One by one, the five other planes that had set out on designated area searches as part of the exercise, had reported back at the airport and had completed their landings. Although by 2:15 p.m. only our Cardinal, C-FWXH, had failed to return. There was still no reason for alarm as there could be numerous simple and acceptable reasons for a delay in return.

Work continued at the Search and Rescue headquarters to brief and finalize plans for the dispatch of another six craft for the projected three o'clock one-hour practice search. The crews of each aircraft were busily making their final flight plans and aircraft checks, coordinating with the search master their designated territories and deciding upon their projected approaches.

At 2:35 p.m., having given a few minutes leeway on the 30 minutes late schedule, the search master was obliged to initiate an official intimation of an overdue aircraft. The planned dispatch of the 3 p.m. practice search was immediately cancelled and the wheels set in motion to undertake a full search. This was not a practice. This was the real thing and an aura of controlled anxiety hung over the Search and Rescue training crews, now part of the official nerve centre of a full search. It was even more distressing that their mission was to find one of their own craft which was presumed to be down.

For Bill Quilley and me, that had been the longest hour of our lives, but worse was still to come. I had already looked at my watch a hundred times and each time gone through the tiring sequence of logic of again trying to fathom why the hands were still at 1:27. We had moved up the slope to a spot about 60 feet from the aircraft where there was a 15-foot clearing. There the sun had made its way through a narrow break in the tree tops to brighten a grassy patch.

It looked like the ideal spot for an afternoon picnic had we been in somewhat different circumstances, but even the grassy patch was deceptive in its appearance of comfort. Hidden in the grass were hundreds of little spikes of growth of young trees that had been left like bamboo shoots, their branches removed by some earlier burn-off. Trying to find some comfortable spot to lie was a torment of jabs by these little spikes.

I had edged in towards a tree and stuck my injured foot up in the air, leaning it against the trunk, this elevation intended to lessen the swelling and so minimize the pain in that ankle. There had been progressive worsening of the pain in my back to the extent that all movement brought spasms of anguish and yet my inability to find any position of comfort made me move constantly.

Worst of all was the neck muscle fatigue setting in from having to hold my head up off the ground. The back of my scalp was a gory mess and because of the condition of my hands I was unable to use them to hold my head up off the grass. My neck muscles were screaming from trying to maintain the weight of my skull in that lying position.

After showing infinite patience with my repetitious asking for the time, Bill finally allowed the edge of his exasperation to surface by answering one of my requests with, "Two minutes since you last asked."

There followed a long silence while I ruminated over that phrase of his and its biting admonition.

Finally, at 2:30 p.m., without my asking and almost by way of apology for his earlier sharp comment, Bill quietly said, "Well, we've been overdue half an hour now. I guess they'll start a search."

For a moment, I was buoyed up by the thought that they'd be overhead immediately, looking for us. I became enthusiastic about the idea of trying to signal to searchers who might be crossing over our location. I maneuvered around painfully until I was in the centre of the cleared spot and opened up my flight calculator which had somehow survived the earlier traumas, sheltered as it had been in my shirt breast pocket. The front face of the calculator still had its shiny buttons to produce innumerable calculations required for navigation. None of its capabilities of converting pounds to kilograms, gallons to litres, and other navigational needs were of immediate practical value. However, the metallic surface did offer a glimmer of hope.

Catching the sun's rays on this reflective surface, I started producing my own brand of signal. I tried to work out some tricky mental calculations to arrive at an appropriate angle at which to hold the shiny surface. My brain wasn't doing too well with the mathematics that this required. To check it out I brought the calculator up near my face and did some tentative angulations to capture a flash of the sun's rays and it dawned on me with horrifying impact that I could hardly see more than a vague outline just inches from my face. I groped around at my face, at my eyes for a while, before I realized that my vision was fine if I pulled down on the lower eyelids. I felt relieved that it was facial swelling rather than direct damage to the eyes that was causing my lack of vision.

Reassured, I got back to the serious business of flailing around with the calculator, searching for the invisible craft that just had to be right above us by that time.

Minutes or perhaps ages later, I tired of the apparent futility of my endeavours and lay back to wait it out.

The inactivity was even more evil than the exasperation caused by my earlier paltry signalling efforts. I knew better than to ask the time again, as I had learned that little lesson the hard way. But I could glance at my watch again. Inside the rim of shattered glass, the hands were compressed into the face of the watch. The second hand was lost, and the little recess that should have shown the date was plugged up with some form of human matter, the underlying bejewelled mechanism of precision now a tangled mess. My reverie took me away from the pain of the present to the joy of the memory of good times in the past. I let myself think again of Jalan Tuanku Abdul Rahman, the main street in the Malaysian capital where I had bought the watch. I could see, in my mind, the darkened jeweller's shop with the slowly rotating fan creating some semblance of movement in the torpid tropical afternoon. So, too, the gentle singsong voice of the tall Indian salesman came back, his turban and flowing robes identifying his ethnic contribution to the cosmopolitan races of that city.

"Very good watch, Sahib. Last you long, long time," I recalled his lilting accent and with a sudden sadness I was jolted back from all that bygone splendour to a tarnished Saturday afternoon where hope was fading by the minute. Was this the end of his predicted long, long time?

As my mood altered, so did the surrounding woodland temperature. A shiver ran through me, the first of many, as I had my first experience of the shattering, uncontrollable shakes of the onset of shock.

A little quiver started up in my spine, then it escalated to a full blown shuddering vibration as my body literally heaved itself from the ground. It was totally uncontrollable and seemed to last for ages until complete exhaustion posed a self-regulating mechanism and let me collapse into a whimpering exhausted stupor.

Thus began my first serious doubts about survival. Bill and I hadn't spoken for quite a spell, though how long I couldn't guess. The minutes were each taking rather a long time. Bill was sitting just a little higher up at the edge of the clearing. He had seen my frantic shakes when I went into shock but was helpless to come to my aid. There was nothing he could do. When I finally settled down, he sensed my need and quietly went beyond his own sufferings and found the strength to offer a timely encouragement.

"We'll make it, partner. They'll be starting out pretty soon now. Just hang in there."

"What's the time now, Bill?" I dared myself to ask.

"Quarter to three, " was his reply. It seemed like a lifetime.

A new anguish displaced physical pain. It signalled full acceptance of the hopelessness of my plight. It dawned on me that I hadn't rewritten my will. I wept silently as I thought of my young sons, Ian and Craig, and of how they would suffer even more because of this one oversight. My recent divorce invalidated my former will, and like so many, I had procrastinated over the simple matter of revising it and nominating my executor. I cursed myself for the thoughtlessness, the lack of caring that would have such horrendous ramifications in inevitable bureaucratic delays. I plummeted to yet greater depths of misery as I thought of this final blunder of omission.

Having decided that a search should be set in motion, the R.C.A.F. Squadron Search and Rescue supervisor, who had been presenting the training sessions, selected local coordinator Robbie Taylor to pilot a search over our designated practice area. She was an experienced pilot with her own plane, more than a thousand hours flying time, a commercial pilot's licence, and she knew the local terrain like the back of her hand. She chose as her spotters Albert Comfort and Ron Krowchuk, both local pilots, each known for his experience and hours on Search and Rescue. Their knowledge of the St. Mary's Lake area and their skill as spotters made them an ideal choice as crew.

They took off from the airport at 2:40 p.m. and flew directly to the ten by five mile area that had been designated for our specific practice search. Robbie piloted her aircraft in the laborious climb to reach 10,000 feet of altitude, some 7,000 feet above St. Mary's Lake. Her purpose in reaching this height was to do an electronic surveillance tuned to the emergency frequency to try to detect any ELT signal from the rugged territory below.

The climb took an exasperating twenty minutes and a further ten minutes of flight along the perimeter of the mapped area to ascertain whether there was any signal coming from the entire segment below.

Having failed to detect any ELT emissions from the valley below, the three experienced occupants of her plane consulted about the best approach for doing a lower level visual search. They agonized over probabilities and techniques of search. What were the most likely or dangerous spots in the search area – the mountain tops, the valleys, or the ridges? There seemed hundreds of possibilities. There was still the faint hope that the plane had deliberately landed because of some emergency and might be sitting on some patch of flat land or even in the lake. They didn't have much time to ponder their decisions on how to approach their search. They felt the urgency of proceeding before the sun started dropping and casting deceptive black patches of shadow.

Suddenly they caught a flash of an aircraft passing in from the west some 2,000 feet below their level. They tried to contact this craft on various wave bands but failed to raise it on the radio. The colouring of that craft was similar to the description of our missing Cardinal but the search crew were unable to discern the lettering on the wing from that height.

Hoping that it was the missing aircraft, they pursued the eastbound flyer who was on a flight path towards the Cranbrook airport. When they had caught up sufficiently to read the markings, they were dejected to find it was not the craft they were looking for.

Robbie sharply turned her plane, anxious at the loss of precious minutes and returned to go over the lake and finalize her plan of search. She would start in the southeast corner and shoot the individual creeks. This was the technique of flying down the length of the stream beds and had the advantage of safety and was an accurate way of covering high probability areas where a craft might have run into trouble.

One of the disadvantages of this particular search technique was that it required climbing to above the mountain tops before each run down the length of the creeks. Recognizing the immensity of the area and the urgency brought on by rapidly passing time, Robbie climbed her craft above the 8,174 foot Grassy Mountain. Albert and Ron were pouring over maps to ascertain exactly which creek to search, and providentially chose Angus Creek. With patience and great courage Robbie guided her plane along the tortuous path of that creek, slowing the craft skillfully until the stall warning crackled ominously. This slow speed enabled her spotters to have the best possible chance of seeing any signs of the lost plane on the wooded craggy landscape below.

Remembering that the lost plane might well be broken-up, the spotters' straining eyes searched fervently for any sign of abnormality in the landscape. They looked for a flash of reflection, a wisp of smoke, a broken pathway through the trees, any indication of the orange and white body work of the Cardinal. As they looked for movement below, the plane hung precariously at its slowest limit of flight.

"Port, nine o'clock, 500 feet, a flash of white," Albert Comfort's eyes had caught just a momentary glint of something alien to the forest's green and brown.

Robbie gently levelled out the flight and kept straight ahead while the spotters tried to landmark the point relative to other topographical features. They flew out over the lake and discussed how to approach the area of their provisional sighting. They felt it was best to shoot the entire valley again so went through the time-consuming process of climbing, spiralling up to achieve sufficient altitude again to start down that dangerous gully.

Descending faster to the approximate area, Robbie then slowed the craft down while the two spotters peered at the general area of the earlier sighting. There was a tense silence. Simultaneously, Albert and Ron yelled, "There it is!" Two pairs of eyes had seen just that one flash of white, then further substantiation in the form of a little trickle of smoke from the same site.

It was still only a tentative recognition that something was there that was not natural for that area of forest. Robbie then took the courageous step of deciding to fly up the valley, following almost the same path as our plane had flown earlier. It was imperative that they fly low enough to give the spotters the optimum visibility, slowly enough to permit the likelihood of a definitive location of the aircraft. As they approached the site, the plane's raucous stall warning once again blared out its message. Robbie edged in closer and closer until at last the spotters could make a positive sighting.

"It looked like three small tents and a campfire," Ron remembered afterwards, but the white and orange segments of wing and unburned tail section with just a trace of indiscernible numerals on the wing told them the fate of the Cardinal.

Robbie and her crew were still, themselves, in imminent danger and only her long experience in mountain flying helped her turn the craft out of the steep creek valley to fly back over the lake. As they turned, Ron gave proof of his intimate knowledge of the local geography. Just some 70 yards from the wreckage Ron could see a previously cut five-acre patch already thickly covered with 15-foot new growth of cottonwood and elder. Beyond this cleared area was a forestry road. He had driven over that gravel road just a week earlier delivering fuel to a logging company some miles up into the next valley, Perry Creek. Ron could not contain his excitement.

"I know exactly where that is. I can get you right there. I'll drive right in," he kept saying.

Robbie, in her methodical and calculating fashion, maintained control. "Right, we've got a positive spotting. We'll keep radio silence until we get back to the airport. It will only take four minutes. It will be easier to dispatch a land crew from the airport."

"Well, well, well. I do believe they're up there," said Bill.

He had seen Robbie's plane making the agonizingly slow spiral climb to achieve sufficient altitude to shoot down the creek. The shadows were becoming longer and there was a chill creeping into the afternoon air. I was frustrated that I couldn't see the plane up there. I could just discern the darkening blue patch of sky trapped in its margins of treetop. Nor could I hear a sound of the aircraft. My mind was becoming a bit suspicious; I had my doubts about many things. I had just spent a long silent time of doubt, wondering if our absence had been noticed, wondering if they were taking it seriously, wondering if they had started a search. Would we be found before dark? Would we be found in the morning? Would we survive the night?

Following all this doubt, I found it hard to be quite sure that Bill might not be just making up this story. "He shouldn't do a thing like that, but perhaps he was doing it just to cheer me up. That would be a miserable way to cheer me up if it was a lie."

"Are you sure you saw something?" I demanded.

"I'm pretty sure," he hedged. "It's gone now, but I'm pretty sure it was a plane. " That qualified reassurance destroyed the credibility of his earlier statement.

I dropped back into silence. There wasn't much point in making an issue of whether or not he had seen a plane. It was back to the waiting game.

My hopes having been momentarily elevated, my mood plummeted back into dejection. Simultaneously, it seemed, the sun's angle dropped another 10 degrees, and so did the temperature. A coldness spread over me as hope dwindled. As if on cue from my psyche, my body went into another dancing fit of shock and my torso and limbs beat a staccato rhythm on the cooling earth.

Bill seemed to know when I needed a little lift and quite uninvited came back with, "Pretty sure they'll have gone up to the top of the ridge to do a run around the peaks to see if we pranged up there. They'll be back, ol' pal. Hang in there."

For an age we sat silent, and time stood still, yet the longer shadows told us time was fast running out. I didn't dare think of how cold it would get at night. Already I knew we'd both lost a dangerous amount of body fluid and the pain was fast diminishing our reserves of energy. The wait went on.

To pass the time I foolishly started a review of my physical state. The hands were obviously much more swollen although I could only see the outline of the fingers if I held them close to my face. They seemed bloated like big burned sausages and although I had the power to create movement, the skin was all so tight that the fingers just wouldn't bend or straighten. The fingers and thumb were spread as if I was holding a basketball. Each digit was' spread as far as possible from its frizzled neighbour to suck in the cold air around it.

I finally broke down and asked Bill the time again. "Three thirty, partner," and as if reading my mind, "Lots of daylight left yet." Then we both fell into silence.

Again I was acutely aware of time. Only two hours. It seemed a lifetime. My eyes were shut down by the swelling around them and the rest of my body was screaming in rebellion. I shuddered again as I recollected some of the stories I'd heard of people being found a week, two weeks, a month, a year after the accident. The ghoulish thought hit me again with real fear for my survival. Again I thought of my two sons, Ian, 12 and Craig, 11, and what their lives might be without me. They had already survived the trauma of my divorce with far greater resilience than I had dared hope. Why did they have to suffer this new tragedy in their young lives?

For a moment, the thought of my imminent death was alleviated in minuscule fashion by my recollection that my life was insured. Even this point of relief was quashed as my pessimism focused on the fine print exclusions likely to prevail in matters of noncommercial flight incidents. I was beyond seeing good in any matters.

We neither saw nor heard the plane pass over on its first low level shoot down the valley, but later Bill exclaimed with rising excitement, "They're up there again but they're far too high. They'll never see us." Even he was alarmed by the search plane's location.

From his restricted tunnel vision up through the trees, Bill could only see the plane for a few moments while it did its final spirals to regain altitude to do its second run down the valley.

We lay still and silent for another age and finally Bill's resolve broke and he intimated he was going to scout up the hill because he was sure there was a roadway in that direction.

His decision brought great fear to my mind for a multitude of reasons. I felt certain we must stay near the plane. Statistically, the likelihood of rescue was higher if we remained near the crash site. That was the thing to do. We could be lost in the woods forever only a few hundred yards from the plane. Who on earth would put a road through this part of the jungle?

It all spelled out the truth that Bill really didn't think they'd find us in the search. We had just that same morning seen the awful result of a spotter who had flown right across a downed plane. How he could have missed it, a huge plane like that out in the open, was anybody's guess. The mixture of fall colours and the colouration of the plane had blended sufficiently for him to fail to see it. It had still been there next spring when the searchers finally located it, with the bodies frozen. The message tagged to the joy sticks said, "We saw you at 500 feet. Could read your letters. Why didn't you see us?"

The chilling truth was that we would never be found. I tried to reason with Bill, but he was adamant that he must try to find the road. He assured me he would still be within calling distance. With his broken leg and his severe burns, but with a resolute sense of purpose and armed with the rightness of his decision, Bill struggled off up the slope. Although I couldn't see him I could hear that he obviously wasn't making much headway. Although his language did become colourful for awhile, he never mentioned the pain or the floppy leg but he did describe the obstacles blocking his way, with words that brought a pain-inducing flutter of a smile to my face. That was the first hint of fun I'd had for quite a while. Inadvertently, his courageous effort was a real tonic. It broke up the monotony, created a very worthwhile diversion, and dispelled the animosity which had developed over the time-keeping. He wasn't trying to save just himself. He was hoping to get help for me too.

"Do you want an axe?" I shouted knowing there wasn't an axe within five miles.

"Now you ask me," was Bill's response from 20 yards away. He had spent five minutes fighting every inch of the way through branches, fallen trees, and dense undergrowth which all tore at his open wounds.

The mood had changed. There wasn't any direct reason for feeling more optimistic, but Bill's move had just done something very positive about our situation. I lost my fear of him vanishing over the horizon because his moves were pitifully slow. I could imagine the pain he was bringing on himself as branches cracked and his comments became even more scathing, but he fought on courageously.

From some 60 yards or so, Bill suddenly hollered, "Well, what do you know? They're up there again." This time, even I heard something. Then the noise faded and the silence returned.

Bill had stopped trying to force his way through the undergrowth, but whether out of exhaustion or awareness of the futility of his actions, I didn't know.

I shouted out to ask if he was coming back down and in a resigned tone he replied "No. I'll just hang on out here for a bit." I didn't know if he had fallen or what was happening but did know I couldn't do anything about it.

Another eternity went by. I had run out of worthwhile things to think of. I went through another paroxysm of shock, but for some unknown reason couldn't muster the strength to worry about it. I fell still again. I seemed to float for a while although I remained conscious.

Before I actually heard anything, I jolted to an upright sitting position with all senses switched off except listening.

Yes, there was a sound. No, two different sounds from different directions. It wasn't Bill. Something. Then I recognized it. Away in the distance that beautiful rhythmical thump of the rotor on a helicopter and simultaneously, in the opposite direction, crushing, branch-breaking people! I looked up, but couldn't even see the opening where the sky should be. I put up my sticky fingers to pry open my lower eyelid and there it was. Blue sky, dark blue now. Great! It was time for action, decision, logic.

"Hey Bill, there's somebody coming," I yelled.

The faint voice of his return was, "Yah, I hear 'em."

I had a momentary concern that we might still be missed. Holding my bloated face, I maintained a little peephole and, forgetting pain, forced myself to my feet. I hobbled, stumbled, and dragged my way back the 60 feet to the plane, or to what was left of the plane. All I could discern was a patch of white. I lunged on to that inclined section of the wing and sprawled myself across it on my back. The beat of the rotors was coming closer and closer. Somewhere to my right, unmistakably, voices of human beings crashed through the underbrush. The rotor beat was right above me now. They must see me. I waved my arms in what I felt was the direction of the rescue craft.

I knew a sudden moment of panic as my pain-racked mind gave a last nightmarish thought, "What if there's gas in the tank in this wing? What if the rotors start the fire again with me on the tank?"

As if in answer to my fears, the chopper moved slowly away and as its sound receded I heard the most beautiful sound of a gasping, spluttering, human stumble through the undergrowth.

My second smile since the crash came when a wheezing voice yelled, "My

God, there's one alive."

With all the formality of a Stanley – Dr. Livingstone encounter I said, "I'm Blair."

"Hi, I'm Lloyd Dean. I'm a first-aid man. You're going to be all right."

My swollen eyes hid the contradicting doubt shown by his facial expression. Years of training had forced him to say those encouraging words.

"The pilot's way up there," I pointed with my grotesque hand.

Lloyd shouted to his partner following him through the bush, "You take the one up the hill to the right."

He gently covered me up with his jacket and just kept talking to me until the stretcher arrived. How he kept on talking and hid his grief I'll never know. Behind me, three feet away in the rubble and ashes, one of the charred bodies that Dean could see was that of his close friend and fellow ambulance partner, John Craig.

By habit, I asked, "What's the time, Lloyd?"

It was 4:56 p.m. In less time than it had taken me to run a marathon we had been found.

Thanks to the courage, determination, and training of a dedicated search group, most of them volunteers, we had miraculously been rescued in just 3-1/2 hours – almost a lifetime.

CHAPTER 6
4:56 Rescue

Calm settled on my mind as if all fear had vanished with the arrival of the rescuers. I was content to lie back and let events take place, confident that those around had all the answers that would ensure my safe and speedy transportation to hospital.

The silence of the forest was invaded by reassuring sounds of activity. A hundred yards away, Albert Comfort and Ron Krowchuk were busily clearing away underbrush and small trees to produce a landing spot for the helicopter hovering above. Simultaneously, others of the rescue force were hacking a narrow trail from that spot to our crash site and also a trail to Bill's location further up the hill.

A buzz of activity went on around me as several rescuers quickly planned my transportation needs. Each member's muted voice still strained with the recent exertion of the half-mile struggle down through the dense brush from the gravel roadway that Ron had identified so accurately from the air. Caring hands loaded me onto the stretcher and gently padded and strapped me to the frame for evacuation by foot along the tortuous recently hewn trail.

The narrowness of the cleared trail dictated that there was room for only one person to carry each end of the stretcher. To try to accommodate my gory scalp,

I had been loaded on the stretcher with my feet protruding off the farther end. Unfortunately, this placed the injured left ankle level with the handles that the stretcher bearer was holding at that end. As he led and pulled the stretcher up that steep path, the bearer at that end kept bumping into my foot provoking reactions from me that left no doubt that I was fully consciousness. I was vocal. That was the longest 70 yards I can ever remember. I thought we'd never make it. In view of some of my remarks, my rescuers would have been justified in dumping me half way!

The helicopter had considerable trouble setting down at the hastily cleared landing zone and as Bill and I arrived almost simultaneously on our stretchers, the pilot realized that he would have to take us out one at a time. As Bill was adamant that I should go first, I was loaded into the small chopper. My smelly and unsightly head was just inches from the pilot's elbow.

Takeoff, though noisy, was from my perspective, uneventful; I later learned that the early evening air currents played havoc with the craft's maneuverability and lift. Once up and away, the flight into Cranbrook, only 12 miles away, took just that number of minutes, although it seemed an eternity. I kept asking the pilot, "Are we nearly there yet?" and each time he reassured me as to the progress of our flight.

"Just over the overpass at the north end of town, " he said, keeping up his ongoing report.

I suspect he kept talking just so that I wouldn't ask the same dumb question, and perhaps he thought that by continuing to talk he might help to keep this frizzled creature alive until he landed and got someone else to take the smelly cargo off his hands.

Finally, I could feel the craft descending and he informed me that we were just landing at the hospital. I could clearly visualize the circle of concrete with its big yellow letter "H" located on the well-kept lawns near the Emergency entrance at Cranbrook and District Hospital.

Even before the rotors stopped turning I could hear anxious voices, and hands snatched open the back door of the aircraft.

My hearing was sharpened by concern and accentuated by the absence of sight. I could make out the distinctive sound of the wheels of a stretcher trolley and staff running alongside.

With gentleness, yet urgency, I was extracted from the body of the helicopter onto the waiting trolley and whisked through the cold evening air. The wheels rattled as we mounted the short ribbed ramp into the entrance-way leading to the Emergency Department. Seeing nothing, I was aware of the changing smells which indicated my route through the small waiting area then into the sterile cleanliness of the Emergency room I'd visited so often in the years I'd worked at that hospital. I could sense the curtains and felt the silent passage of the trolley as it moved onto the rubberized anti-static flooring. It was 5:30 p.m. and the tranquility of an autumn Saturday evening was about to be disturbed. It would be transformed to a scene of urgent endeavour. Many of those present had been my co-workers and close friends. It was not an easy time for anyone in that room.

The myth of physicians' lazy weekends, days off, and after hours leisure was again exploded. Dr. David Lenz was the general practitioner on call for his clinic that evening. One glimpse inside that emergency room finished his hopes of attending the Sailing Club dinner that evening. His confident stride faltered before he reached my side. My bloated features made me unrecognizable. Difficult though it was, he managed to remove from his mind the thoughts that he and I had raced against each other just the previous weekend in the final Regatta for windsurfers.

It was reassuring to hear his calm young voice direct the team that held together the threads of my life and hear him request additional help from a wide range of other experts. I was not aware of a great deal of pain then, as they had quickly started me on pain-relieving injections, but I pleaded for a drink. The dehydration resulting from hours of fluid loss had caught up with me and I felt certain just one little drink would be enough to satisfy my raging thirst. Dave firmly insisted that I couldn't have any fluids. He found the time and patience to explain that I'd be needing surgery as soon as possible. Although this explanation was logical, I was furious that I couldn't even get a sip.

The team gathered. I heard a myriad of voices, many familiar to me, and others unknown. I asked someone to phone my close friend, Bill Gordon, as there were one or two odds and ends that required his urgent assistance.

The admitting personnel scooted in and out, trying to satisfy the bureaucratic requirements by filling in the appropriate forms with details of date of birth, next-of-kin, address, and my medical insurance number. From all corners of the city and surrounding countryside emerged general surgeons, orthopaedic surgeons, radiologists, laboratory technologists, radiographers, extra nurses, internists, operating room staff, and housekeeping staff to clean up the mess I was making.

It was a Saturday I'll never forget – a time to remember the countless numbers who care for the needs of others.

CHAPTER 7
6:05 Disturbed Chef

6:05 p.m. found Bill Gordon indulging in one of his great leisure pastimes, gourmet cooking. The menu for that Saturday evening meal was Boeuf Bourguignon and the strident unwelcome ringing of his kitchen phone came at a crucial moment in his culinary preparations.

"Inopportune" would have been the polite way of describing the disturbance and indescribable the muttering as he wiped his hands on his "I Love Gourmet Cooking" apron. With uncharacteristic briskness, and his Aberdeen guttural "r" rolling, his displeasure was clearly recognizable by the brevity of his response, "Bill Gordon here."

Accustomed to periodic contact from the hospital, a penalty of his position as Chief Regional Laboratory Technologist, Bill's eyebrows instantly arched with annoyance when he heard the words, "Hello, Bill. It's Admitting at the hospital."

His sharp intake of breath was a precursor to his expectation to impatiently explain again that one of his laboratory staff was on call for any emergencies. The breath blew out like a deflating balloon as he heard the next few words. A million images flashed before his eyes in response to one short sentence. "Your friend, Blair Farish, has been in an airplane crash. He's in Emergency and is asking for you."

Without a moment's hesitation he responded concisely with, "I'll be right there." He slammed the phone into its cradle.

The Boeuf Bourguignon got the cold shoulder and was left to frizzle on its own. Not even stopping to wash his hands, he grabbed his car keys, shouting to his wife, Maureen, as he dashed out the door. Giving her only scant intimation of the awful news, he promised to phone when he had time. With purposeful disregard for the speed limit, he arrived at the hospital in four minutes. Parking askew in the Emergency Department's "No Parking" zone, he defied the world at large to mention this indiscretion.

His stride slowed slightly as he saw the faces of the Admitting personnel, and their silence gave him mute forewarning of what was beyond the frosted doors of the Emergency Department. Most of the permanent staff of the hospital were well aware of the close friendship between Bill and me and their empathy was evident as they saw him enter those doors.

He took a deep breath to control his feelings and quietly slipped into the throng of professionals, each busily engaged in vital activities around the bed. Even with almost thirty years of hospital experience, he was unprepared for what he saw. He looked at the other vacant beds in the Unit to see if he could possibly be mistaken. At that time, mine was the only body there, but my watermelon-sized face and head and bloated features made my face unrecognizable even to my best friend. With courage and calm dug from the deep reserves of inner strength, Bill quickly realized that I could not see him. His unmistakable Highland brogue broke through the cacophony of sound around me.

"Hello, Blair. This is Bill." With characteristic understatement and appropriate humour for the occasion, he said, "I see you've got yourself in a wee spot of bother."

I was delighted to hear that familiar voice.

"Hello, Bill. Sorry to drag you out from whatever you were doing."

"Och, I wasn't up to much anyway. Just doing a spot of cooking."

"Aye, I've been doing a bit of that myself, you'll notice." The levity of this little exchange was a tonic for all in attendance.

Orders and instructions were repeated to ensure that they had been heard correctly and thus avoid misinterpretation: "Intravenous #16 intra-catheter left arm running wide open. Start Ringers lactate with #18 in right forearm. Demerol 20 mg intravenous. Apply saline cloths to burned areas. Lab tech Blood work drawn. CBC, HCT, electrolytes, and cross-match for 2 units of blood. Blood pressure 100/60. Gravol 25 mg intravenous to lessen nausea."

"Well, Bill, I have a couple of little jobs for you."

Amidst all this technical jargon and turmoil, I'd had time to assimilate my thoughts and recited a list of chores. Even if my agenda was at odds with that of the staff, they at least found out that I was thinking lucidly.

"My Subaru is still out at the airport. The keys are under the back seat and my flight briefcase is there. I'd be anxious that nobody took that because I'll be needing it again. You could just park the car at your house, Bill, for a week or so until I get back out of here. Then there's my dog, Yogi. You'll have to pick her up and take her to the kennels for a few days. She'll not like that very much, but she'll know I'll be coming back. And then you'll have to tell Diana, my secretary, that I won't be in Monday and my physiotherapy clinic will have to be closed for a few days. Get in touch with Ian and Craig, and let them know I'll be in dock for a little while. Now make sure you don't alarm them, and above all I don't want them in to see me while I'm not looking my best."

Getting this load of instructions off my chest seemed to tire me out more than I'd expected. As I fell quiet, I heard in the recurrent brisk medical orders around me that everything was "stat." This was the medical jargon dictating that the job had to be done immediately or sooner.

It dawned on me that things weren't going as well as my impatient nature would have chosen. I was not yet showing any signs of getting better. In a hesitant and uncustomary coarse voice, I finally managed to express something that I had been purposely suppressing, but my tone betrayed the dread of my true suspicions.

"Oh, and Bill, let's get something quite clear. I do not want my mother, in Scotland, to be informed of this wee mishap unless, unless things go badly." The pauses accentuated and proved my fears.

Staunch in his friendship and ever ready to oblige, he answered that he'd attend to all these matters directly. He, too, had been smitten with a raspiness of voice as he responded to my final request.

It was as if a huge burden had been taken off my shoulders and the confidence that my wishes would be attended to allowed me to bring my attention to more mundane things that related to my immediate physical well-being. Results of various tests were beginning to speed back.

The inability to see brought a whole new challenge to communication. I was impressed by the readiness of all around to introduce themselves verbally prior to embarking on whatever measure was next involved. It was reassuring to hear those voices and names linked, to help me cope with each new procedure as it happened. Dr. Dave Lenz got my undivided attention as he patiently explained what was happening and what I should expect to feel as he inserted a Foley catheter.

"It'll be a little bitty uncomfortable as it passes up into your bladder," and his warning preceded an excruciating jab which made me forget all other aches and pains for just a second.

The catheter made possible accurate measurement of the outflow and helped in calculating total fluid loss from my body.

About this time, I realized that I had a conspicuous absence of clothing but it seemed an inappropriate moment to make a fuss about nudity.

With all this activity going on, the clock had ticked its way through another forty minutes. The helicopter had again taken off and returned to its temporary landing area near the crash site. After a brisk loading and speedy return to the hospital landing pad my severely burned and injured pilot was brought through the Emergency doors to the adjoining bed.

The commotion broke up the concentration around my bed. As he wheeled past, his glance took in the numerous tubes going in and out of my body, and his encouraging words were again a tonic.

"Hi there, old partner. Hanging in there, are you?"

I recognized the husky voice and with that inner reserve of strength we all unknowingly have, I replied, "Sure, no problem, Bill. How're you making out yourself?"

"Just fine," he answered, which we both knew was a lie but again it helped boost us both.

From an unknown location, still more staff appeared to help cope with the new challenge of yet another seriously injured patient. Amongst their other calculations to assess the severity of our burns, estimates of the depth of the burns were being tabulated.

First degree were areas of superficial skin damage which would regenerate and clear up without need for replacement by grafting. Second and third degree deep burns would need urgent grafting to minimize continuing fluid loss and to provide a matrix of replacement skin and scar tissue to create healing, thus covering the underlying tissues. Body surface area can be calculated estimating a whole arm to be 9% of the body surface area, a whole leg as 2 x 9 or 18%, the trunk as 4 x 9 or 36% and the head itself as 9%. Using this rule of nines method, both of us were estimated to have approximately 30% total body area burns.

Had our accidents happened 50 years earlier, even with the best medical care available our chances of survival with 30% burns would have been slim. With the advance of medical science, skill, and early hospitalization in up-to-date Burn Units, it is now possible to survive with even up to 90% surface area burns.

Shortly after the other survivor's arrival, another new dose of pain killing drugs was administered through an add-a-line sidetrack on the intravenous drip into my arm. I was wheeled away to X-ray for pictures of suspected skeletal trauma. Views were taken from multiple angles to visualize head, neck, chest, spine, pelvis, hips, knees, feet, and ankles. I'd made my provisional diagnosis some four hours earlier and was not reluctant to expound on this to anyone who might listen. There was, at best, a polite murmur of concurrence. The answer, "Could well be," was hardly the enthusiastic gratitude I'd expected for laying my professional judgment on the line in this important case!

While it might have appeared to be of little comfort to me to be right, I did gloat immodestly when the X-rays confirmed my guess as to the skeletal diagnosis. The lumbar spine fracture appeared stable and certainly there was no sign of nerve damage from that spinal level involving the lower limbs, so it was felt that the time was right to do something about the dislocated left ankle.

As I was already plied with analgesics to kill the pain emanating from a myriad of sources, my foot was skillfully maneuvered into a better anatomical position and supported with a plaster of Paris splint to prevent me from undoing the good work. This manipulation was an interim correction pending a surgical repair at a more opportune time.

My vehement demands for "a drink of anything" were all to no avail. Doctors and nurses can be stubborn people.

Bill Gordon's unobtrusive but constant presence was confirmed by his welcome response, "I'd slip you a wee Scotch in that intravenous line if I could, but they'd get awful mad at me."

The loss of body fluid, the ongoing energy expenditure to fight off pain and anxiety, and all the bustle of activities around me were finally taking their toll and I started slipping in and out of consciousness. Those dedicated workers continued to pour copious amounts of fluid into my veins to try to make up the shortfall caused by the hours when body fluid had oozed out through the burns. My fluid imbalance was life threatening at this time. Had I been able to consume thousands of calories per day I couldn't have kept up with the loss of energy caused by the burns. Over the next three weeks I was to lose 40 pounds from my 175 pounds marathon-trim physique.

As I was lulled into oblivion, the work went on around me. In one of my few lucid moments, Dave gently told me that I should be moved to a specialist burn unit. Despite my protests that I would be just fine staying in Cranbrook, arrangements were made to transport both survivors by air to the Foothills Hospital in Calgary.

Bill Gordon finally returned home at 10 p.m. He, too, had lived a lifetime since he'd abandoned his Boeuf Bourguignon. In the half hour after seeing me off at the airport, he picked up my car, collected my dog, and returned home stunned, sad, and with a feeling of disconsolate helplessness. He'd collected what remained of my charred clothing and personal effects. In a fit of desperation and need for something purposeful to occupy his mind, he absorbed himself in trying to clean up my blood stained, scorched running shoes.

He worked with furor on this chore, hoping to exorcise the dread from his mind. The prognosis was one of meagre chance for survival. Somehow it seemed that by salvaging that grimy pair of Nikes he might improve the odds on my future return to running. He kept at the thankless task for a disproportionate time.

He was not alone in his strength-sapped frame of mind and body. Dr. David Lenz was suffering similar distress. Ten years in medicine had inured him to the demanding switches of environment from hospital trauma scenarios to the expectations of home life and bouncing small children. That night, however, David's return home was with heavy heart and a slow tread.

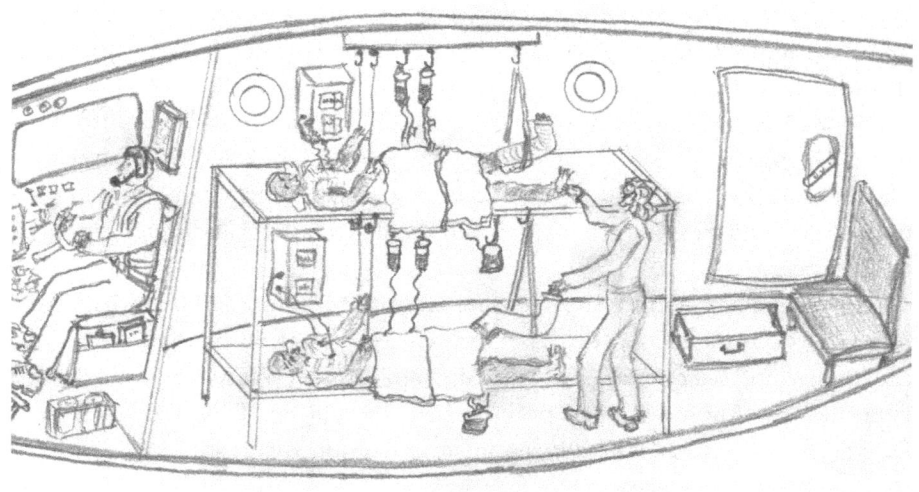

CHAPTER 8
10:50 Flying High

The extent of our burns had been determined at 30% of our body surface area, and there were further concerns of possible inhalation burns into the lungs. Dr. Lenz and his team of local specialists had decided that our best hopes for survival and future care would necessitate our immediate transfer to the specialist Burn Unit in Calgary Foothills Hospital in Alberta.

Although this involved using another province's hospital facilities, it was less than half the distance to British Columbia's major burn unit in Vancouver, almost 600 miles away from Cranbrook. This choice of Calgary would also make the travel for visiting friends more feasible, and was the usual choice for patients in the Columbia/Kootenay regions who required more specialized medical care than was available in the local hospitals.

Having communicated with the Foothills Hospital Burn Unit to ensure their ability to admit two more patients, the search was then on to locate a plane and pilot to transport us.

A twin engine eight seater plane was finally traced through Emergency Services Registrar and flown in from Osoyoos. Thankfully, some pilots let their names be held on a standby list for just such mercy flights.

When it became evident that the two burned transfer patients would require a nurse in attendance, Pat Strang instantly agreed to accompany the patients on their flight to Calgary. Many years of experience as a nurse in the Emergency Department of Cranbrook and other hospitals made her an excellent choice for the demanding job involved. She'd been in attendance during much of the four-hour stay of her two charges in the Emergency Department, and so was fully informed of their medical status and of their anticipated needs during the one-hour flight.

Additional time was needed for the transfer to the airport by ambulance, and further unavoidable delay occurred in removing seats from the plane so that it could accommodate the two stretchers. I was in a coma, sporadically alternating from peaceful and still to violent and flailing, to the extent that I had to be strapped down.

Equipped with a wide range of potent medication to cope with any anticipated emergencies, Pat set off with the unenviable task of keeping us alive during the hour's bumpy flight over Canada's highest mountain range in the black of night.

None of his suffering, anguish, and trauma could deter Bill Quilley from reverting to his longtime flying enthusiasm. With his head just behind the pilot's seat back, Bill carried on an animated chatter with the pilot.

"You'll be taking Victor 08, I guess," said Bill, his mind readily analyzing the flight path that he would have piloted over to Calgary.

"And I guess you'll be going at 14,000 feet," he added. And so the conversation continued.

On the premise that it's not advisable to disagree with your patient tied down to a stretcher, the pilot continued to at least acknowledge Bill's instructions. "Pretty close, my friend," replied the pilot. "It's good to have you in the right-hand seat even though you're horizontal."

The flight was predictably turbulent as the plane passed over the towering craggy peaks and 5,000 foot deep splits of valleys.

The 9,000 foot high backbone of the Rockies took a heavy toll on Pat and her two charges. Changing inclines of position during takeoff, altered pressures, and bumps and dips of flight created havoc with her patients. Working conditions were far from ideal as Pat was wedged into the cramped space between the stretchers.

As my face and head continued to swell Pat had to cut the bandages to lessen their constricting pressure. She was kept busy with constantly monitoring my racing heart rate and alarming blood pressure, and keeping the intravenous drips flowing as the bags of life-giving fluid swung precariously on their temporary hooks on the aircraft ceiling.

It was a night she'd never forget. Her contribution that night was typical of the oft-unrecognized dedication, valour, and skills of her profession.

Yet another mercy mission complete, the pilot brought his charges into a safe landing at Calgary where a local ambulance team swiftly transferred us to the Foothills Emergency Department.

During the first short while in the Foothills Emergency Unit, Pat helped by supplying the local team with accurate history and details of previous treatments. Gradually, as a new team swung into high gear and took full charge, she left to face the emptiness of a sleepless night in a staff quiet-room, awaiting a commercial flight back to Cranbrook the next morning.

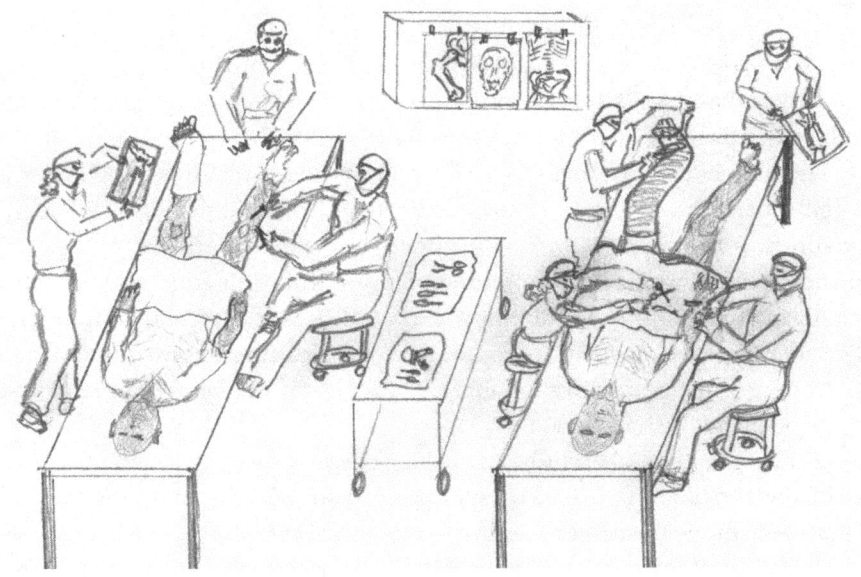

CHAPTER 9
23:29 Saturday Night Fever

During that half-hour before midnight, Saturday, October 1st, 1983, patient #591671 was somewhat less than his normal talkative self. I was conscious but noticeably feeling the effects of a hectic day. The flight over the Rockies and subsequent transfer by ambulance had all taken its toll. Because of the state of the burns on my hands and wrists, the admitting clerk clipped the customary identification wrist band on my uninjured right ankle. During the next three months of my stay, this name tag would be examined numerous times each day by different visiting staff and doctors.

Had I been more aware of my environment, I would have been alarmed at the number of individuals around my bed. An admitting assessment was performed by a team of doctors, nurses, and support personnel. They initiated a complete recheck of vital signs, blood pressure, pulse, respiration, and numerous other tests to supplement and update the information that had been brought with me from Cranbrook Hospital.

This new analysis included further X-rays, laboratory tests, cardiographs, and requests for other specialist evaluations. A flurry of activity continued around me as residents in orthopaedics, plastics, internal medicine, and anesthetics contributed their knowledge in determining recommended action appropriate to my status.

Dr. George Hamilton, senior resident in Plastics, appeared just minutes after my arrival. His careful, detailed assessment of my burned areas gave no indication that it was almost midnight on a Saturday night. Hospitals and their staff evidently work on a 24-hour-a-day basis.

The fingers on both hands were by then swollen like tight skinned sausages, recently barbecued. The skin had been stretched to its elastic limits and ongoing swelling was causing pressure on the underlying veins and arteries. Compression of these vessels was likely to occlude the blood flow with consequent probable loss of my fingers. It was imperative that a release be performed immediately. This technique is known as "escharotomy," the opening of skin and fascia.

George explained the rationale and urgency for this procedure and briefly described what he had to do.

"I'll have to just make a little slit on each of your fingers to lessen the pressure and allow the blood to flow through to your tissues. We haven't time to put you under anesthetic for this procedure so I'm afraid it's going to be pretty sore."

I was again impressed that he had bothered to be so thorough in his explanation to me, so I gave my unreserved authorization. I had every confidence in him.

"Well, George, if it's got to be done, let's get at it," I said, including myself as part of the team.

I hadn't fully appreciated the implications of my participation in this procedure, and even with the forewarning given, was not ready for the scalpel as the first careful stroke split the skin on the side of the little finger. A brief scream left my lips before nature found its way to limit my suffering and I passed out.

In the subsequent much quieter atmosphere, George was able to perform a required release of pressure on other fingers. He then continued his thorough analysis of the extent of the burns, documenting the areas of second and third degree skin loss and making predictions on which areas would require urgent grafting.

For some time I drifted in and out of consciousness, waking up enough to answer, with surprising clarity, questions from various staff as they investigated my injuries and state of health. A resident in orthopaedics reevaluated the areas of skeletal damage and concurred that my spinal compression fracture was stable, but that further repair was needed on the fracture dislocation of the left ankle. It was imperative that this next surgical step be undertaken as soon as possible and he, too, was thorough as he explained his plan and elicited my verbal authorization to go ahead. Months later, reading a copy of the hospital charts, I found a scrawled "X" that was witnessed as my consent for surgery.

With the extent of evident facial burns, there was considerable likelihood that there had also been damage done by inhalation of smoke and heat. The resident in anesthetics was next on the list of investigators. Although there was evidence of some burns inside the mouth, this initial examination did not reveal any significant damage into the windpipe or lungs.

During that first two hours of this range of examinations and tests, five separate further dosages of morphine and other pain suppressant drugs were administered. The record sheet of intravenous solution intake compared to urine output, with resultant balance of fluids absorbed, read like some unwanted accounting statement. The dreaded bottom line, in red, showed an undesirable deficit. I was still losing body fluid through the burns at a dangerous rate.

Various tubes brought much needed fluids to my body, and to minimize my nausea and retching a nasogastric tube was inserted to drain fluids from my stomach. Oxygen was also applied via nasal tongs.

The surgical repair of my left ankle was scheduled for 2 a.m. Sunday. In the interim the Burn Unit staff attended for their first look at their future full-time client. Their function was to use their special skills in assisting with an initial debridement of the burned areas. This involved removing the obviously destroyed areas of skin and patches of clothing that had been burned onto the flesh. In my usual stubborn manner I informed the resident anesthetist that there was nothing wrong with my breathing. My voice was hoarse from the dryness and the inhalation of the fumes earlier in the day, but I was still naively unaware of the life-threatening extent of my injuries or unprepared even to consider this possibility. I felt that my presence in the Foothills Hospital was synonymous with survival.

I knew everyone around me was busily contributing to my welfare, but certainly did not realize that I was offering my last few coherent statements prior to a ten-day period of inexplicable loss of consciousness.

Perhaps this was my body's natural protective reaction to the trauma. This loss of consciousness provoked prolonged and diligent investigation by yet a wider range of world-renowned specialists in that hospital. They had a challenge on their hands brought on by much more than just a Saturday Night Fever. I had been in Calgary only two hours!

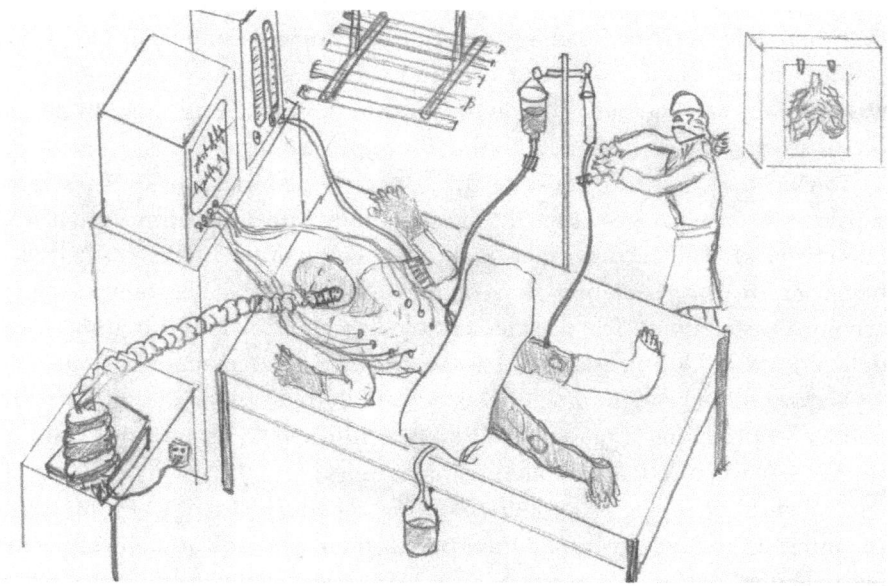

CHAPTER 10
Glasgow Scale 0 – 15

Frequently, during my life, there have been times when those around me wished for my silence. As that Saturday night stretched into an all-night session of activity, my last minutes of conscious awareness of my surroundings were fast dwindling.

A battery of further tests was performed, including further X-rays of my left ankle and my spine. A review of these by the orthopaedic team, and more consultations with internists, anesthetists, and other specialists, confirmed that surgical correction could be performed without anticipated threat to my other body systems. The extensive plastic surgery that I needed would have to be postponed till a later date.

Surgery at such an unreasonable hour must have been the last straw in my body's tolerance to outside interference. Although the ankle surgery lasted only 30 minutes, it involved the relocation of joints in their proper positions and repair of damaged ligaments, thorough sluicing out of the last remnants of Kootenay soil, sewing up and encasing the limb in a toe-to-knee plaster cast.

After surgery was completed, I was moved to the Trauma Unit. The anesthetic team decided to leave the endotracheal tube in place as there was still suspicion about the severity of damage to the throat and windpipe from smoke inhalation.

A new challenge, in addition to the existing multiple damage to my various body surfaces, was my reluctance to regain the expected level of consciousness following my visit to the operating room.

The great hangover after the middle-of-the-night theatre episode was to last for ten days. My only knowledge of these times comes from the detailed records written by a long list of specially-trained staff who cared for my pressing needs. For this period in the Trauma Unit on the tenth floor of the Foothills Hospital, my body was entrusted to a group of medical personnel who are often unseen by their patient, and so unknown by name. Sadly, this also means they were seldom thanked for their great work. As I hovered between life and death, I did my best to be obstructive and try to undo much of their good work.

Most of the time I sank into blessed oblivion but occasionally clawed my way to the surface with as little care and thought for those around me as a drowning man might have in his frantic search for air.

The measuring system used to record the depths to which I was sinking was the numerical Glasgow Scale of consciousness. It was ironically appropriate that they made use of this system to keep tabs on the fighting Scot in that bed. The use of graded levels was established by a medical team in that great homeland city whose name it bears. The Glasgow scale runs from zero to 15, covering a range from the deepest levels of unconsciousness to normal. It was a yardstick that permitted those around me to tolerate my many pain-induced antisocial actions and words.

My misbehaviour was summed up succinctly by one exasperated nurse's writings on my chart, "He must be feeling better. There were less obscenities today."

The ongoing battle with this recalcitrant patient began in the Intensive Care Unit at 4:40 a.m. that Sunday morning on his return from the operating room. I was initially kept on heavy dosages of morphine and Pavulon to diminish pain response and induce deep sedation to lessen the probability that I'd crash around and cause more damage to my existing injuries. My windpipe was intubated with a large breathing tube connected to an automatic ventilator. My airway was thus considered protected, lessening the possibility of choking or swallowing. A nasogastric tube allowed suction of any accumulating gastric material and minimized the likelihood of vomiting.

Needles inserted into the veins of both arms led to plastic bags and bottles of blood plasma which had been matched to my grouping. Saline drips were maintained to infuse fluids to compensate for loss through the open burn sites. A catheter was in place to allow an uninterrupted flow from the bladder and facilitate measurement recording and observation of colour, and thus help in assessment of kidney function.

Head, arms, hands, and legs were bandaged with gauze coverings and the lower part of the left leg had a plaster of Paris cast to the toes. The eyes, which were swollen shut, were covered with moist dressings to try to soften the dried-up cracking eyelids.

A further array of wires and leads connected me to heart monitors and blood pressure recording instruments. Consequently, the end of the bed was a maze of oscilloscopes, screens, and resuscitation equipment. All these items had warning bells and lights. Overhead, a four-foot-long infrared heat trough maintained the optimum air temperature. It was at an uncomfortable level for the staff working and visiting that unit, but minimized my requirement to produce body heat.

Nurse Mary was a veteran of three years in the Trauma Unit, a work area where the stress and mental anguish of the job were not conducive to professional longevity. Burnout regularly took its toll of staff.

Although she had only two-and-a-half hours until the end of her shift at 7 a.m., her work, on that occasion, was uninterrupted by my body reaction, as my level of consciousness was established at three on the Glasgow Scale. This score had been determined by three factors: the absence of reaction to light when she flashed her pen light on the pupil, no response to deep pressure on the toes or the prodding of non injured areas, and no evident attempts at verbal response.

It was a demanding regime, trying to carry out the long list of contradictory postoperative orders. To minimize the likelihood of pressure sores, I had to be turned from side-to-side each hour. In my unconscious state this was appropriately known as "log rolling." Simultaneously, as if by some feat of contortion, my head was to be constantly elevated, and my recently casted left leg kept above hip level. A cartoonist would have shown me tied up inches from the ceiling with the little caption, "Everything elevated."

In addition to all these passive gymnastics, 28% oxygen was administered; Ringers lactate replacement fluid was run in via the intravenous drips at 375 cc's per hour; morphine was injected half-hourly into the add-a-line side entry on the IV tube; Gravol was ordered if I was nauseated; temperature and pulse were constantly monitored; Vitamin C, multivitamins, Valium and Pavulon were given; urine output was observed; blood cultures and match were done and six units of blood were held for emergency use.

In her spare time, Mary was also required to spread Flamazine ointment to the deeply burned areas of the body and Polysporin to less damaged areas of the face. As an afterthought, orders included, "Routine burn dressing." To give this busy nurse a bit of a break the "NIL P.O." order told her she did not have to feed me by mouth. It was lonely, high-pressure, and thankless work. Her only hope of reward was that one day the results' of her care would be seen in a walking, talking, laughing human being.

She hardly had time to think that her patient might have a home, a family, a joyous busy life somewhere. She had no idea what her patient normally looked like, as the swollen, crimson, scorched skin distorted the facial features unrecognizably. She knew only that I was 45 and had been in a plane crash 15 hours earlier on the other side of the Rockies.

For those few fleeting hours she might well have enjoyed the silence. During the next ten days outbursts of anguished vocal and physical violence, uncharacteristic of the patient's normally temperate speech and conduct, assaulted her.

Her forgiveness could only occur commensurate to her understanding and interpretation of the vacillating score on the Glasgow Scale.

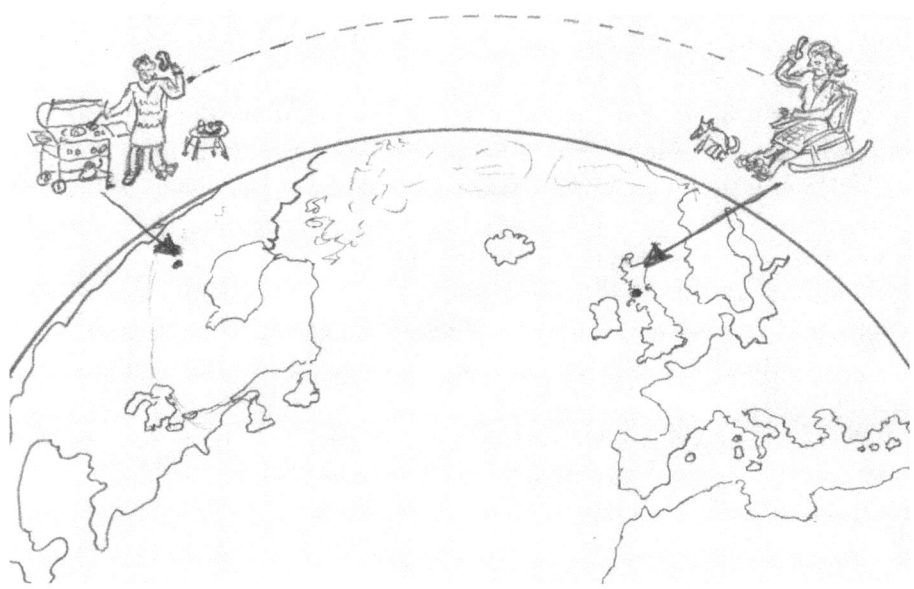

CHAPTER 11
2:10 The Speed of Bad News

Sunday, October 2nd, 1983, dawned crisp and clear, showing promise of another glorious fall day. Indian Summer was a welcome bonus, staving off the inevitable arrival of winter.

In contrast to her normally hectic days as a school vice principal, Evelyne Craig always looked forward to her Sunday mornings as a gift of leisure. Unrushed and undisturbed were the trademarks of those luxurious, slow-starting days. Even her two dogs, a sheltie and a schipperke, knew to be patient on these mornings while Evelyne lingered over her second cup of tea and a good novel.

The ringing of the phone at 10:30 that morning portended bad news. Even before she answered its ring, Evelyne was less than pleased with the disturbance. She had already decided that this intrusion into her peaceful state had better be important. Many years of teaching had inured her to accept viewpoints and habits that were at odds with her own, and had trained her to tolerate such interruptions. The caller's need of some information elicited her normally pleasant response, tinged with an unmistakable hint that the enquiry could have waited until Monday.

After several minutes of discussion, the speaker jolted Evelyne into full wakefulness by saying, "I suppose you've heard that dreadful news about Blair's plane crash? He's in Calgary. Do you think we should send a card?"

Flying and Toastmasters were two special interests that Evelyne and I shared. Our enthusiasm for both these pursuits over the previous four or five years had instilled mutual respect and a close friendship.

The news came as a terrible shock. She was incensed that the caller had mentioned the tragic accident as an afterthought, having prattled on about some inconsequential trivia.

At her immediate change of voice, the dogs slunk to their baskets. A flurry of questions shot out at staccato rate. To add to her worry, no solid answers were forthcoming. The only available news had been derived from a local radio news broadcast earlier that morning, stating that there had been an air crash. Two people had died and two others, seriously injured, had been taken to hospital.

Thanking the caller, Evelyne hung up with uncharacteristic abruptness, her brain already racing several steps ahead.

With the kettle on for a new cup of tea and armed with paper and pencil, Evelyne embarked on what was to be an exasperating search for information. "No news is good news," was not the theme for the day.

Her first call to the local radio station brought the first rebuff, "There would, no doubt, be further information at the next news broadcast at noon."

In her persuasive manner Evelyne showed she was reluctant to wait that further hour and a half to hear the news and her tone and words obtained a rereading of the previous hour's newsline.

Evelyne jotted down the disquieting details but there was no update on the condition of the injured. The call to the airport was next, bringing about hesitant reiteration of what she already knew. Details were scant, and the officials at the airport were unable to provide names or other details of those involved.

The next communication was with the Cranbrook detachment of the R.C.M.P. The officer was firm in his insistence that no further details could be provided at that time.

Evelyne's investigations not being too productive, it was time to start using some edge on this matter. A call to the hospital proved that organization's adherence to patient confidentiality. At last, with a flash of insight, Evelyne remembered the Flying Club, but this just yielded the same details heard on the local radio station. Pressuring her contact into admitting that he was involved with the previous day's search and rescue programme, only brought down a tighter veil of secrecy. He left her with the final closure of further communication, the ultimate silencer, "No further comment on this matter."

Evelyne was stymied. She knew of my close friendship with Bill Gordon but was reluctant to call him in case she found herself as the bearer of bad news and with such scant information was reluctant to spread further the disquieting rumours.

At 11 a.m. she finally phoned Alan Conway in Calgary. Evelyne, Alan, and I formed the Toastmaster flying trio who had made a memorable Cessna flight to Phoenix, Arizona, two years earlier. The conversation was short. It was typical of two pilots relaying information of takeoff time, flight direction, wind direction, altitude, and destination. The information was given and as if Alan had been asked to calculate fuel consumption and estimated time of arrival, he replied that he'd go to the Foothills Hospital straight away and find out the answers.

Having done something positive to track down more accurate information, she then phoned Bill Gordon to see whether he knew of the accident and had any further information. She was somewhat relieved to find no answer and remembered that Bill would still be at his morning church service. Needing to do something concrete to fill in time, she drove the six miles to my country home, planning to break in if necessary, and at least feed my dog Yogi and take it back to her city home.

When she arrived in the driveway, she was surprised to see two other cars there and activity in the house. Maureen Gordon and my former wife, Pip, were already there busily tidying up the place and closing the house up for a protracted absence. The women shared their news and comforted each other as best they could. Their presence in that house was proof of the dormant reserves of strength, friendship, and commitment inherent in people around the world, needing only a spark to bring forth the glow of extra caring so evident when tragedy strikes.

For Evelyne it was reassuring to know that she was a part of the supporting group who would do everything possible to help. This team's combined efforts would prove invaluable on my long road to recovery.

Evelyne went home to await Alan's promised call. It was a distressing conversation, but accurate facts were preferable to rumours.

It was not to be a quiet Sunday for her. The news, or lack of news, was spreading fast, and just as she had been anxious to fill in the gaps in her own awareness, the sparsity of detail also concerned others in that community where I enjoyed a wide range of friends and acquaintances. As my friend, and in her capacity as the Area Governor for Toastmasters in the Kootenays, Evelyne was the obvious person to contact. Calls started coming from far and wide in addition to dozens of local anxious enquiries. Her phone was to become remembered for its busy tone on that and many subsequent days and weeks.

Evelyne took it upon herself to quash misinformation and rumours that had already started spreading regarding the severity of my injuries. Slowing down the speed of bad news and encouraging the spread of hope became the tools she used to pass many anxious days of waiting.

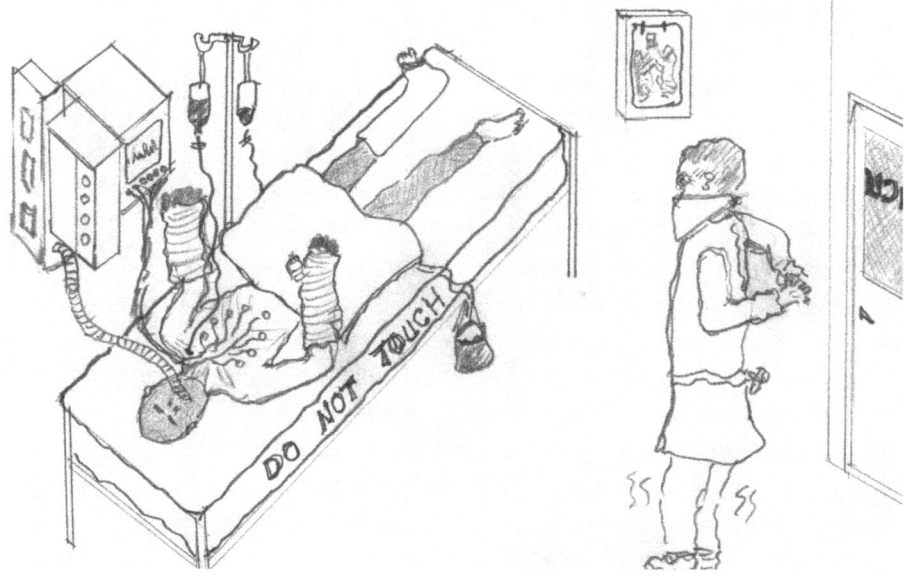

CHAPTER 12
Turbulence at 11:00 Hours

Turbulence is one of the facts of life for those who choose to fly small planes within sight of the eastern margins of the Rockies. After 500 miles of towering peaks and deep gashes plummeting to river valleys 5,000 feet below, the terrain briefly becomes the rolling country of the Alberta Foothills for 70 miles just prior to Calgary. Near that city, the winds aloft are vengeful from their roller coaster journey from the Pacific.

Flyers in the Calgary area have accepted the unpredictability of weather conditions as part of the challenge of staying aloft. To Alan Conway, coping with sudden change and bringing order to the unruly elements triggers his methodical engineer's mind.

His Sunday morning tranquility had been shattered by the 11 a.m. phone call from Cranbrook. It started a sequence of events that was marked by meticulous attention to detail. There was little need for discussion between Alan and his wife Jan, as their love and understanding of each other provided immediate acceptance of the sudden change of plans for that day. Caring for others is part of their life.

In ten minutes, Alan was at Foothills Hospital, prepared to overcome any obstacles that might block his way. His opening statement gained him access to the ward clerk in the Trauma Unit.

The well-trained front-desk staff, enured to the constant deluge of enquiries and visitors at that busy hospital, had already declined comment to numerous callers anxious to obtain information about my status.

With nary a touch of conscience, Alan stated, "I'm the next of kin to Blair Farish who was admitted here last night." He thus circumnavigated the traditional first obstacle.

Although no legal or familial ties bound us, years together in the Toastmaster organization, a shared love of flying, soccer, and hiking the high country, had formed a bond between us as close as any two brothers. Our immigrant, new-Canadian status, also added closeness.

As a recent divorcee, I had no legal adult next of kin in Canada, so Alan, in effect, became my next of kin.

Urgently needing more information about me, the staff in the Trauma Unit welcomed Alan with open arms. No better source could have appeared. Other than the patient admitting form transferred from Cranbrook Hospital and other meagre information sifted from the contents of my wallet, they knew little of my personal history.

Alan was escorted into a tiny waiting area where a nurse met him. Laurie was anxious to meet someone who knew something about the burned flyer. I was her full-time charge. It would help greatly if she could document some additional information about her patient.

Her first important task was to check Alan's credentials to ensure that he could rightfully be permitted to visit me. How much could he contribute to their piecing-together of my personality profile? In his quiet Canadian-Irish accent and the proof of his sincerity showing on his face, Alan's acceptance as part of the team took only a matter of minutes. His preparedness to be there and to obtain any further information that might be needed was the vital link that would help so much in the days ahead.

Gently, Laurie prepared Alan for his role in the team. "Blair is badly burned and won't look much like what you remember. His face is very swollen, he's all bandaged up and unconscious at the moment so won't be able to say anything to you. He's got tubes sticking in and out of him just about everywhere," she said, with a flicker of a smile to bring a little levity to this heavy conversation. "Your help can be of great value to us in his continuing treatment. While he won't be able to answer you, he may hear what you're saying, so just speak to him as you normally would. It's very important that he hears voices that he recognizes."

Although Laurie could see that Alan was anxious to get in to visit me, she knew that he was dreading what he might see. It was a bit of a relief to

Alan to have a further delay brought about by the need to answer some of her questions. He gave information as best he could about my pre-accident general health and pursuits and was delighted to see her brighten as she noted my five to eight mile daily runs and nonsmoking habit. Although she knew from the existing records that I was a physiotherapist in private practice, the unconscious body in her charge gave no indication of what accent I might eventually use in my speech. During the next 10 minutes of their conversation much information was recorded about my interests, pastimes, travels, family, and habits. These were pertinent facts that helped to build a full identity of the person underneath the charred, unrecognizable features.

Laurie explained the next step prior to entering the sterile environment that held her patient. Alan was warned to avoid touching me or the bedding or any parts of my immediate surroundings. He was also required to wear a surgical mask to minimize the risk of passing any germs from his breathing or an inadvertent cough or sneeze. He had to wear the traditional hospital long-sleeved high-necked gown, tied behind his back. This was to be the dress code for any visitor and all hospital personnel who might come into contact with me.

At first, despite his anxiety to do everything possible to ensure my safety and progress, Alan was a bit self-conscious about this paraphernalia. It was reassuring to see Laurie go through the same stringent preparation before entering the isolation unit. As a last forewarning, she mentioned that the room had to be kept at an optimum high temperature and would feel uncomfortably warm to the visitor. He should feel free to leave the room at any time if he was feeling distressed by the heat.

As her hand reached the door she paused. A twinkle came into her eye as she gave a last snippet of information. "It gets a little smelly, too, sometimes!"

With dread, Alan realized that there was no more time for preparation. He steeled himself for whatever might be ahead and followed her into the room. He hadn't far to walk. Even before he took in the unbelievable sight of my features, he was shocked by the conglomeration of apparatus and the lack of space. While the cramming-in of so much equipment made for speedy access to urgently required items, Alan had envisioned more space. Perhaps what he really hoped for was room to step back from the immediacy of what he saw.

His eyes took in a body and involuntarily he looked around that small room to search for his close friend. Even his thorough forewarning, his acceptance that things would look bad, his awareness that I'd probably be unrecognizable, fell short of preparing him for that first moment of disbelief.

The face and head were a huge bloated watermelon with little slits where eyes should be. Crusted bumps of tissue were the ears, and a pumping respirator maintained oxygen exchange through the heavy rippled tube that disappeared into my mouth. The arms and hands were swathed in bandages as were the thighs and right leg. The left leg was raised on an inclined support and a plaster cast encased the foot and lower leg.

As Laurie had forewarned, intravenous tubes brought life-giving fluids into the jugular vein in the neck and the femoral vein in the groin. A catheter tube led its murky contents to a collection bag clipped to the edge of the bed and cardiograph lines sprouted like tiny antennae leading to their beeping monitor screens.

Alan was not aware of any other living presence in the room. His breathing stopped. His eyes took in the shocking sight. Experienced in such moments of horror, Laurie was standing just aside, observing Alan rather than her patient, and ready to help should this traumatic experience be too much for the visitor. She let him stand and have his moment of agony and then gently took control of the situation by settling him in a bedside chair. Even though I was unconscious and unable to respond, there was the hope that I was hearing voices and finding some benefit from the tone and words used.

In a louder voice than she had been using earlier to speak with Alan, she addressed me, "Blair, here's your friend Alan to visit you. He heard about your accident from your friends in Cranbrook. He will be here to visit with you for a while to help with your recovery. It's nice to have him here to help me with some of the jobs we've got to do to get you better. He looks pretty good dressed up in his mask and gown. I think he'll make a fine nurse."

And so in her skillful way she brought some relaxation to what had been the most turbulent moment of Alan's life.

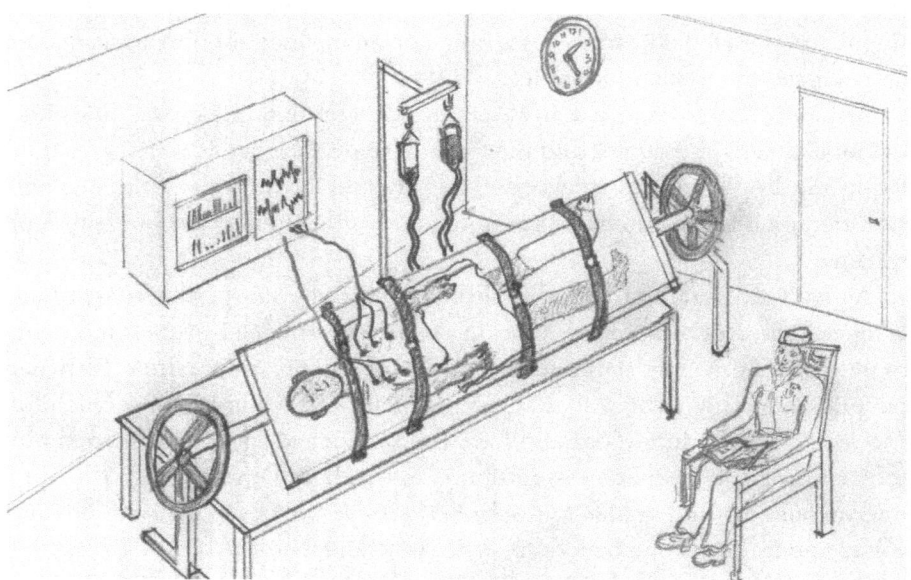

CHAPTER 13
Lost Days 1 – 8

"Critical but stable" was one of the infuriating descriptions given on inquiry into my well-being. One long exhausting 12-hour shift merged into the next, with a purposeful overlap period to allow time to communicate verbally as well as in written material, the happenings of the previous work span. There was a steady flow of specialists assessing, ordering, interpreting, hypothesizing – all trying to explain my body's reaction. For several days my low level of consciousness required the continuous maintenance of life through a respirator but gradually my own breathing pattern started to trigger the cutout on the machine and forced me to breathe independently.

As I fluctuated from the comatose state through different levels of response, unintelligible utterings and moanings were the only indications of a human, albeit antisocial creature, within that charred body. Even those noises gave a glimmer of hope for the people whose caring hands worked so hard to bring me back to life.

My mystifying reactions and failure to respond provoked sheaves of requests for specialist consultation. Neurologists were invited to try to explain my persistent loss of consciousness. Pathologists responded with their interpretation of the bizarre findings in the laboratory reports on my blood chemistry. All tried to determine locations and reasons for infection, increased temperature, and cell count aberrations. The eruption of a skin rash required the expertise of a dermatologist. Radiologists interpreted the almost daily X-rays to determine lung status. Internists and anesthetists were invited to assess my body's general readiness for further surgery.

The entire team was coordinated by the Trauma Unit director, a specialist physician whose task was to lead the total team required for care.

As each long day and night dragged by, the staff continued to pour in fluids, feeding me a high calorie/high protein diet through a tube directly into my stomach. Gradually I responded, though showing little gratitude for what was being done for me. As my Glasgow Scale level crept from three to five then eight, my ingratitude was vented in a tirade of obscenities.

It was even more stressful for visitors not accustomed to the traumas experienced by medical personnel. Suffering and embarrassment brought on by my atrocious vocabulary and behaviour tested the tolerance of my friends. Only in retrospect, with the forgiveness of time, did this time become amusing. I still shudder when friends describe those early days.

As I clawed my way up the Glasgow Scale I also groped and tore at anything interpreted by me as an obstacle in my way. The nasogastric tube was a regular focus of my attack and despite heavily bandaged fingers and hands I thrashed around and finally tore it out.

Sensing the pressure caused by the encircling bandages on my hands, I did my best to whip the ensheathing gauze from my wounds.

With the strength of the demented, I tried to clamber out of bed. Efforts at restraining me became more stringent as my strength increased. For a long desolate week Alan suffered with me. He spent innumerable hours at my bedside. I now know his very presence helped.

The nursing staff advised him to constantly talk to me, even though I was unlikely to respond. This one-way communication would encourage me, as the staff felt there was some chance I was able to hear his words. He patiently described many of the procedures that were being carried out and explained the necessity of those which obviously provoked great pain.

During my gradual resumption of higher levels of consciousness, I developed a habit of receding into a deeper comatose state at the sound of the nurse's voice, or environmental sounds which portended a painful procedure.

Alan would speak in a stage whisper, "The nurse has gone now. You'll be just fine again." The dramatic response to this almost implied that I was a sham.

In retrospect, this occurrence may have been responsible for one of the numerous diagnoses used to try to explain my protracted loss of consciousness. I am now aghast that it would be described as psychiatric, but the other more honourable hypotheses offered included cerebral anemia, toxicity, contusion, and infection. Each theory caused a spate of further tests including brain scans, spinal taps, further blood analysis, and a spree of contradictory recommendations for positioning, medication, and other treatments, all to no avail.

Dr. Robert Lindsay, the plastic surgeon in charge of my care, was a regular visitor. Although he assessed that, for optimum result, skin grafting should be proceeded with urgently, he deferred to the advice of other specialists who recommended waiting, to improve my chances of surviving surgery with its life-threatening dangers due to my state of depressed consciousness and general systemic poor health.

One area in which Alan was of great help was in the provision of details needed in the reconstructive surgery projected as part of my cosmetic repair by the plastic surgery team. Asked if he had a photograph of me, Alan recalled a group picture taken just some three months earlier as we had climbed Mount Fisher near Cranbrook. He retrieved the negative for this picture and rushed it to the photo shop near his office, asking for an enlargement of the segment showing my face. His explanation of its need and urgency brought forth, "We'll see what we can do." Alan gave his office number to the clerk and returned to work. Twenty minutes later he heard the miraculous words, "That special photo you needed is ready."

Senior Management at his work at Canadian Western Gas had listened sympathetically when Alan had told them of my accident. They had authorized Alan to take off whatever time he felt was needed. On news of the photo's availability, Alan left word at the office that he'd be gone for an hour or so. He rushed over to the photo shop and thanked them profusely for their thoughtfulness in giving priority to this piece of work. The photo was placed on my treatment chart in the Trauma Unit within an hour of the original request. That enlargement was to be of significant value in the reconstruction of my features in subsequent surgical procedures.

Somehow, with seemingly inexhaustible energy, Alan managed to juggle the requirements of performing the majority of his work duties, with unconscionable time at the Foothills Trauma Unit and still find some time to be home with Jan, his wife. The next ten weeks put a heavy strain on their lifestyle as Alan continued to visit the hospital every day. Jan, also, was a regular visitor and they opened their home to travellers from Cranbrook who needed a place to stay when they visited me.

In that first week, a further vital role was to convey accurate, if not good, news to my close friends. A network was set up to minimize long distance phone calls. Alan gave direct news each day to Bill Gordon who would then relay the news to Pip and my sons. Additionally, Evelyne Craig and Diana Cavers, my secretary, would be informed and each disseminated the information to other well-wishers who inquired.

This conduit of accurate information was most helpful in combating the insidious horror and exaggeration of the rumour mill.

Though I was not aware of their individual contributions at the time, unseen members of a huge team held together the threads of my very being. Their support coaxed me back to life and fortified me so that I could undergo the reconstructive surgery and rehabilitation that was to make me whole again. Only the medical chart tells the story of the painstaking effort that was put in by those countless hands. The list of the thankless, repetitive, inglorious tasks performed is a monument to the people who made it all happen.

"Log-rolled every two hours," "White cell count unchanged," "Temperature/pulse settling to normal," "Lower lobe X-rays unremarkable," "Fracture stable," "Nutrition intake acceptable in the circumstances," "Vital capacity improving slowly," "Splints remodelled," none of these notations were earth shattering news but still were vital parts of my overall progress during those seemingly interminable lost days. The clock ticked on.

CHAPTER 14
Gathering of the Clan

Saturday, October 8th, was an emotional time in that Trauma Unit. From far and wide, close friends had journeyed to my bedside. As in days long ago, the clan would gather around the ailing chief, so those near and dear to me migrated to the Trauma Unit. At level eight on the Glasgow Scale, I was halfway to my normal status. I was sufficiently conscious to spout obscenities at all who appeared to be producing the pain that I was experiencing, yet occasionally sufficiently lucid to recognize voices and respond favourably. One moment I was pleasant and placid; the next, a source of shudders or brief respites of entertainment.

My former wife, Pip, an experienced Registered Nurse, stayed several days in the Unit, assisting the staff with my care. I now sadly find she was the target of some of my most repugnant remarks. She had remarried since our divorce, but her presence in that Trauma Unit was a wonderful example of the continued caring that can occur between two people who have gone their separate ways after the breakup of a marriage. Her ongoing contribution in that team of supporters was inspirational to others present.

A longtime close friend, Cliff Fowler, had flown in from Vancouver just to be at my bedside. Our friendship went a long way back as we had trained together as physiotherapists in London in the late fifties. Our army service together in Germany and Singapore, and our paths crossing numerous times in the subsequent almost 30 years, had nurtured a close friendship between us. Cliff's distinctive Sheffield accent was one of the first sounds I recognized.

In one of my momentary flashes of alertness, I brought sniggers of joy to those around with, "Hi, Cliff, glad you came. About time. Get me out of this bloody place."

After this order I was again swallowed up in the murk of unconsciousness. Bill Gordon was back again for his third visit in a week, putting unbelievable miles on his brand-new car. His anguish at having been served two speeding tickets in one week on his travels to Calgary provided levity to that strained gathering. Catching me in a moment of consciousness, he bemoaned his foul luck, using his driving misdeeds as blackmail to make me get better quickly, before he accumulated more demerit points.

Another close friend from Cranbrook, Peter Norman, had also travelled up to give his support. His presence, indicated by his turning on his thickest Liverpool accent and idiom, brought a few ribald responses from my cracked features.

Completing this gathering of the clan was the ever-present Alan. His soft Irish accent rounded off that blatantly British bunch.

Hearing the diversity of all those distinctive accents, the nursing staff encouraged each of them to keep up the stimulus that those voices could provide. Going into that Trauma Unit in pairs they would bombard me delightfully with their individual dialects. To drag me out from the depths, Cliff favoured reminiscing about our sojourns together a quarter of a century earlier in Singapore. Provoking my reaction, Cliff started to say, "Do you remember that night in the pub in Raffles Square?" He was briskly interrupted by Alan, who anticipated the likely debauched response. "Oh, don't start him on that again! You'll have us all thrown out of here and himself included!"

Peter Norman's contribution was to egg me on to get back to my house at Six Mile Crossing. He had joined me for a few summer barbeques and indulged in the delights of my outdoor hot tub. He proposed that I invite a couple of those pretty nurses back to Cranbrook. A suggestion like that would have brought anybody back from death's door and was just the thing to wake me up from my deepest comatose state. I extended a loud and ribald invitation to everybody within hearing range.

These exchanges evoked a mixture of sadness at what they saw and joy caused by the frivolity of my responses. There were tears of gratefulness for my recovery and yet concern for my long-term prognosis.

That gathering of the clan will be easily remembered by all those who were present. It was my 45th birthday and the gift they brought was their presence that day. Their reward was my gift of recognizing each of them and my sometimes shocking responses and reactions. That day was the turning point in my recovery. The staff who had patiently waited and tolerated my abuses started nurturing more socially acceptable responses.

Having hidden the weariness of scribing "delay surgery another 24 hours" on each of the previous days, Dr. Lindsay unleashed his convictions on the 9th of October. In his painstaking legible calligraphy, he wrote, "Surgery definitely tomorrow – Thanksgiving Day." It was October 10th, a holiday Monday, but holidays don't count in the urgency of a patient's medical needs. The clock had ticked on relentlessly. It had become imperative to proceed with skin grafting in the hope of achieving the optimum result.

The success of my response to my close friends' visit was still the talk of the Unit when another positive incident occurred on that Sunday. A dear elderly couple, Harry and Berta Moore, had travelled almost 200 miles from their home near Radium on the other side of the Continental Divide. Harry, disabled with a gross arthritic hip awaiting surgery, made his ungainly shambling way on his two crutches. The ward clerk met him at the doorway to the Trauma Unit. The gentle denial of his entry to the Unit, on the grounds that only "close family" were being admitted brought forth an unexpected reaction from the elderly visitor.

Harry's voice lifted a note or two and, sounding scratchy with exasperation, spelled out the facts with indisputable honesty. "Well, no, I'm not family, but that lad's like a son to me."

The impasse held for a moment and a hush descended. The head nurse approached, having heard the start of the strongly one-sided altercation. She whispered discreetly, "Let them in."

"When you're within spitting distance of either side of 80," Harry later crowed, "you've got some experience behind you to deal with these young things."

Draped in the required visiting-gown, and admonished firmly to avoid touching any of the instruments or the bed or me, Harry and Berta spent their moments of anguish and conveyed their well wishes for me. Like so many others, their presence and the well wishes of others afar, all helped to nurture my recovery.

With a tear in his eye, a lump in his throat, and an illicit jab at the mattress, Harry managed a parting shot that I'm certain should have produced reaction, "Now hurry up and get better, young fellah. We need you back there in the Kootenays."

Sadly, I was having one of my of semi-comatose days, and missed all the fun.

The four-and-a-half hours in the operating room Thanksgiving Day made it a holiday to remember.

That surgery involved farming large areas of skin from the unburned portions of the thighs and right lower leg. These grafts were used to put a closing covering over the skull and forehead. Considerable further meticulous work provided new skin to cover my nose and rebuild and design the tops of the rims of the ears. Extensive grafting had to be done on the backs of both hands, from the wrists distally onto the fingers. The fingers were immobilized by driving four-inch-long wires through the entire lengths of each digit to hold them still to allow the new grafts to adhere firmly.

The propriety of choosing this date for surgery was proven by my rapid improvement in overcoming the trauma of anesthesia and the surgical procedure. I spent a short period in the Recovery Room following the operation, then was returned to the Trauma Unit for my last day there.

Although my state of consciousness continued to improve, I was never sufficiently conscious to express any thanks to the staff of that unit for their great work and forbearance. My removal to a new location occurred at 11:00 on Tuesday the 11th of October. After an interminable time lost in consciousness, finally, I was being sent to the Burn Unit.

CHAPTER 15
Unit 31 at Last, the Burn Ward

Despite the urgency with which I had been transferred from Cranbrook ten days earlier with the express intention of entering the Burn Unit, I had been woefully delayed en route. I would not have chosen to dillydally in the Trauma Unit for ten days nor voluntarily have made the side trips to the Operating Room, but my arrival in the Burn Unit on October 11th was clearly evidence of my progress.

I began to have a more regular stream of visitors, many of whom were not impressed by my progress. They had not witnessed the earlier days of horror. My appearance and behaviour had improved much from those early days of total dependency on the respirator and deep loss of consciousness.

Much of my face was left un-bandaged to allow natural healing. The patchwork of grafts on the nose, forehead, ears, and most of the scalp was still not a pretty sight. The gash on the back of my head had been grafted also, but was still oozing and had a patch of bandaging to cover the open wound. The hands and wrists were bandaged, completely covering the grafted mosaic and the hands were immobilized in that optimum healing position: wrist extended, knuckle joints bent to almost 90 degrees, and the fingers held straight and separated.

The plastic splinting material used to hold the hands in this painfully necessary position held the thumb away from the palm, a position ideal for making picture shadows of a snapping dog.

The lower half of the left leg was still top heavy with its plaster cast although it had been bivalved, a split cut down each side to lessen the pressure that had earlier been causing some restriction in the blood flow to the toes. From knee to thigh on that casted leg and toe to thigh on the other leg, the limbs were now tightly wrapped with elastocrepe bandaging. This wrapper covered the underlying burn dressings and "opsite" patch, the special plastic-like covering that minimized the loss of body fluid from the donor sites, where healthy skin had been removed for transfer to the burn sites. The deliberate graduated pressure imposed by these bandages was also to create constant flattening of the grafts to help prevent ridge formations.

To add to my picture of health, there were still the inevitable tubes in and out. I had intravenous fluids pouring into me to try to combat the fluid loss and thus restore my already vast loss of weight. My earlier attacks on the lines threaded into the veins at the elbow had caused considerable damage to those sites and so the infusion was now directly into a vein in my neck. I was unable to see this entry and consequently it had better survival potential. Even the nasogastric tube for direct fluid feeds into my stomach was safer now that they had my hands well trapped in the splints.

The catheter was still in place. However, my restless, clumsy rolling from side to side did little to permit free drainage of urine as I repeatedly rolled onto the tube, blocking it.

I was still on heavy dosages of morphine every four hours, if I could last that long, interspersed with Valium when I became too agitated.

The entry on the chart described me as, "Conscious but confused, speech slurred, disoriented to place and time. He wants to go home and is trying to climb out of bed." This was not a picture of tranquillity and added to the distress of visitors.

Coincidental with my arrival in the Burn Unit on October 11th, nurse Tammy had started work on Unit 31 in her first placement as a graduate Registered Nurse. She had already completed an eight-week rotation during her training on this very Unit, but this was her first experience as a regular nurse. My ramblings and incoherent speech, my unguarded and uncontrolled shouting in response to pain, and my constant endeavours to clamber out of bed were all unexpected complications to her busy day. She cared for three patients in that segment of the Unit. Somehow she had to try to fit in two-hourly checks of temperature; pulse and respiration; dressing changes; blood pressure readings; regular medication; feedings; bedpans; and answer the recurrent warning buzzers on drip lines when there was change in their rate of flow.

Alan arrived at 4:30 in the afternoon. It was his first visit to the Burn Unit. He was by now a veteran at the hand wash and gowning prerequisites for visiting those in isolation units. I managed to come out of the haze of semiconsciousness to welcome him with a battery of complaints and demands. He took it all with characteristic calm. Tammy struck up a conversation with Alan, anxious to find out more about my normal behaviour. "Is he always like this?"

"No," he answered solemnly, "he's sometimes much worse. You'll have to keep a very close eye on this one."

Capitalizing on Alan's offer of help, Tammy decided to try to get me out of bed. It would help me to move my joints and make a change in routine. She carefully explained what she planned to do. At first, even though I had been trying to clamber out of bed, I still resisted the whole business of anyone else trying to move me. I still had the suspicion that this was the precursor to some diabolical pain-provoking action. Once I got the idea my enthusiasm overpowered all reason. I disregarded the restrictions imposed by the indwelling catheter, the intravenous line or the drip bag on its mobile stand.

All went surprisingly well. Team work achieved my transfer to the padded wheelchair. With the feet elevated on the leg rests, and some blankets providing coverage greater than that of the scanty hospital gown, I was trundled off into the corridor and did a marathon ten yards along to the small solarium.

All this new environment was quite frightening in its own way but I kept up the tirade of instructions which at least brought a glimmer of entertainment to my helpers. Taking notice of my surroundings I asked, "What happened to him?" A young lad, swathed in bandages, was sitting in a cumbersome vehicle similar to my own. As if the young man wasn't able to answer his own questions, I enquired from Tammy what had happened to him.

"He was racing a trail bike and crashed. It burst into flames, burning him," she told me.

"Bloody stupid thing to do," I spat out a scathing response.

This ended my first visit to the solarium. I was whisked away by Alan while Tammy apologized to the recipient of my assault. I was still not ready for public exposure, and Alan was relieved to usher me back into the confines of the Burn Unit before I could do more harm.

Alan's trials were not yet over. Pushing one-handed on the ungainly chair he steered it towards the Unit door, while at the same time wheeling the intravenous stand. The inevitable nudge against a wall was enough to dislodge the ratchet holding the footrest. The dead weight of my leg in the cast caused the foot to crash to the floor, bending the bandaged knee. This elicited shock waves through my body, which provoked an explosive reaction.

Alan was beside himself with apology, but nothing could placate my wrath and staff appeared from all sides to check the source of this outburst.

My overreaction was quashed by a firm scolding from Judy, the head nurse, who had tolerated enough of my tantrums for one day. Suitably admonished, I sulked and whimpered. I was bundled back into bed and collapsed in exhaustion, giving those around me a reprieve, temporarily.

When I emerged from my stupor, and with Alan's encouragement, I made my first attempt at drinking through a straw. I gulped and spluttered those few mouthfuls like a baby learning a new skill. Intoxicated by the few ounces of orange juice, I surveyed my realm.

A vague outline of a figure on the next bed was intriguing. "What happened to him?" I demanded.

Alan was still shell-shocked from the catastrophe caused by my derogatory remarks in the solarium just ten minutes earlier, and was evasive in his response, "Oh, that's Bill, from Kimberley. You remember Bill?"

"Never heard of him," I lanced back at Alan. He shuddered at the unexpected fervour of my response. I was clearly irritated that he might insinuate loss of memory amongst my other ails. Bill was uncomfortable as the focus of this conversation. Alan tried to placate both parties.

"Well, Blair. I thought you would remember Bill. You were both on the Search and Rescue together..."

I exploded into an upright sitting position, lunged over, almost falling out of bed, and launched into a terrible attack.

"You're the bloody pilot! A right mess you got us into!"

Consternation broke out. Alan was speechless with embarrassment. Two nurses appeared from nowhere and whipped the screen around to separate me from my target and, as Alan and Tammy tried to quieten me down, Peggy, the second nurse, whispered gently to Bill that she was sure I hadn't meant what I'd said. It was just the drugs that were making me do and say such things. As the steam gradually fizzled out of me, I began to realize how objectionable I had been. I reverted to whimpering self-admonishment. I was filled with the extremes of excitement at the progress shown by the first sip of nutriment by mouth, and yet ashamed of my uncharacteristic thoughtlessness and antisocial behaviour. I craved the forgiveness of those around me. It was the first of seventy days in the Burn Unit.

"We all get a bit touchy when times are tough," I heard Bill respond gently. He had already come through a similar topsy-turvy state of poor self-control when he emerged from his earlier state of diminished consciousness.

Bill had spent only two days in the Trauma Unit but had been more cooperative, quickly regaining a conscious state. He had already spent a week in the Burn Unit. His two excursions to the operating room had provided grafting over much of his face and extensive burns on his arms and shoulder and hands. His fractured right leg was cast from toe to thigh and he was still confined to bed.

With heavy heart, and exhausted with the trauma of his three-hour visit to the Burn Unit, Alan took his leave. He couldn't guess just how much his presence had helped. I had used him as a buffer – a recipient of my anguish. Sadly, those who are kindred spirits must often take the brunt of our feelings in a way we could never dare try with someone less close to us.

Moments later, I hardly felt the prick of the needle as they administered an opportune dose of tranquilizing medication. A rough jab with a blunt needle would have been more deserved but with their unending supply of understanding the nursing staff had dealt with yet another mini-crisis which marked my first day in the Burn Unit.

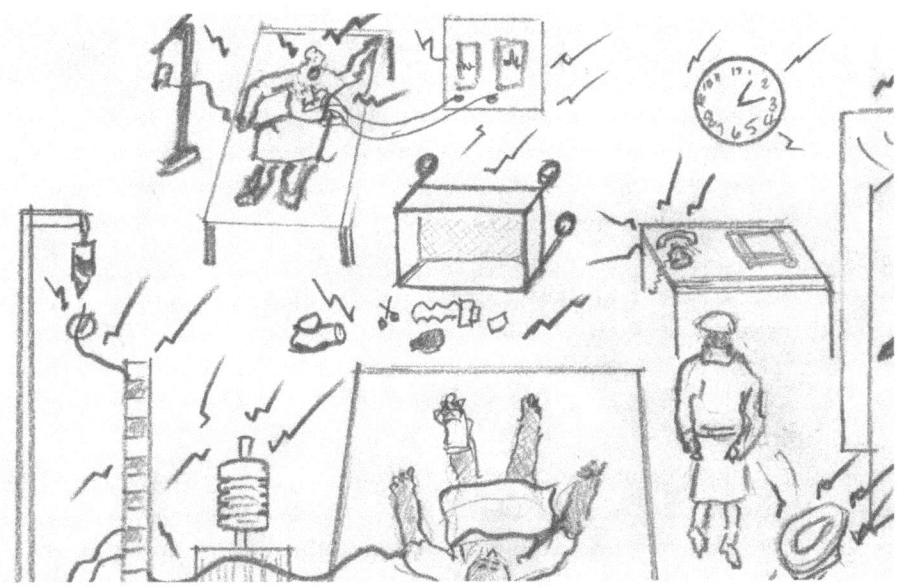

CHAPTER 16
Noisy Time Day & Night

As my awareness of the environment grew, so also did my intolerance. I was not in the mood to look on the positive side and see the daily progress in my condition.

The nursing staff deserved every praise that might be lavished on them – the same could not be said of the physical layout of the Burn Unit. It would have been inappropriate to describe the Burn Unit as anything more than temporarily tolerable, a state that had continued for many years, awaiting the long-promised remodelling and renovation "when funds became available."

Located on the Plastic Surgery Wing of the third floor, the Burn Unit's proximity to the Rehabilitation Unit was one of its redeeming features. Although it adjoined the Plastic Surgery Unit's nursing station, the Burn Unit did not have sufficient physical separation to offer either privacy or the isolation required by the infection-prone clientele that it housed.

The corridor leading to the doors of the three and four-bed wards in the Burn Unit was clearly marked "Isolation Area," but this assumed the public's willingness to read and heed notices.

My arrival to the three-bed segment of the Unit placed me near the entry door and directly opposite the cramped little nursing station which doubled as conference desk, dressing station, and drug cupboard.

It was easy to see that the Unit was in its last years in temporary quarters. This was a make-do location while a better one was being planned. The three-bed unit was where the new patients were first located. In many cases, they were in great anguish and consequently very noisy. At the time of my arrival, I had two roommates. Bill Quilley was very quickly moved as a result of my verbal bombardment and Tom replaced him, a convenient new target for my abuse. The other long-term resident in that ward was Ernie, a cantankerous old gent whose severe leg and body burns gave him cause for an unrelenting tirade of complaints.

Contrary to what one would have hoped for in such a place of healing, the feature I found most disturbing was noise. The unrelenting hubbub of suffering and required procedures was itself traumatizing.

As I gradually emerged from the silence of semiconsciousness, the contrasting onslaught of sounds brought out the worst in me. I just wanted rest. My body felt constantly drained of energy and absolutely craved peace.

Even in the relatively quieter long hours of darkness, there was no peace. Old Ernie was a disruptive force even when asleep. He muttered and moaned all night and snored when he wasn't talking, although sometimes he managed to do both, simultaneously. Tom, in the next bed, needed oxygen at night and a humidifier which puffed and hissed into his tented environment.

Each of us was on drip feed or intravenous lines with their alarm monitors ready to activate at the slightest change of flow speed. These sophisticated gadgets drove staff and patients mad with their recurrent "beep, beep" alarms contributing to the cacophony. The toned-down ring of the phone at the main nursing station and the auditory patient alarm bell with its accompanying flashing beacon to gain the nurses' attention were further annoyances.

The daytime onslaught of commotion was a trial to all who had to endure it. Ernie suffered noisily but also had a belligerent nature and one of my early recollections was his abuse of the hard-pressed nurses. Ironically, I lashed out at him with righteous indignation. Despite my own verbal abuses I berated Ernie's intolerable attitude. The paradox of my efforts to try to change his ways, while I still had sporadic sessions of bad behaviour, brought a quiet smile to the faces of the staff. Theirs was exemplary tolerance and cheerfulness.

It was difficult to distinguish between the disturbance of sound and the movement of traffic throughout the Unit. The constant convoy of medical personnel, each garbed with the anonymity of his isolation gown flowed through the door just inches from the bottom of my bed. I soon labelled my location as "the bus stop." I was furious at the constant waft of air as the door opened and closed. Although I had long periods of semi-comatose escape, the predominating feeling was of being constantly disturbed.

Much of my care involved disruption of my search for peace. The seemingly full-time job involved dressing wounds, changing drip bags, checking monitors, administering medication, feeding, checking pulse, respiration, and temperature, tying me back into bed as I tried to clamber out, blanketing me as I whined about cold, and denuding me as I fussed about over-heat, changing splints, reshaping splints, re-bandaging splints, X-raying, and breathing exercises. All these were constant irksome chores I refused to recognize as essential.

Even in those early days, visitors were a welcome intrusion and while my staying-power was distressingly short-lived, I did enjoy the moments when I recognized visiting faces and tried with mixed success to put on a chirpy response.

Visitors to the other patients were not viewed by me in the same encouraging fashion. Tom's condition had deteriorated seriously and he had the mixed blessing of local Calgary family, friends, and business associates, all anxious to visit him. While the staff were stringent in their adherence to "only two visitors at a time," I sometimes felt that they should institute a two busload visit-limit in a day. The endless stream of his well-wishers were less adept than the nursing hospital staff at slipping discreetly through the door with minimal disturbance to me. They'd either leave the door open or swing it closed when they realized their oversight. This correction blew a gale onto my naked feet. From time to time I would explode with uncontrolled wrath.

To placate me, poor old Tom was finally trundled out into the solarium where his visitors could extend their sympathies and pass on their encouraging words to him unimpeded. I was oblivious of the trade-off to satisfy my demands for peace and quiet. Tom was being subjected to extra suffering and exposure to possible threats of disease in the less sterile environment of the sun room. A well-meaning nurse gave me a gentle rebuke, reminding me that Tom needed all the help and love he could get. At first I muttered my continued objection but finally as my selfishness dawned on me, I reverted to remorseful weeping.

Throughout all this noise and turbulence, exasperation and pain, one factor was predictable and dependable. That was the unfailing good nature and unbelievable patience of the Burn Unit staff.

Work on a Burn Unit is a career selection that is incomprehensible to anyone who has not made that choice. It guarantees exposure not only to heart-rending visible suffering and frequent verbal abuses, but also to very demanding elements of patient care.

There is little respite in any one eight- or twelve-hour shift. There is no escape from the hemmed-in feeling caused by isolation to prevent infection spread, cramped quarters, and the idiosyncrasies of the patients.

Not only must the staff bear unnaturally high room temperatures, maintained for the patient's needs, but they must tolerate noises, smells, and sights more horrible than most could imagine. Additionally, they share part of the mental suffering of each patient.

To the uninitiated it would seem a thankless career, but surprisingly, placements on staff in that Unit are coveted and competition to gain those cherished positions permits selection of high calibre staff.

The head nurse, Judy Sleath, embodied these desirable qualities and was a shining example to her staff. Not averse to contributing the occasional spicy anecdote to bring a ripple of levity to those around her, she nevertheless had that talent of exuding a firmness that left no one in doubt about who was in charge, yet endeared her to staff and patients alike. Her blend of skill and knowledge, with a preparedness to deal with mundane chores like the capsized bedpan, brought her much deserved respect and admiration. She surrounded herself with a staff of delightful and unique personalities each contributing in a very special way in the team. They formed an unpretentious but marvellous team.

Although other visiting hospital staff would only have to endure short exposure to the sufferings on that ward, the staff nurse on duty was required to tolerate the unremitting anguishes of her patients for her entire shift. The personnel from other departments performing tasks there would know they'd have a reprieve from the sights and sounds as soon as they left. They would enjoy regenerative respite as they travelled to the next location.

Although some of my suffering was brought on by my belated recognition that much of my behaviour was atrocious, I was unable to mend my ways. I fluctuated from euphoric moments of fun and frolic to self-indulgent, obnoxious behaviour.

Blending the maturity and experience of some of the longterm nursing staff with the youthful exuberance of the newer faces, the team offered a diversity of individuals that brought a constant freshness to the ward. Nursing assistants, orderlies, porters, and cleaning staff all contributed their talents and personalities.

It is to the great credit of that local team and to all the hundreds of other hospital personnel who visited that Unit during my 10-week stay, that I never heard a harsh word or a suspicion of dissension among them. It is surely proof of their common goal of caring for the sick.

The days seldom started well as there was no such thing as awakening refreshed and rested. Although the nurses' notes frequently described "slept well," I regularly felt as though I'd had a disturbed night. The thankless job of wakening us in the morning became a challenge for the nurses, immediately after the short morning staff meeting to catch up on the current state of each patient. The merciful removal of the night splints from my hands made mornings worthwhile.

By nature a chirpy morning person, I never got into my stride in those early days. My sufferings made me consistently grumpy on awakening in that Unit.

The long-awaited remodelled Burn Unit was completed four years after my departure. Individual private rooms now house each patient. This provides better isolation, minimizes the risk of cross-infection, and improves soundproofing, thus negating my constant complaint of noise. But gone, too, is the camaraderie, the sharing, the constant bantering, and that word or glance that lessened the pain. Perhaps it was good noise.

CHAPTER 17
8 – 9 Hot Tub Time

The clock moved at an infuriatingly slow pace in the middle of the night, but took on an urgent surge of new life each morning. In spite of the lethargy of the patients and their reluctance to embark on a new day of predictable pain-inducing activities, each day presented a busy agenda of tightly programmed events for each of us.

While there was some token choice left to the patient in selecting the sequence of events for the day, that flexibility still had to fit in with the staff's busy interlocking calendars.

The visit to the whirlpool bath, or the "hot tub" as it was unaffectionately described, became a vital but much dreaded part of the start of each day. Although the actual time spent in the water was only about 30 minutes, the regime of preparation and subsequent dressing after the bath monopolized a two-hour segment of each morning. Having become aware of the pros and cons of early or late bathing, I preferred to grab the 8 a.m. time slot as my tub time, choosing to get this portion of purgatory over as early as possible.

The use of hot soaks in the treatments of burns has become a recognized method of achieving daily cleansing and removal of dead tissue. It is often used in the early debridement of loose nonviable tissue, and assists in lessening the threat of further infection. During this hydrotherapy, an opportunity is made available for thorough and accurate wound assessment by nursing staff and surgeons, permitting regular review of the progress of the healing tissues. Although many forms of apparatus are available to provide these hot water soaks, a popular functional unit is the Hubbard Tank. Named after Dr. Hubbard, an American surgeon, the unit has the shape of a keyhole to permit full body immersion of an adult and allowing the arms and legs to be extended while floating in the up-to-12-inch depth of water. The narrower dimensions at the "waistline" of the tank's shape permits the attending staff to be close enough to be able to treat and handle the patient's entire body without moving their own position.

The Hubbard Tank had great use in the '40's and '50's when its design permitted treatment of polio-paralyzed clientele, using the benefits of buoyancy of water to compensate for the patient's inability to move against the force of gravity. It was shown then that some degree of independent movement could be performed by even grievously disabled patients, providing a psychological boost to assist them in facing a lifetime of paralysis.

The stainless steel structure lends itself well to the need for aseptic nursing technique and in most burn centres is a highly utilized modality of treatment in the daily care of the patients.

In my early days prior to regaining full consciousness, I had made several trips to the Hubbard Tank but my first fully conscious visit was as memorable as it was terrifying. I had become aware that something dreadful was about to happen, indicated by the nurse's insistence that I should have a pain relieving injection before going to the tub. The majority of the outer layers of bandaging and all my splints were removed in the ward ,and I was then wheeled from my resident location in the Burn Unit. My first trip along the short hallway leading to the Rehabilitation Medicine Unit felt like a big city at rush hour. I was just not used to all that traffic.

The view from my horizontal position was primarily of ceiling tile, recessed ceiling lighting, and an abundance of insulated piping and duct work. Most alarming of all was the lively attitude of the two physiotherapy assistants as they whisked me along that busy freeway.

Their exuberance and air of confidence did little to cheer me up as I failed to share in the fun of near-miss crashes with other passengers and assorted vehicles.

From my helpless situation atop the narrow stretcher, that first journey provided enough horrifying stimulus to my peripheral vision to make me forget all the woes I might have felt from my physical indisposition.

As we approached the hydrotherapy section, the gurgles and steam of the filling Hubbard Tank brought forth my anxieties about cauldrons. There was a distinctive aroma of antiseptic fluids and general cleanliness. It was reassuring that I would not be prone to infection while I inevitably drowned in that bottomless tank.

As with all new segments of my treatment and care, a full explanation of the rationale for the use of the hot tubs was given to alleviate my obvious concerns. By this time I had begun to recognize that these informational chats were usually the prelude to a dreadful act. It was my first meeting with physiotherapist Abby MacLeod, with whom I would subsequently develop an unabated verbal, physical, and mental tussle which would last three months. It would end in a draw, neither party having conceded one inch in the battle. It was a delightful impasse of two stubborn individuals, but one in which I quickly recognized the depth of her professional skill, combined with a disarming bubbly personality.

As the efficient and experienced team took over the procedure of transferring me into the tank, I was alarmed that my only contribution to the activity was just being there. As the covering sheets were removed, it dawned on me that little effort was being made to clothe me in a conventional swimsuit. To placate my indignation, a flimsy hand towel was draped over those private areas I felt should not be shown in public.

I gathered from the little asides that my state of consciousness had been assessed as improving. Although I had apparently made this trip before on several occasions, I had not hitherto expressed any concern over the degree of nudity involved in the procedure.

It was evident by my strong verbal reaction to all that was happening that I was well aware of my environment. Wheeling me under the gantry of a hoist, the staff proceeded to attach four long metal rods to the eye hooks on the metal stretcher on which I lay. Even this simple operation threatened my exposed and defenceless body as I was fearful that they might inadvertently strike my injured and fragile burned areas during the process.

The constant assurances that they had done this once or twice before did little to lessen my fears.

Lying there on my back on that hard metal surface, I was at least fortunate to have no open areas of skin destruction on my back or the back of my legs. The only open wound on the weight bearing surface in this supine position was the patch on the back of my skull. They had supported my neck on a rolled towel to keep this fragile segment from being further damaged.

I had a certain amount of pain in my lower back where the stable vertebral fracture reacted to the pressure and unaccustomed firmness of the trolley, which was as devoid of padding as was my scrawny torso.

I was appalled that they would consider dunking me in this steaming water with the left lower leg still encased in its plaster cast and was reluctant to share their optimism that all would be well. It looked as if they had done all this before, as they quickly sealed the cast in a large plastic bag, taping it to my skin just below the knee.

For a moment I eyed the hoist apparatus with suspicion and trepidation. It looked reminiscent of something I'd seen in a slaughter house used for raising and transporting carcasses. My last vestige of confidence vanished when I saw the diminutive assistant who was about to operate this contraption. Seeing the fear in my eyes, she leaned forward and made sure that I heard her words above the noise of the running water.

"It'll be a bit noisy when this hoist starts up, but you'll be just fine. The stretcher might tilt a little but we'll make sure you don't fall off."

With that reassurance she moved to the end of the stretcher and pulled on the starter cable of the hoist. The raucous air compressor mechanism produced noise similar to a mechanic's air driver ratchet used to tighten the nuts on car wheels. The onslaught of noise amid the tilting and lifting of the stretcher was just appalling. I was certain I'd slide off the slippery surface of the stretcher. I felt a mixture of anger and exasperation that all the fine work that had already been done on my behalf and all my suffering would be to no avail, as I'd surely be killed falling off this stretcher.

With equally frightening suddenness, the wretched noise stopped. I swayed precariously for a moment close to the ceiling, although in reality only four feet from the floor, which had disappeared from view. Then with a heave, they dispatched me along the length of the gantry. I watched untrustingly as the double wheel support mechanism rolled along its slender track. Two hundred feet above the slopes of a ski hill, a similar mechanism would bring no fear, but two feet above a Hubbard Tank, all faith in such gadgetry evaporated.

With a final lurch, the horizontal movement ceased and without warning the din started again as the hoist took me through a power dive into the abyss of swirling waters below.

Plummeting at one inch per second, I was seething at my total inability to control the lunging fall. It reminded me of the first practice spin in the Cessna. The language of that occasion returned.

"Tut tut, Blair. That's no language to use in the presence of ladies," was Abby's shouted admonition while the machinery continued its noisy descent.

As the carefully tilted head of the stretcher was guided down to seat in the supporting hooks at the top end of the tank, I again showed my absence of confidence in their handling of this craft. If my physical contribution to this so-called treatment had to be nil, at least I was not going to miss out on contributing verbally. As the 100 degree Fahrenheit water gave its first sensory sting on my upper arms, I bellowed more in exasperation than pain.

"It's far too hot," I shrieked, but they had either lost the switch or were deaf. The mechanism continued in its quest to drown me.

As the water swept over my body, there was a feeling of shock at the onslaught of even that light pressure on some of the burned areas. It was a soothing feeling, but I wasn't going to tell anyone that. My main concern was to keep the plastic-draped cast out of the water.

The noise stopped. Nobody spoke. Momentarily, I enjoyed the respite from threat. For a few seconds, I was allowed to wallow in this blissful state. Abby came around to where I could see her at the side of the tank and said, "Did you enjoy the ride?" Her eyes twinkled. My suspicious mind was not going to be taken in by all this front of frivolity.

Masked, gowned, gloved, Abby was not the bearer of glad tidings and joy.

"Don't they usually give anesthetics for this type of surgery?" I tried.

There was a polite responding giggle from the audience. Progress had been made. I'd spoken a whole sentence without swearing. There was hope for me yet.

Indicating that there was work to be done and a busy schedule to be kept, hands zoomed in over the edge from all sides. The metal hooks were removed from the stretcher and with a quick blast of shocking noise the hoist was zipped up to the ceiling and whisked along the beam out of harm's way. It was some relief to know that the machinery wouldn't fall on me, but I concentrated on the more dangerous appearance of scissors from which the brown antiseptic fluid still dripped.

With my casted foot perched precariously on a supporting splint to keep it out of the water, I half floated, half drowned in the 12 inches of water. Given time and peace to think about it, I could have enjoyed an undisturbed soak in that pleasantly warm water, which was heated to just a degree or two above my body temperature.

The water was at a carefully predetermined level of salinity and loaded with germ fighting antiseptics. A 10 kg bag of salt had been added to the water to bring its pH level up to approximate the body's normal level. "About as salty as your tears," I was told, to minimize the flow of ions, the life-saving electrolyte, which had leaked so freely from my burned body.

The scissors began their terrifying work. The rolls and rolls of elastocrepe bandages that had provided supportive pressure on my legs had been removed in the ward, except for some that were stuck to my body by oozing body fluid. My Scots inclination was appalled as they cut off the adherent bandages.

Bellowing my reaction, I said, "These things cost $6 each."

I was mollified by the response that it was cheaper and safer to put on new wrappers than to go through the elaborate process of cleansing and sterilizing them for reuse. The underlying "cling gauze" bandages were starting to loosen and float off in the bath. Those coverings were carefully snipped and teased away from the fragile wounds, with momentary reactions from me when the occasional one was reluctant to give up its hold.

The bandages were gathered from the water and dumped unceremoniously in the ready plastic bags fixed around the bath.

"Okay, scrub," ordered Abby, watching my dismayed reaction.

She bubbled over in her comforting hearty laugh which was to be the trademark of her exuberant style.

Sterile scrubbing sponges, newly removed from their sealed plastic containers, offered different textures on each surface. I enquired about the reason for this and was further educated with a practical demonstration. Selecting an uninjured area of my shoulder, it took little time to show me that the orange surface was more soothing than its partner. The rougher green surface was only sparingly used on stubborn areas where it was required to remove unwanted dead tissue.

Scrubbing was not really an appropriate name but those sponges were used to remove devitalized tissue, helping to remove the threat of bacterial infection. Trying to avoid causing excessive bleeding, those gloved hands stroked, rather than used circular motions to cleanse the weeping tissues.

The process was not devoid of pain, but it was evident from the concentration and care that was put into the work that it was a vital procedure. I tried to tolerate the surges of pain with stoicism, but more frequently was heard bawling and swearing.

The open wound at the back of my skull was evidently a particular challenge for Abby. With persistence, she kept at that stubborn area. Attacking with tweezers and sponge she revelled in her quest to remove the remnants of imbedded Rocky Mountain hillside soil. Midway through this procedure my surgeon appeared, to take advantage of the unfettered view and make an inspection of the progress of my burns. Dressed in his white lab coat, the face mask presumably to avoid inhaling any of my bugs (doctors don't carry bugs), he kept his distance. With hands tucked safely behind his back he peered with that 20/20 vision that could detect any errant graft. He defied them to fail to take.

I was delighted to show off my progress but voiced my concern about my skull's tardy healing. "Yes, that spot's a wee bit stubborn," he said, transferring warmth in his Aberdeen accent, accentuated a little for his fellow-Scot patient. "You're doing very well. The grafts are taking just fine."

"Will I need more surgery?" I asked with no great enthusiasm.

"We'll just have to do a little patch up on that thigh and a few spots on the fingers, but nothing like you've already had," he reassured me. "One, or at most two surgical procedures. We might even do one of these under local anesthetic if you like."

I was pleased with this prognosis, and the thought of surgical intervention under local anesthetic gave me the idea that I could supervise the procedure and ensure that it was done properly! Despite his characteristic economy in time and phrase, he lingered a moment longer to direct a few words of thanks and encouragement to the physiotherapists before slipping away.

"Now, wasn't that good news?" Abby declared. "We told you you were doing fine but you didn't believe us." I felt abashed and quietly conceded that I had not given those able staff the credit they deserved. This was the start of my realization of their unstinting contribution to my recovery. As did others, I, too, would proclaim lifelong indebtedness to their skill and dedication.

In the swirl of attention, time had quickly passed and I had endured, if not enjoyed, almost 30 minutes in the tub. Having completed the scrubbing and picking at all the offending patches, Abby and her assistant stood back to survey their work. Now was not the time for rest for me, but rather a time of participation. With all the restricting dressings removed from my fingers, arms, and legs, it was exercise time in the tub.

With much cajoling from the onlookers, I sweated as I tried to move joints that had been idle for weeks. After 25 years of plaguing others to exercise, it was a bit of a shock to be on the receiving end of such firm tutoring.

The soothing softening of the warm water had eased the immobility a little, but already the ogre of natural stiffening due to inactivity had tightened up the capsules of the joints. As I struggled to produce movement to satisfy Abby's insistent "Just a tad further," I could visualize minute tears and splits occurring in the adhesions formed in the gristle around each joint.

The muscles, too, had wasted away through inactivity. My 40-pound weight decrease wasn't all fat loss, and my arms and legs were scrawny.

"Not too bad an effort for a physiotherapist patient," was my effort at self-praise.

"A normal patient would have done much better," I was told, keeping me down to size. "You'll do much better when you're out on dry land, back in the gym by 11:00." I groaned at the prospect. When would I get time for just two minutes' rest. Fatigue haunted me constantly, disappearing in the middle of the night, only to be replaced by insomnia.

I had been lulled into a sense of security by the pleasant warmth of the pool and buoyancy of those soothing waters, but now I had to get out.

To preoccupy my mind, already tensing for the upcoming horrors, Jenny remarked, "Look, your cast didn't fall in the water at all today."

I focused on it, and realized that it had sat, totally unassisted, throughout the submersion routine, but now I was certain it would falloff its perch at any minute.

My reverie was shattered by the machine-gun chatter of the hoist as its operator gave it a three-inch surge. The ominous ratchet sound was just as foreboding as it had been on its earlier circuit.

The roll of the approaching hoist along its I-beam support was hypnotizing. I watched, transfixed, with only eye movement possible to follow its surge, until it was poised dead centre above my helpless body. The din started again as the grab chains came lower, but I was ready this time and started issuing my orders to prevent the inevitable goring of those metal rods.

"It's all right, Blair. We won't let the hooks hit your wounds. Yes, we'll keep your foot out of the water. We won't let the stretcher tilt. No one has fallen off yet today, but then you are our first patient this morning."

I was sidetracked but reluctant to be outdone I started my tirade about the lack of support of my neck pillow.

With all the hooks in place, the uplifting process began. Slowly at first, with water deluging off all sides, my body heaved through the surface bubbles like some submarine reluctant to show itself above the waters.

Abby's hands lay gently and firmly on my shoulders in what I mistakenly thought was a moment of special caring. The clatter of the hoist continued before I realized her devious intention. With the head end of the stretcher still held just at water level they continued the dreaded contraption's upward drag until the foot end of the stretcher was tilted up at a steep angle above the water. The din ceased and so did all movement.

"We've got to let you drip dry," was the explanation. "We can't let all that water go on the floor, can we?"

Seething and starting to shiver, I tolerated the inevitable wait. It felt like every window in the place was open. The water continued to run off the edge of the stretcher. Abby's hands maintained their firm support of my shoulders. Without them I felt I'd have been launched down that slipway to vanish into the cavernous plug hole that had already consumed most of the murky water from the tank.

With a jolt I started up toward the overhead machinery. I was beyond caring. Exhausted and already frozen, I knew nothing much worse could happen. The vertical movement ceased and simultaneously I was launched laterally to the right with a heave and accompanying whirl of roller bearings. As if all haste were imperative the downward movement started again with its corresponding racket while I was still in the last sideways glide. This all translated into a parabolic swoop which careened to an abrupt stop as my buttocks and shoulder blades were slammed on the wet stretcher as it suddenly ground onto the waiting metal trolley.

As Abby unhooked the hoist's attachments from the stretcher, she forced a glimmer of a reluctant smile from me with her comment, "Right on target with that landing. Whew! Lucky I guess."

The shivers were really starting when I was given a delightful surprise. They bundled me up with three lots of sheets which had just been removed from a nearby warming cupboard. The finishing touch involved covering my skull and leaving just my nose and eyes exposed. I felt wonderfully comfortable. Now, that was tender loving care!

Already an assistant had started the onerous job of scrubbing and scouring out the tank in preparation for the next swimmer. She cleaned up my mess, disinfected, sterilized, and removed all the evidence of the past half-hour's ordeal.

From the comfort of my cocoon, I muttered a sleepy thanks, as I was whisked off on the return journey to the ward. By the time we passed the main swim pool area, most of the drips had stopped and the rapid transportation through the corridors was just a blur of faces and figures. The constant chatter of exchanges between the porters and staff members en route was an example of the positive camaraderie that occurs in these great institutions. It was a soothing, comforting murmur that lulled me almost to sleep.

I closed my eyes momentarily and drifted until my senses detected change. I was back home in the Burn Unit. My nostrils were assailed by a multitude of distinctive smells. Invading my peaceful state, they reminded me that some unpleasant things were about to happen. I glanced at the wall clock. I shuddered. Nine o'clock. The first half of the two-hour morning ablution and dressing schedule was over. Cold was creeping through the dampness of the stretcher beneath me. This would prevail for some time until I was bandaged and returned to the welcoming warmth and dryness of my bed, after completion of my dressings. I was already exhausted and didn't know where I'd find the energy to cope with the next hour, but I had achieved the first goal of my day. I'd survived tub time 8–9.

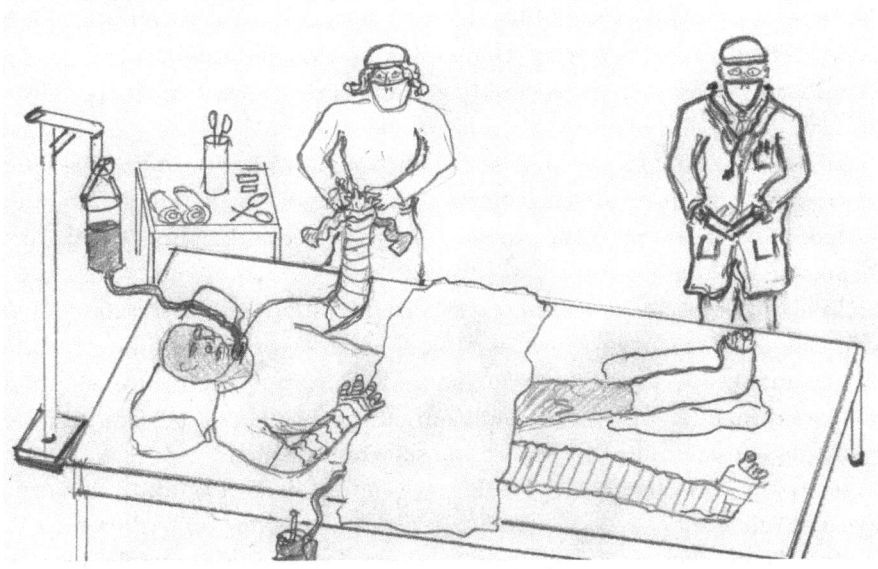

CHAPTER 18
Dressing Time 9 – 10

The glide back to the ward from the whirlpool episode had been a joyous dream journey. I was conscious of unbelievable exhaustion brought on by a combination of the heat of the water, the energy-sapping pain, and anxiety, yet I had a feeling of accomplishment at having overcome another of the many hurdles posed by each day.

With the soothing comfort of those layers of warm sheets, I had been lulled into a brief state of oblivion. All too soon, there had crept into my dream an insidious increase in the discomforts of the fast cooling wetness and hardness of the metal of the stretcher beneath me.

Arrival back at the Burn Unit brought a quick reawakening of the painful reality that was each hour. The welcome mat was out in the form of the nurse awaiting my arrival to start the whole process of dressing my wounds. This venture was not something to look forward to with relish. By agreement and careful scheduling, I had already had my first pain injection at 7:30 prior to the trip to the healing waters. As a precursor to the anticipated discomforts brought on in the dressing process, I was ready for a further pain-relieving needle. Gone were the days when such infusion of medication could be done into the add-a-line side tracks in the intravenous tubings. Now it had to be a good old fashioned stab in the rump. That morning I had the pleasure of meeting a new nurse, so would be able to rate her skill as an injector, using my quick-check one to ten scale. Depending on the medication, I had found that most intramuscular drugs could be administered in a virtually pain-free manner.

Having been duly forewarned of my idiosyncrasies and whines, Christine was prepared. She provided a commendable buttock stab rating four and proceeded to placate me with two small cartons of orange juice to slake my ever-present post-bath thirst.

I finally got my much deserved reward of a brief snooze while she completed the final setup of my dressing trolley. Although she was on a tight time schedule and was anxious to start on my one-hour-long dressing procedure, she had been forewarned by the previous shift's nursing staff. "He's really cranky if he doesn't get a few minutes rest before you start his dressing."

The room had taken on a whole new appearance and aroma since my departure one hour earlier. My roommates had either gone off to Physio, O.T., or to their scheduled time in the spas. The room had been thoroughly cleaned, and tidied. The conglomeration of night splints, extra blankets, and breakfast trays had disappeared.

"Okay, Blair. Time for action." With a gentle shake on the shoulder she brought me from my blissful state of dreamland. The awakening was dismal. The cold wetness of the stretcher beneath me started my first petulant demand.

"The other nurse usually slips a dry sheet underneath me," I said, trying the usual blackmail.

"That seems a great idea," she responded, and I was taken aback by her cooperative and friendly approach.

"Now where would you like us to start this morning with your dressings, Blair?"

While this was a crafty way of making me responsible for where the pain would start, it also allowed me a moment to procrastinate before we finally got down to the rotten chore.

"Start with the arms," I suggested. "Right arm is first today."

Christine moved the dressing trolley to that side of my stretcher, had a final hand scrub, dried off with a disposable paper towel, and donned the new sterile surgical gown. Next, carefully grasping the folded-back edge of the sterile surgical gloves she slipped them on. Her technique would have brought praise from her nursing instructor of years earlier. I was an old hand at watching these matters. Impressed by her performance, my confidence began building up.

The covering towel of the dressing trolley was folded back just enough to expose the required items. Christine proceeded with efficiency, a master of her art. Various lotions and creams were applied for their known benefits. Flamazine, a silver sulfadiazine compound, was by far the most commonly used ointment. It was an antibacterial agent that also minimized natural drying of the wound, keeping the healing tissues soft, and thus helping to lessen joint stiffening. Other potions such as Dermabase were used to keep the healed tissues pliable, while Polysporin was aimed at specific centres of infection and recalcitrant healing spots. Several layers of gauze were then placed over the larger unhealed sections of the hands and arms. Christine chatted away in a delightful manner, but my natural wariness made me try to ensure that everything would be done just right.

To hold all the various pads and covers in place she started on the laborious process of individually wrapping the fingers with the two-inch rolls of "cling" gauze. It was essential to keep those fingers independent and allow for the subsequent exercise programme to maintain their desired mobility in joints where movement was available. Some joints were purposely immobilized by long spikes of wire protruding from the ends of the fingers. These were the intramedullary nails intended to hold the fingers in a fixed position to allow for the undisturbed "taking" of the grafts. The wire in the left thumb had inadvertently

been driven in further than had been intended. This had been brought about by my frantic flailings in the early semi-comatose state. The nail's disappearance below the skin's surface at the tip of the thumb was to have entertaining ramifications later, and my consequent enthusiastic efforts to mobilize the stiff joint in the phalanges in that thumb brought no results.

Christine's friendly manner and evident skill quickly had the dressing completed surprisingly painlessly. I was forced to provide grudging praise.

"I see you've done this job before," I quipped and the ease with which she took my compliments developed a bond between us.

To ensure that there would be no chance of transferring any of my "right hand" bugs to other areas, the gloves came off, and Christine wheeled the trolley round to the other side of the bed. She was careful to avoid touching any part of it which held the dressings or materials to be used on me, before she went back to the sink for another scrub and donned the second of the six pairs of gloves that would be used in my dressing routine. As she started work on my left hand, the head nurse came in through the door. She was already masked and offered her help.

Head nurse Judy's expertise at this business had been proven during her earlier sessions of applying my dressings and other care. I gleamed at the chance to check Christine's technique compared to that standard of excellence for which Judy was renowned. A bit of competition would go down well.

Judy went efficiently through the scrub, gown, glove routine and gently lifted off a narrow section of covering sheets from my left leg. Side by side the two nurses went about their tasks with enthusiasm.

My anticipated testing of these two, one against the other, received a severe setback. Even with their skilled gentle approach, providing the required padding and dressing brought forth unpredictable stabs of pain. I had been able to concentrate and deal with these shots of pain emanating from one source at a time with only minimal abuse or verbal reaction. This newfound double-pronged attack was too much. My hitherto mild rebuffs became a noisy lament.

"So we're getting your complete attention I notice," Judy tried to appease my wailings. She seemed to sense that I was evaluating their relative skills, so while keeping on at the necessary bandaging attempted to distract me.

"Who did it? Was that Christine or was that me, this time?" The extra seconds they had both been working had brought the pain to a grievously unpleasant level.

"Both of you," I shouted with more disgruntled reaction than I had intended. They both downed tools simultaneously while I muttered an apology for my outburst. Now that I was back in the land of the fully conscious, I recurrently had remorse for my explosive reactions. Judy took a break for a moment or two while Christine finished off the final wrappings on that left hand and arm. Then as she stood back to survey the finished masterpiece, Judy continued and completed the leg bandaging without further reaction from me. To maintain the even counter-pressure to minimize the bumps and ridges that might be produced by the healing scars, three rolls of six-inch elastocrepe bandaging were rolled from toe to thigh on the uncasted leg, and knee to groin on the other. The careful tensor wrapping, using the traditional herringbone pattern of overlapping layers, was used to ensure that every area was covered, leaving "no windows" around the ankle and to provide an even pressure over the length of the legs.

Judy slipped off her gloves and gown and said that she'd pop back in five minutes to help with the transfer back to my bed. The subsequent dressing of the right leg continued without incident or aggressive reaction.

The transfer back onto the newly made bed was a moment I dreaded. The nurses held the stretcher firmly against the bed
so that I couldn't possibly dive down the chasm that I feared might appear between the two structures. I crabbed sideways with a lurching four-point elbow and heel-only contact system. It was another safe landing to mark up in my flight log book!

With my neck comfortably supported in its supporting pillow, Christine completed the dressings on the open wounds at the scalp.

"Healing over nicely," she said. They always said that, but I knew there was still a huge crater there, weeping vital tissue fluid. The sheets continued to be stained every time my head sagged down to contact the mattress during my sleep. By morning I was glued to the sheet. I felt as if I was tearing the back of the skull off as I tried to dislodge my head from the bed.

"How big's that hole in my head now?" I asked in a cross voice.

"There are only two tiny little peepholes about half an inch across each," she said.

I was a little angry that she would belittle the gaping wounds and was surprised at a later stage when they finally gave me a double mirror viewing which showed that the wounds were one tenth the size that I had imagined them to be. The dressing routine continued on to deal with the nose, face, forehead, and scalp. These areas were healing well, and were given their appropriate covers of oleum to maintain their baby's bottom softness and flexibility and to allow me, one day in the future, to again wear the smiles and grins and frowns that were my true nature. The news had obviously gone around that my ears had best be left to last. The ears had taken the brunt of the exposure to the devouring flames six weeks earlier. Crusted bleeding remnants had been skillfully debrided, grafted, and stitched. I was amazed to find that in the top rim of the ear eleven tiny stitches held the fragile grafts in place. The right ear had lost a considerable amount of its natural contour. The traditional cupping rim which provided an acoustical shell receptor to direct sound to the inner ear, had been lost beyond restoration.

Rolling the graft to squeeze out any underlying bubbles of fluid brought my anticipated disgruntled reaction. I steeled myself to cope with the pain in those last few titivations, and at last Christine stepped back to survey her work. After some final adjustments to set my arms up in the elevated troughs that would hold them aloft, I stole a few minutes' rest before the next attack. I had contributed nothing to the whole process except my verbal assailings but I was perspiring due to the effort I'd exerted just tolerating their well-meaning efforts.

Individual jars of Dermabase, Flamazine, and ointments, all duly inscribed with my name, were put into my locker to minimize the exposure to light. Some ointments that needed refrigeration were replaced in the nursing station fridge. The cleanup completed, the trolley was removed. I gulped down another two quick drinks of orange juice as tranquility returned. It was always a question of which of us, the nurse or the patient, gave the greatest sigh of relief when the job was completed.

The brief respite of sleep was disturbed by moans and grunts as each of my roommates returned from his session in the whirlpool and went through a similar dressing procedure. I might have guessed that the peacefulness would be short. A deputation from the lab approached with their evil intent.

"Good morning, Blair. We were in earlier but you had gone for a swim." They drew the screens around me.

"What'll it be today then, ladies?" I tried to humour them.

"Oh, just a few drops of blood and a little urine will do."

Finding the blood from my arm vein was a little painful but was nothing compared to the anguish brought on by producing the required specimen. It wasn't that there was any pain or difficulty in passing the required fluid, but with my hands completely wrapped up in bandages the vexation was caused by the humiliating dependence on others for accurate placement of the plastic paper cup to collect the specimen. Added to this was my concern at not being able to stop the flow once it had started.

As with so many things, the anticipation was worse than the act. The lab staff finally drew back the curtains, having carried out their delicate needs in a discreet, professional fashion. Recognizing my discomfort, their sympathetic understanding minimized my concerns.

Even so, as they left I quietly fumed at my state of dependence on others. I glanced at the clock and groaned again as I saw it was almost time to go to Occupational Therapy. If only I could steal five minutes' undisturbed rest. The day was still young, but I had achieved one more tiny goal. I had again survived – dressing time from 9 to 10.

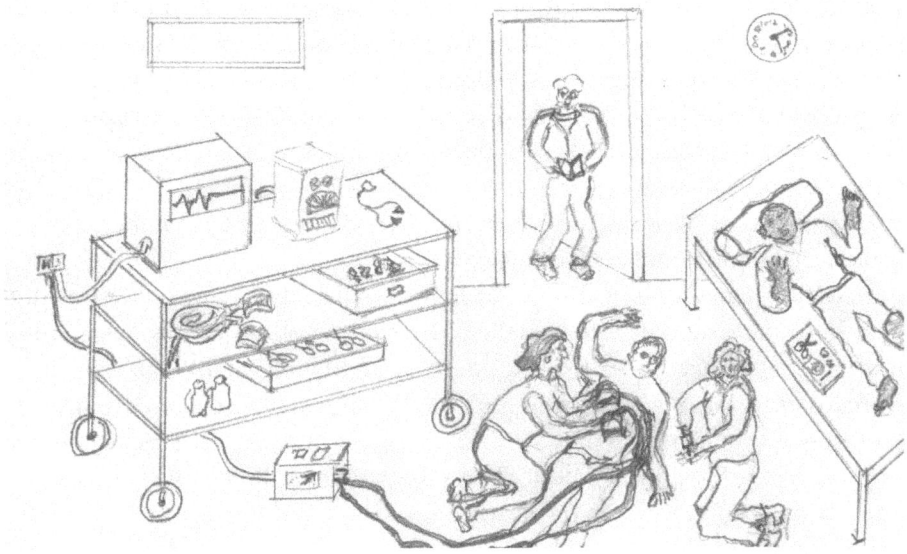

CHAPTER 19
Code-4 Time of Death

It was just two days after yet another venture into the wonderful world of surgery. I'd been blessed with a new grafted patch over my left knee, a replacement of a small area that had failed to take on the right thigh, and an assortment of other minor corrections on the fingers and on one ear. The focus of my attention was a 4 x 4 patch covering the area high on my left thigh from which the available graft material had been farmed. This donor site with its special "opsite" covering, to facilitate quick healing and to minimize fluid loss through the large new open area, had the dubious distinction of having a dozen metal staples holding its edges in place. I had been horrified when I first saw this patch. I was told that the staples were faster to insert and remove, and that they were very expensive. This made them much more acceptable.

I should have been happy with the progress being made. With luck, when these new grafts all took well, I'd be leaping ahead.

There had been a change in my independence and freedom. Prior to that most recent session of surgery, I had been able to limp and stumble around and certainly maneuver quite successfully in a wheelchair. My hands had not been capable of the propelling, but I had developed a very satisfactory mobility using the "heel-drag" method of pulling the chair along with my one uninjured foot.

All that freedom was gone. The five-day "complete bed rest" dictated as a post-surgical regime, made me solemn and exasperated with my bedridden state. I was again subjected to the delights of eating and dressing changes in bed, and horror of horrors – bedpans. It was just a matter of time before nature's inevitable needs would force me to succumb to what I regarded as the ultimate degradation. In consequence, my fellow ward patients were taking book, betting on how long I'd last.

"Three to one Wednesday, five to one Thursday, and a ten to one certainty Friday," the odds told their miserable story.

Fred was a master at rubbing salt in this wound. Fred's presence was due to one of life's simple little mistakes. His truck's refusal to start, one frosty morning, prompted him to use the time-honoured method of pouring gas into the carburetor. With a friend manning the starter switch, their communication had miscued, and the ill-timed firing of the engine caused Fred to deluge the can of gasoline over himself. The subsequent explosion of flame caused deep burns to his face, arms, and upper body but had done little to quell his exuberance.

Despite his 50% body burns, Fred was mobile. He could walk all over the place and, of course, he took great relish in lording it over my new bedridden status. It was one of the delightful fringe benefits of a four-bed ward that we'd trade off harmless insults and goad each other in many little well-intentioned ways.

"I think I'll just make another trip to the toilet, Blair. I'll do one for you while I'm in there," was Fred's laughing farewell. There was no truce in his impish one-upmanship. He went off to answer nature's call.

The evening duty nurse started on my dressings. My bedridden state immediately post-surgery, dictated the need to soak some of the dried-on dressings with saline solution, to allow their removal without pulling off the underlying new grafts. It was a slow uncomfortable procedure requiring extra care. Eventually, both hands were clear of bandaging and had been delicately wiped with a sterile scrub sponge to remove small areas of dead tissue.

Nurse Jill's experience showed as she deftly put the finishing touches to cleaning my wounds. A regular staff nurse on the rotation of days, evenings, and nights, her maturity at mid-30's showed in her quick changes from serious conversation to comfortable levity and her contributions of a vast repertoire of anecdotes set a light mood in the ward that evening. From our sheltered spot behind the curtain encircling my bed, we were about to start on the ointments and wound redressings.

Fred eased the ward door open, moved in and back-heeled it closed, with the classy no-touch-technique of a veteran. He announced his return with his humour aimed in my direction.

"What a bowel movement!" he exclaimed, "and I did it all by myself."

A thud startled us and John in Bed Three called out, "Quick, Nurse. Fred's fallen."

Jill disappeared around the screen, inadvertently leaving it partially open, and through the gap I could see Fred, prostrate and still. One glance at his fallen form sent Jill scurrying to the door to call for assistance. In seconds, with the help of two other nurses, she had him onto the bed and in the ensuing whispered exchanges by those capable women, the three other patients in the room fell into an ominous silence. One nurse rushed to the nursing station phone to dial the emergency call to the switchboard.

As if in echo, a muted call came over the loudspeakers. "Code 4. Burn Unit. Code 4. Burn Unit."

In the preceding weeks of my stay I had heard many such demands which were part of any large acute hospital system. In the middle of the night that insistent speaker had dispatched the emergency resuscitation team to various critical situations.

This was the first time I'd heard it announced for the Burn Unit. The three nurses were working frantically on Fred's still body. Years of training and experience with resuscitation had not lessened their dread of such times.

Further down the corridor a door clattered open, wheels rippled along the tiled floor, running feet and breathless voices came closer and then burst through the door to Unit 31. Six members of the resuscitation team arrived with their "crash cart." Fully loaded with vital equipment and materials, this trolley carried the wide range of items needed for emergencies such as heart attacks and brain hemorrhages, or other life-threatening happenings. Two other pairs of running feet announced the arrival of two more members of the team.

As their trained automatic reaction took over, individual members started investigations and procedures. Without invitation, Jill embarked on a brief history about the patient.

"Two weeks ago, 50% body burns, second and third degree, 40 years old."

I lost the following sentences as the alarming thought struck me that Fred was younger than me. Fear gripped me as I wrestled with this new devastating logic: Fred's mobility, his ability to go to the toilet while I was confined to bed, and my sudden awareness that he was younger than me. This focused and exaggerated my own vulnerability and chances of survival.

The door swung open again and my reverie was interrupted. The senior trauma resident quietly took charge. The essentials of the story were again relayed to her and she guided that team in life-restoring maneuvers. We three roommates were hardly daring to breathe for fear that it would disturb that electric atmosphere.

Only snippets of words were discernible, as the team worked with intensity.

"Draw up 20 cc's. Inject straight in. No pulse."

"No pulse," intoned another quiet voice.

"Clear for shock."

There was a moment of activity. Someone stumbled over something and another formless body backed against the curtain surrounding my bed. There was a muted thud and a gasp and a quick voice, "Pulse, pulse, pulse, pulse."

There was a stirring amongst the staff and throughout the murmurings, although the words couldn't be distinguished, there was clear hope portrayed by these sounds. A rasping cough started and then a pleading voice that I'll remember forever.

I couldn't believe my ears as Fred's struggling words gasped out their message, "What's happened? Am I going to die?"

As if a conductor had orchestrated their response, in unison each caring professional around the bed uttered a quiet word of hope and encouragement. Just as quickly, their few words fell silent as each held their breath in dread. "No pulse, no pulse, no pulse," that same quiet voice broke the silence and intoned the awful news.

"Another 20 cc's. Stat." "No pulse, no pulse." "Clear again," that command was given with utmost brevity yet it was understood by all.

As time slipped by the sounds grew more urgent and yet the measures being performed only elicited increasing dejection in the voice, "No pulse. No pulse."

Suddenly, the hubbub was split by a yelp of pain and a muttered curse and an immediate embarrassed apology. A young nurse had inadvertently injected a spring-firing syringe into her own hand as she was hurriedly preparing the instrument for urgent use. Someone helped her back from the fray and sat her on the chair at the end of my bed. She was oblivious to my horrorstricken stare. Her white face was drenched with perspiration and shock. She covered the bleeding hand with a gauze swab. In evident disbelief she again inspected the puncture wound in the palm and the exit hole still bleeding on the back of the hand. Her head tilted back, her eyes closed tightly to hold in the pain, a stream of tears rolled silently down her cheeks.

I felt so helpless, my hands still bare in their undressed state held aloft as I had been trained to do. I could do nothing to support that young woman in her moment of need, but I shared her anguish.

Gradually, time ran out for Fred. They had exhausted their repertoire of life-saving measures. Fred was gone.

Instruments and apparatus were collected and put back on the trolley. The team leader broke the painful silence with a whispered word of thanks and praise.

"Thanks, guys. We did our best but lost, this time. We'll do the review at eight."

She thus scheduled the necessary discussion of their team action, trying to learn from the sequence of events and aiming to be ready for the next similar emergency.

In the adjoining nursing station the phone rang. The front desk staff forewarned the arrival of the family members. There was a hurried consultation and a resident was allocated the unenviable task of meeting the immediate family. Their late night visit was the response to a call half an hour earlier, indicating a serious setback in Fred's condition.

As hurried footsteps burst through the doors at the end of the corridor leading to the ward, the resident steeled himself to face Fred's relatives and give them the news.

Then the weeping started, indicating to us all that the news had been relayed. It continued in paroxysms of anguish as they came in to the ward to be at the bedside. In life, Fred's burned features were a sight to avoid, but the added mask of death must have been devastating for his young daughter and her husband.

As if from nowhere, the hospital chaplain appeared and slipped quietly through the door to join them. His very presence brought a lessening in their grief and each of us in that room drew comfort from him as he prayed.

Gently, the Padre guided that newly bereaved couple from the room and soon after, Fred's body was placed on a stretcher trolley and discreetly moved away to the morgue. The empty bed was wheeled out into the corridor to allow the last bit of tidying up and the removal of the bedside locker.

The horror of the past three hours hung heavily in that room, and every little sound had its own sad meaning. One of Fred's bedroom slippers was dropped and rolled under the curtain. My eyes riveted onto that fur lined moccasin. It looked so very empty. It told me Fred was gone. A hand snatched the slipper back without a word. Next, there was a little scratching sound as scotch tape was torn from its attachment on the over-bed light fixture. A sob escaped as the nurse quickly gathered up the redundant "Get well soon" cards that had hung above his bed.

The ensuing silence was finally broken as Jill made an apologetic, tired appearance at the end of my bed. My naked hands were still aloft as she had left them and I was wide awake, somber and very afraid.

"I'm sorry," she started to say, but her need was greater than mine. She broke off, lost for words as she came along the edge of the bed. Tears were brimming in her eyes.

"Scoot off for a cup of tea and a cigarette," I whispered. With a wordless nod of thanks she left.

Ten minutes later she returned, her composure restored, to continue with my dressings. Only the fatigue lines on her face belied the encouraging little smile she had miraculously conjured up for me. We were both anxious to maintain silence, respectful of the inner turmoil that we shared. Her years of training and experience had once again helped her to contend with the tragic happenings of the previous three hours. In managing to carry on with the immediate tasks, her fortitude shone through. This was so vital in helping me deal with the devastating proximity of death from which I had been separated by just a flimsy curtain. It was Jill's inner strength, her very presence and loving care that got me through that "Code 4" and time of death, the night the clock stopped for Fred.

CHAPTER 20
Physio Time, 10-Minute Km

Eons ago, I had had a brief educational exposure to the treatment of burn patients. That was during my training in London, England. A two-day visit to a centre specializing in the care of the severely burned had given me scant but memorable impressions of the horror of that specialty. During that brief interlude, I vowed that I would not be involved in the care of those poor souls. I just didn't have the heart to face such glaring suffering day after day.

By some quirk of good fortune, more than a quarter of a century had elapsed before I was again to witness physiotherapy in the care of a burn patient. It was the ultimate irony that I was on the receiving end of the treatment.

Within 48 hours of my accident, even while still on the ventilator machine to ensure regular oxygen exchange into my lungs, a physiotherapist was in attendance to assist with suctioning of accumulations of phlegm from my lungs and to perform some passive chest vibrations, somewhat akin to artificial respiration techniques used on the unconscious. This helped to force out stagnant pockets of air that were not expelled by the ventilator.

As my flaccid unconscious state gradually changed to a more violent semiconscious level, I alternated between maximum uncooperation, defiance and exemplary respiratory excursion.

There was little need for any invitation to keep my joints mobile; rather, a great concern was to keep me from flailing my limbs around and trying to keep me tied into the bed.

On transfer to the Burn Unit, concerns over my ability to breathe diminished although routine checks of my vital capacity were maintained with unpredictable levels of cooperation on my part. I tended to express my indignation at being required to blow into a silly little mouthpiece to see how far I could force a bunch of plastic balls up a measured perspex tube. I had forgotten that I had frequently forced and cajoled patients to do exactly that same exasperating exercise, but was now unimpressed with the value of the whole performance when it was my turn.

Nor was I beyond extolling the virtues of this procedure when a fellow sufferer in the neighbouring bed required the services of my colleague. I provided my professional contribution in ordering the poor patient to breathe deeper, cough louder, to spit further. I was oblivious of the titters, as the physiotherapist and a few of the nurses enjoyed the irony of the situation.

Physiotherapist Abby MacLeod was to be my mentor, blithe spirit, pace setter, and task master. Providentially, her skill, dedication, streak of stubbornness, quick-surfacing sense of humour, and infinite patience were qualities that endeared her to me and engendered respect from me for her professionalism.

Abby's periodic visits to the ward were carefully synchronized so that she would apprehend each of us patients at the exact moment when we were failing to comply with her orders. As with many of the patients suffering with burned hands, a constant irksome requirement was the need to elevate those limbs. This was to minimize the swelling likely to occur should we let the hands down for any length of time. The word would be spread marginally ahead of her arrival, "Hands up," and like some chorus line, misshapen bandaged limbs would immediately be elevated.

This pantomime always triggered in my mind the theme tune of the Club Med organization with their catchy rendition of the "Hands Up" song. Regretfully, the decor and personalities in Foothills were a far cry from the windswept, sun-drenched beaches, and allure of Mexico or the Bahamas.

Abby tolerated my relatively passive involvement in the morning whirlpool tank immersion, but my subsequent two visits per day to the Physio Department demanded action on my part. Within three or four days of my move to the Burn Unit, always after a much too brief rest, it was physio time. Routinely, I would be trundled off to the Rehab Unit in one of those cumbersome lazy-boy chairs for my mid-morning physio session. Encumbered with a mobile drip stand, with an ongoing transfusion leading into an arm vein, hands supposedly held aloft, legs elevated, and constantly terrified in case people might bump into my helpless form, I was exhausted by the time I arrived in the open exercise area.

I didn't recognize it at the time, but being placed in a general patient area as opposed to the isolation of the Burn Unit was the first step in my acceptance of a painful socialization program. There was a camaraderie and mutual support amongst that diverse patient population, much akin to the denizens of a military establishment. A semblance of rank and respect was quickly established amongst the patients, proportionate to the severity of wounds, evident disabilities, and above all duration of suffering or stay in the hospital.

Although I was not in particularly good shape at the time, I quickly assessed that many there were very much worse off than I was. This was my first positive recognition of real hope for my future, although this theory of relativity was apt to fail me when I dared allow myself a more objective analysis of my condition.

In the intrigue and excitement of meeting new people on that first occasion, my exhaustion was forgotten, and the spark of new friendships kindled.

My concentration span on those visits was distressingly short. After a brief chat with those around me, the work of exercising fast-stiffening limbs and digits began. This was aimed at combatting the contracture of scar tissue, with its potential for creating disabling joint limitation and disfigurement. Stretching and strengthening exercises were invariably painful procedures. A routine injection of analgesics prior to visiting Physio provided some lessening of suffering but the exercise sessions were nevertheless justifiably dreaded.

To give some respite and make the half-hour stay more palatable, Abby would leave me for a few minutes to attend to the needs of some other suffering soul. Her admonishment that I continue some specified exercises, with the threat of unmentionable consequences if I stopped, did little to delay my immediate sagging into exhausted sleep. In just moments, I'd be gone from this world. My head lolled on my chest but my hands still feebly tried to maintain the "hands up" pose. As I slumped, the blanket would slide off, and the skimpy hospital gown revealed its secrets.

Understanding the causes of this lapse from activity, Abby woke me with a mild rebuke, discreetly adjusted my coverings and, with an appropriate touch of humour, started me on the next uphill mile to recovery. A few more stretches, a few more resistance exercises, and an ongoing cajoling of "Just a tad more," would keep me trying. My eyes would glance at the clock above the door and the moment the hands reached 11:30, I would start my harangue about the urgency of returning to the ward for lunch. It became quite a game for Abby to conjure up different inducements to tease a few extra minutes from me, and while my mind was frantically searching for good reasons to get out of the place, she would have somehow coaxed another degree or two of range of movement from my stiffened joints.

The all-too-brief half-hour after-lunch siesta was always disturbed by my scheduled travels to Occupational Therapy, and then another session in Physio at three o'clock. Thanks to Abby's perseverance, each day I'd sputter through the series of activities she planned. By quarter to four I'd again become a clock watcher, but I had the misfortune to have had assigned to me a physiotherapist who was never in a rush to leave work regardless of her four o'clock finishing time.

"Don't you have a home to go to?" I'd explode in exasperation at five past four.

She'd deflate my antagonism, quipping, "Gee. Is it that time already? Time flies when you're having fun," and as a reward for my questionable behaviour she'd personally wheel me back to the Burn Unit where she'd tarry a few minutes longer, even finding an orange juice to tide me over until supper arrived at five to five. Friends again, we'd exchange a few mutually refuelling kind words. Those extra moments of caring by her were very special for me.

As the weeks progressed and I finally had a walking heel put on my cast, the big moment arrived when I could step on my left foot. The 24 hours of waiting for the cast to harden after the fitting of the heel piece was an unendurable lifetime; I was so keyed up for the great moment of walking that the staff were anxious to get it over and done with, to quieten me down.

Abby was present for the great happening, to assist the two nurses who were on guard for the inevitable disaster that everybody except me anticipated. I'd lost almost 40 pounds in those few weeks but all their forewarnings were of no avail as I prepared to launch myself from a sitting position on the edge of the bed.

Trying hard to disassociate myself from the helping hands around me, I assumed that my body would react automatically when my feet hit the floor. The anticipated reflexes that should have triggered the appropriate antigravity muscles failed to materialize and even the rescuing support team were caught short, as I buckled to my knees before they could hold me.

I just couldn't believe that my body would fail me so. My euphoria of the moment was such that I was mildly amused by the proof of my loss of physical prowess. Much later on it dawned on me just how serious was my weakness, but at that moment the ceremonial 20-step walk around the confines of the ward, albeit assisted by my entourage of helpers, was the first great accomplishment of my rehabilitation. It was hardly a marathon, but I was unquestionably mobile!

The euphoria was short-lived when next day my visit to Physio provided the opportunity to go it alone along the supporting parallel bars. I still needed considerable support. The bars were lifted to their maximum height so that I could rest my unbandaged elbows on them for support. At first I just stood up from the chair, half dragging myself to the erect position. Surreptitiously, Abby placed the full length mirror at the other end of the bars. This was designed to help me achieve a better postural stance and discard the slumped, crooked, stance I was using.

Struggling upright and, on her instructions, looking ahead, I was frozen into immobility. It was the first time I had seen myself since the crash. I was devastated at the sight of a bent, frail, old man; but for the presence of other patients, I would have burst into tears.

Sensing my turmoil, encouraging words came from those nearby.

"Go for it, Blair! Your first hundred yard dash. You can do it!" Above all, Abby's gentle grasp on my upper arm gave great emotional, if not physical, support.

Dreading and hating what I saw, and yet almost hypnotized and drawn forward by that haggard spectre in the mirror, I staggered along the 15 feet to the glass and stopped. Oblivious of those around, I concentrated with all my strength on the face glaring back at me. Entranced, I peered forward, suddenly aware that my glasses must still be lying broken at Angus Creek. As if from a great distance, Abby's voice forced my thoughts to rationalize and accept what I saw.

With immense gentleness she asked, "Well, what do you think, Blair?"

I stared on, searching for the right words, and finally got it all together. The tension had built up in the room as those around had retreated into a respectful silence. After an age, with a bit of a sigh and an accepting shrug of my shoulders, I managed to intone, "It could have been worse."

The spell was broken. I had taken another gigantic step on the road to recovery. With a weight lifted off my shoulders, I turned around. Inviting Abby to leave off her supporting grasp, I made it back unassisted. As I slumped into the chair a little cheer went up from my supporters. Buoyed up by all that praise, I lunged up again and trudged back along the bars. I had straightened up considerably on this trip. I looked my reflection straight in the eye, and knew I'd be okay.

Having got the bit between my teeth, my adrenaline up, all my exhaustion was gone. I tramped back and forward along those bars until Abby dragged me into my chair.

"It's quarter to twelve, Blair. Way past your lunch time." I glanced at the clock, unbelieving. "Time flies when you're having fun," I got back at her. As she wheeled me back to the ward we both enjoyed the silence, each treasuring the moment of progress that had occurred. She was much more aware than I of the huge hurdle that we'd overcome together.

As the days stretched into weeks, so the attendances in the Physio exercise area became more prolonged and involved new challenges. My legs continued to be bandaged in gauze "cling" dressing and miles of elastocrepe, to maintain even pressure from toe to groin, so I was, consequently, unable to do very much in the way of specific leg exercise. My thighs had withered away to half their former size, but the various wounds and gaps in the skin were gradually closing. The donor sites, from which the grafts had been farmed, were also healing over well.

The primary focus of the mobilizing exercise sessions was to restore movement to joints in the fingers. They had enjoyed prolonged immobilization to allow the tiny grafts to become firmly adherent, especially over the knuckles. When the long wire prongs, which had been inserted longitudinally through each finger during the surgical procedures, were eventually ready for removal, the dreary bending of joints began. Degree by painful degree, we achieved it – together.

Much of this restoration of movement in my fingers was gained by slow manual stretching done by Abby. As I sat, tolerating her ministrations, she delicately yet persistently gained range. Like a wrestler working over the little finger to gain a submission, she had pushed each joint that one degree while I sat and sweated with the pain and fear. I hollered, "Enough!" This would give her the signal to tease another minuscule movement, before stepping back to survey the progress.

She often worked with two or three of us patients in a little group, and we would suffer along with each person on the firing line, as he became the recipient of her "tender loving care."

With much of the hand surface still heavily bandaged, it was difficult to make much use of the extensive equipment available around that exercise area. I took pleasure in helping some of the more grievously injured patients who were wheeled down, still in their beds from other wards, and I encouraged them as they worked on pulleys and weights. It was clearly not only an exercise time for them, but a time of diversion and change in environment. It was an equally rewarding change for me to see patients from wards other than the Burn Unit. Hearing the graphic tales of their prolonged bedridden state made me grateful that, within a month, at least I was up and independently mobile in my wheelchair.

Although there was encouraging progress, each tiny new achievement cumulatively building on previous improvements, a day came in mid-November which boosted my self-esteem beyond anything to date.

I had been eyeing the treadmill for some time, but Abby had cautioned me that I couldn't get onto it until I got my Jobst panty hose. These were needed to give an even, total support to the grafts and donor sites on the legs.

Additionally, I was having considerable swelling in the left ankle and foot as I had not been observing the orthopaedic consultant's cautions about overuse since the plaster cast had been removed.

The day came and, dressed in my fancy new panty hose, shorts, and running shoes, I finally took my first tentative steps on the treadmill with unaccustomed enthusiasm.

With the motor running at its slowest rate and the rubber matting on the platform inching round at a snail's pace, I stumbled and limped my way, lunging sideways against the support handrails as each step on my left foot shot pain throughout my whole being.

The elasticized Jobst stockings seemed to get tighter with every step but I was on the road again.

Abby stopped the machine after a mere minute and said, "That'll probably be enough for your first time. Try it again this afternoon."

Like an addict who has had his first teasing taste, I was hooked.

"I'm not getting off this thing until I've done one kilometer," I said with an unintentional vehemence.

Seeing my hyped-up state and reluctant to spoil my obvious joy of the moment, she cautioned, "Just another two minutes, at most, or you'll be sorry." She set the little timer accordingly. Advising me to lie on the bench to cool off after my exercise period, she left to attend to some other work, saying she'd return.

Like a mischievous child, I waited until she was out of sight. I angled down until I could maneuver the clock dial to ten minutes, hurting my unwieldy bandaged fingers. A full two-hand effort on my part was needed to turn the little dial that Abby had so easily set with finger tip adjustment.

Hypnotized by the monotonous rumble of that motor, I lunged into a contorted stumbling pace, eyes glazed and fixed on the distant Bow River as it meandered through the suburbs half a mile away. Through the plate glass windows in front of me, the crisp November chill was invigorating and I became entranced with my own pace, oblivious of the sound around me. My heart was pounding, adrenaline surged and the taste of victory was in my mouth. Soon I had that distinctively bitter surge of saliva in my mouth, and could feel the start of body sweat as I reran the marathon. Mile after glorious mile I just floated along, but some irritant was invading my peace. I glanced left, thinking another runner was passing. She had an ominous look, hands on hips, mouth puckered up, and her exasperated explosion brought me to a dragging stop.

"Get off!" she spat, and just then the timer bell rang. She cracked into a smile, her wrath evaporating as she sensed my unbelievable satisfaction in the achievement of that 10-minute escape.

I struggled over to a bench and collapsed, joyous, as I sweated and steamed. It took ages to cool and whether she knew she couldn't cope with my euphoria or that my sweaty body did not encourage closeness, on that one occasion I got away without doing hand exercises. By the time I had staggered back along to the Burn Unit, I knew I was going to pay dearly for my 10-minute frolic. My ankle was pounding inside the now brutally tight, stockinged foot and the left knee, whose large burnt area had healed over so beautifully, had been grated horribly by the movement of the elastic stocking. The snugness of the body section of those panty hose was clammy with sweat.

The news of my foolishness preceded me to the ward and with less than normal gentleness I was disrobed, bathed, and gently reprimanded for my indiscretions.

When the nurse left, I lay back, my thoughts soaring with victory and oblivious of the scolding. There was hope. I kept gazing at the ceiling, not daring to break the spell in my aspirations for future running by seeing the hands, the puffy foot, the blistered knee, or the scraggly limbs. The ecstasy of it all! I knew I'd run again. "Ten whole minutes," I reminisced. A smug smile crept onto my face, and was still there when I struggled painfully to O.T. after an ever-so-brief after-lunch nap.

Later that afternoon, the reactionary pain and stiffness in my ankle and knee made the discomforts in my fingers seem mere trivia. I gloated on, while Abby performed her routine efforts to mobilize the stiff joints of the fingers.

My mind was far away, thinking of running distances and times. Abby was sufficiently understanding to let me dream of that memorable first kilometer run in Physio Time.

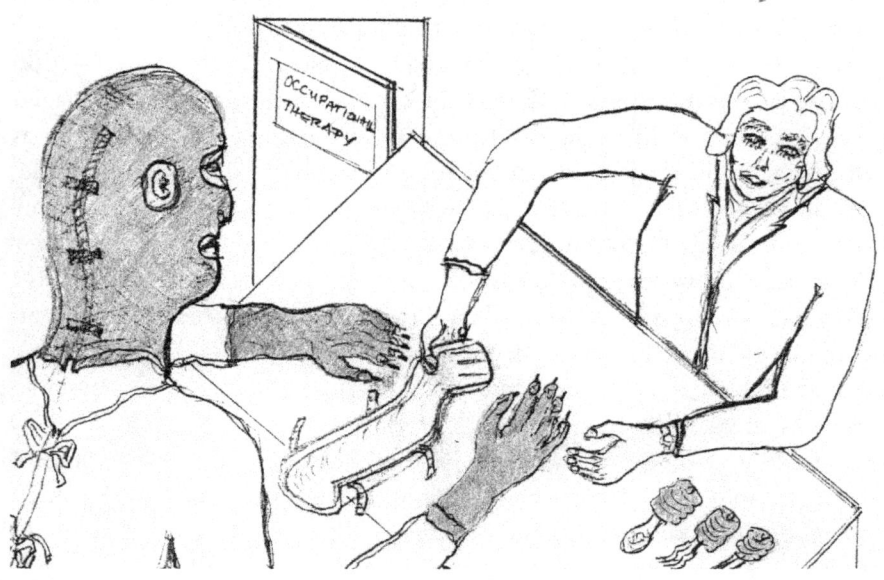

CHAPTER 21
O.T. Time

Although I had spent many years of my professional life working in close proximity to and often sharing working space with Occupational Therapists, I had little awareness of the depth of their knowledge and diversity of their skills. I gained better understanding of one specialist area in which they are involved during my three-month personal immersion program. It started within 24 hours of my arrival in the Trauma Unit and my personal instructor was Occupational Therapist Delilah Bailey.

Delilah's task on that first day was to provide hand splints made from a thermoplastic material. Sansplint was chosen for its capability of quick and easy softening by simply dipping it into boiling water for a few seconds. It was ideal malleable material which would form and quickly harden into the desired shapes.

It was imperative that my hands and fingers be held in positions likely to minimize joint contractures. The splints were helpful in keeping the wrists extended, the knuckle joints bent and the fingers straight while maintaining the thumb pushed out and away from the neighbouring digits.

When I had been at my lowest ebb of consciousness, Delilah had had the opportunity to treat me without my regular antagonism. In the ensuing ten weeks, each time some unpleasant pain-provoking change or modification to my splints was indicated, the onus for this change was to be hers.

As I had reluctantly emerged from my ten-day "big sleep," an early recollection was of the pain involved in the shaping of night splints which were bandaged on each evening to immobilize and protect those painful hands. As soon as I had managed to adapt to the splint and found them almost comfortable, Delilah would see fit to make further modifications to them to better hold my joints in a more suitable position.

Long and loud were my petitions that the splint was absolutely perfect, as I watched it disappear into the boiling cauldron and emerge seconds later as an unrecognizable floppy piece of plastic. The moulding and bandaging onto my protesting limb was a recurrent fight in which, despite her diminutive physique, Delilah was always victorious.

A humbling lesson for me was watching another patient with severely burned legs have full splints which ran from his toes to his buttocks. The shallow trough encasing the full ankle complex and the knees held his legs in a brutally straight position. His anguish made my plight seem trivial.

As time went by and I started feeding myself, I was grateful for O.T. assistance in improvising various forms of gadgetry to help me in this usually simple task that I now found so difficult. Building up the handles of various implements such as spoons, by enlarging them with a sponge rubber casing made them of better use for me, despite my feeble grasp. These helpful modifications offered me a sense of independence at an earlier stage than my temporarily disabled hands could provide, and did much to lessen the desolation that my hospitalization and physical limitations were causing.

An article of immeasurable value in providing comfort was a special collar designed by the O.T. staff. A thick, contoured trough carved out of heavy duty sponge was the perfect neck support to hold my weepy head wound clear of the pillow and doubled as a rotation restrictor for my neck, stopping my tendency to roll onto my fragile, reconstructed ears.

Delilah contributed meticulous care and patience in the measuring for all my Jobst's garments. Gloves, a face mask, and panty hose of specially designed elastic support material were an essential part of my wardrobe for the next two years. It was only when I finally visited the Jobst factory in Toledo that I became fully appreciative of Delilah's insistence on the accuracy of the multitude of measurements required.

Prior to the arrival of the Jobst gloves some interim gloves were made in O.T. The soft supportive stockinette material fit well, yet accepted the bulges of the finger bandaging and remaining wire spikes protruding from the tips. Even the first wearing of those temporary gloves was a boost to morale, as it was one more step of progress.

My pride in those new white gloves was so great that when my cumbersome efforts at self-feeding brought about the inevitable spillage of food on them, I childishly viewed the mishap as an immense tragedy.

By a quirk of scheduling much of my occupational therapy time in the department was spent in the early afternoon. My first few visits to O.T., spent slouched in the mobile lounge chair, proved to be little more than a diversional change of scenery. Even at that, I saw little of those surroundings as I emerged from sleep reluctantly for only a few moments, then my head would again loll and my limbs would gradually lapse from their required "hands up" position. Their leaden weight dragged them down to repose on whatever supporting surface they might be guided by gravity. Sometimes they would only drift onto my lap, while at other times they would descend till the hand almost touched the floor. The staff were a great team and took turns at cajoling me back into another brief moment of wakefulness. Other patients who had been through that tired stage were tremendously supportive as well, no doubt remembering the helplessness and futility that they, too, had experienced.

Gradually, as my energy returned and I was able to tolerate a more productive session of therapy, I was introduced to exercises designed to re-establish function, strength and mobility.

The superficial simplicity of some of those exercises mocked my inability to perform them. I just could not cope with the frustration of being unable to twist a wooden roller bar or pull a tiny weight up on a child-sized meccano pulley system. Worst of all was my tantrum provoked by being asked to play checkers on a board on which the pieces were attached by Velcro. Although the whole purpose of the exercise was to make me work my fingers, when the hook parts of the material became stuck onto the tubinet gloves it was all just too much for my patience.

In answer to my demands for something more manly to perform, I was eventually let loose in their small rehabilitation workshop.

As I had spent many years remodelling houses, building fences, greenhouses, and innumerable forts for Ian and Craig in their early days, I looked at the potential in that workshop and just knew that I'd found my escape den.

Delilah stood back and gave me free-rein to prowl around that small shop. She was well aware of the outcome long before it became evident to me that I couldn't hold a hammer or saw, touch any power tools, and had to avoid dust or oily surfaces. Within minutes I beat a sad retreat from what had appeared an idyllic diversion.

I should have learned from this lesson, but still plagued the staff for something a little more appropriate, something more imaginative to keep me busy. Eventually, we compromised with yet another project that was doomed before the start. The challenge was a chess set. I did manage to achieve the simple task of putting the first line of pawns in place, but that was the end of my success. Attempts at placing the major pieces got no further than the king, as several pawns were scattered by the cumbersome padded glove, inflexible fingers and my uncoordinated grasp.

Frustrated by my performance, I watched, with envy, as other patients accepted the activities recommended by the O.T. staff. My stubbornness nurtured its own grief.

One facet of my visits to O.T. that was particularly acceptable and helpful to me, was Delilah's guided tour through segments of a huge photo album. This showed pictures of other patients who had undergone the whole process of recovery. I found the chronological sequence of progress reassuring. She gently de-emphasized the disability aspects and enlarged upon examples of ability shown in the pictures. I found hope and dared to think that one day I might get back to my practice.

Each Wednesday a hand clinic was scheduled for the whole afternoon. This was the opportunity for former patients to return as outpatients. Their varied hand conditions were re-assessed by their surgeons and other rehabilitation team members. A steady stream of these patients arrived in Occupational Therapy for readjustments of splints or the provision of new imaginative gadgets to help them in their everyday activities. From time to time a former burn patient would come into O.T. on a purely social visit. Many were happy to be shown off by their proud therapist as an example of how well things could turn out. I was introduced to several who had had extensive burns and struggled with disbelief when Delilah pointed out their functional abilities and minimal residual scarring. She emphasized that many of those patients had earlier suffered more serious and extensive burns than mine. After a few of those success story presentations, I developed a discouraging habit of asking how long it had all taken to achieve this visible miracle. I was devastated one day when the proud displayer said with excitement, "Only two years."

As time dragged past, a gradual change was occurring. I was stumbling along in my dot-and-carry walking pattern, expertly maintaining "hands-up." Noticing a first-timer sprawled in a half-asleep pose in the mobile lounge chair that I had long since vacated, I stopped and took the time to offer a word of encouragement. As she managed to drag open one bleary eye, I endowed her with my monumental experience in such matters.

"They're really good folks in here, you know. You'll be surprised how they'll fix you up in no time." For a moment she held me in vague focus before her head sagged forward and the bandaged arm slumped over the edge of the chair, a useless appendage. Gently I lifted the floppy limb and placed it caringly on the pillow in her lap. I felt an inner warmth reawakening: the joy of helping others and the diminishing of my prolonged self-centred and demanding ways.

Delilah's patient tolerance of my persistent complaints about gloves and especially the vise grip tightness of the face mask was a feature that engendered in me great admiration for her personally, and for her chosen profession. An example of the teamwork in that department was the ready offering of help amongst the staff in many of the treatment programs requiring more than one pair of hands.

Much of the precision, dexterity, and strength that I take so much for granted today, is thanks to the contribution of Delilah and her fellow professionals. I hope that my belated acknowledgement of their help will offset my apparent ingratitude during my time in O.T.

CHAPTER 22
12:27 Jobst Time

Conrad Jobst's birth in 1889 in Erlanger, Germany, occurred in a decade when three other fellow countrymen were receiving recognition for their inventive genius. Their names, Diesel, Benz, and Daimler have subsequently remained the hallmark of automotive engineering expertise.

It was thus not surprising that workmanship and efficiency became the byword of Jobst's chosen career in engineering. He is credited with more than forty patents in a diverse range of products. Precision and attention to detail were features that connected his disparate pursuits ranging from toothbrush manufacture, automobile sunroofs, precision gun sights, oceangoing ships' propellers, high fidelity instrumentation, and finally, the product that would hold his name, the Jobst pressure gradient support garment.

By happenstance, Jobst's inventive genius and imaginative engineering mind focused on a health concern that had plagued him all of his adult life. He suffered from chronic congestion in the leg veins causing recurrent ulcers on the skin. By the late 1940's, he had observed that spending time standing in his swimming pool brought considerable relief to the circulatory stasis in his legs. It was still a long step from his recognition of the mechanical benefits produced by the surrounding pressure of water, to the final acceptance in the hallowed halls of medicine, of his prototypes of elasticized leg support stockings. He endured many rebuffs in his attempts to present his newfound knowledge to the medical fraternity, but finally found support during a visit to an aeronautical engineering laboratory. His own investigation revealed that carefully graduated diminishing pressure at progressively higher levels on the leg provided optimum support, producing beneficial results while still avoiding any circulatory restriction. His theory supported the findings of researchers investigating the needs for pressure suits used by airmen in high altitude flights in postwar aviation.

After many exasperating delays and setbacks, Jobst finally established a small scale production plant in Toledo, Ohio, in 1950. From a modest beginning this organization mushroomed into the world-renowned Jobst Institute, and continues to provide a product that Jobst had first designed to benefit his own painful and debilitating condition.

During the next decade the demand for increased productivity at the Jobst factory in Toledo continued in response to the orders from around the globe. Sadly, his death in 1957 prevented Jobst from witnessing the monumental expansion in the use of the garments he had pioneered.

In the early '60's, leading researchers showed that the application of external artificial pressure helped minimize the ridges that can occur in scar healing. Additionally, they observed that thickenings that had already occurred were subsequently lessened and flattened by prolonged counter-pressure.

As has happened in many great medical discoveries, coincidence of need for a new, even surface skin pressure system for scars, and the existence of Jobst material, united to bring about a miracle for burn sufferers.

The Jobst pressure gradient garments, already credited with undisputed benefits for venous insufficiency, were shown to be an ideal support medium in the treatment of recovering lower limb burn scar patients. It wasn't long before the same principles of accuracy of measurement were adopted in the provision of support garments for other areas of the body, including the great challenges of the undulating contours of the face and hands.

I was very excited at the prospects of getting into my Jobst stockings as it seemed everybody had been telling me that it would be a big step in my progress. I had built up some unrealistic expectations of the miracle that would occur the moment I put them on. In my mind, I imagined an immediate move from being a disabled pain-wracked burn victim, swathed in bandages, to becoming suddenly almost cured, in the new Jobst outfit. It was time for a touch of reality.

News came from the Occupational Therapist that the Jobst's production team had again amazingly beaten the clock. My outfit arrived only five days from the time I was measured. How this miracle of efficiency had occurred was only divulged during my visit to the Jobst Institute three years later, and my indebtedness to that great organization was belatedly brought to my awareness.

I had been impressed with the O.T.'s precise measurement session just those few days earlier, even though I squawked and complained about the time taken to complete the job and the apparently unnecessary fastidiousness of her technique. She had insisted on measuring the circumference of my limbs at every inch, from toenail to the top of the thigh. In my state of chronic fatigue and pain, all this bothersome attention to detail seemed excessive and unpardonable. The recorded measurements were sent off by express mail and at the time I took it very much for granted that this marvel of science would be immediately available. I was unaware of the distant team who would play such a big part in my recovery.

More than 2,000 miles from Calgary Foothills Hospital, in an unpretentious brick-faced building on the banks of the Ohio River, a dedicated team of professionals met my personal needs and produced a pair of made-to-measure Jobst pressure gradient stockings. From the moment of receiving my statistics on the patented measuring tape system, they created the garments individualized to my unique dimensions and dispatched the final article within two working days, thus honouring a guarantee of production of which they could be deservedly proud. Almost 20 members of the 500 staff at the Institute were involved in the crafting of my super-stretch panty hose.

Jobst clerical staff received the mail order and documented the information, allocating a patient number and transposing the figures onto computer screens for easy and efficient storage and retrieval. Design engineers then made up the pattern doing automatic corrections where measurements failed to reveal anatomical idiosyncrasies, such as the curve of the heel or kneecap. The final pattern was drawn up into several separate segments, allowing preset extra measurements to accommodate a millimeter or two here or there for the seams of the component parts.

Another staff member entered the coding to select the appropriate strength, thickness of weave, and elasticity of the fabric to be used. From the dozens of bolts of material, only one would suit my individual needs, providing the required gentleness of support for the delicate healing grafts, yet also offering adequate pressure to support and minimize the post-fracture edema in my dislocated left ankle.

The next step in the process was the placing of a miniaturized outline of these segments of my suit onto a computer screen. With video arcade skill, a technician juggled the individual pieces of this screen jigsaw puzzle to fill the screen completely, leaving no blanks. This guaranteed the maximum utilization of material when the screen picture was transferred and enlarged with mathematical exactness to true garment dimensions, ready for cut-out on a selected four-foot wide roll of elastic fabric.

A laser beam then zipped out the programmed patterns in seconds, its ultra-violet beam cutting out hundreds of individual segments of many different patients' garments. Every single cutout had tiny code numbers attached to enable the sorters to manually collect and envelope each order before sending it along the production line to the seamstresses.

Even the thread selected for use in sewing each garment was chosen for the particular elasticity requirements of that garment and, before the tiny code numbers were snipped off, another staff member checked to ensure that the components used were all correct. More caring hands were involved in checking the workmanship and passing the item along the production line for further documentation, billing, packaging, addressing, and mailing out by express post, all within the promised 48 hours.

As if aware of the urgency of my needs even the U.S. Mail and Canada Post made their contribution and transported the miracle item in an unbelievably short time to its Calgary destination.

The package had my name and patient number on it, so there could be no doubt that it was intended for me. The first onslaught of doubt occurred when the package was opened and out tumbled a tiny pair of miniature panty hose. They had obviously been designed for a skinny cabbage-patch doll.

Seeing the alarm on my face, one of the nurses demonstrated the elasticity of the fabric by stretching one leg to show that it would fit my limb.

"There, you see. They'll stretch," she said.

I was far from convinced.

There were a few moments of indecision while the two cheerful young women determined front, back, inside, outside of the garment. The clear instructions for application, wear and care, provided a step by step eight-point agenda for putting on the garments.

Despite the disparity between my size 11 feet and the three-inch long foot portion of the stockings, the nurses' obvious confidence and experience in such matters made the reading of the instruction sheet unnecessary.

There was some confusion, delay, and debate on where to start but finally, as a team, we attacked the left foot, only recently removed from its plaster cast, and still grossly swollen. Pain and exasperation combined to provoke from me an unstemmed outpouring of insults and ingratitude addressed to those long-suffering nurses. The sounds of this altercation attracted an unexpected crowd as another nurse and an orderly appeared. My friends and fellow patients were disappointed that the curtains denied them their customary ringside viewing of this performance, and so they made their impudent contribution.

"Are they raping you, Blair?" guffawed Jim from the next bed. In the ensuing hilarity, it suddenly dawned on me that I was making an awful fuss.

My interference and impatience caused the mistake of trying to get the smaller right foot stocking on my swollen left foot and making a mockery of the meticulous measurement session of five days earlier. My contribution to the whole farce was solely vocal. My hands were still swathed in bandages, each finger sticking out in its bizarre, spread position. Uninformed as I was, even I knew that spiky wires and panty hose were incompatible, and in consequence I doubled up on the verbal contribution to make up for the dearth of manual assistance that I could provide.

After what seemed a lifetime but was really only a few minutes, the garments were squeezed up around the heels and up to the knees. To complicate the procedure of donning the new garments, there were still layers of gauze bandaging over the burned areas. These covers were required to separate the medicated skin care lotions from the elastic tissue in the garments. There was also an extra pad on the supersensitive left knee, which had been gashed as well as burned.

The panty hose unrolled past the top of my thighs. Although I had been measured at hip, buttock, waist, and lower rib cage, I now had new doubts about total fit.

My normally trim abdominal contour had not withstood the loss of 40 pounds unscathed and showed a saggy belly. In a bit of a rush the panty hose were yanked their last stretch-distance until the top rim perched precariously near my nipples. With tact, the nurses had chosen a rear view onslaught at this stage, and were anxious to ensure that adequate upward stretch was maintained on the thighs and buttocks. From my helpless viewpoint, I knew that the garments were snug, to say the least, around the buttocks and pelvis, but were a bit wrinkled over the navel. The top rim hung on my clearly defined lower four ribs but as soon as the nurses' hands were removed, the rim slipped down rib by rib, until it found a point of support at the level of my belly button.

This dilemma was corrected with shoulder straps. They suddenly appeared past each ear and with the benefit of a "cross-your-heart" technique at the back, the ensuing uplift was complete.

The support straps were temporarily attached with safety pins. I gazed in doubt, if not wonder, at the apparition. Although it wasn't exactly what I might have chosen, I was ready for the road or perhaps more ready for ballet. I made a few tentative moves and, snug though the fitting was, found I could bend where I was supposed to bend. With a token pas de chat (at least an inch off the floor) I received an accolade and survived the next big step in my recovery. Donning a gown on top of the revealing new outfit, I lay back to rest after the exertion of dressing. With the screen swung back to reveal the new accoutrements, I assured my fellow inmates that it hadn't been too horrendous a procedure. After a few experimental flexings involving my ankles and my knees I began to realize that these Jobst items weren't too bad after all. By the way everybody talked about the past success of the garments, I knew that all was going to be well.

Unfortunately, the simple, usually gratifying, experience, of an unassisted visit to the washroom took on a whole unexpected complexity. The casual dress code of the Burn Unit with the in vogue gown, open at the back, made for certain ease of such visits even for those with grossly limited use of bandaged hands. I was totally unprepared for the delays in the procedure with the Jobst panty hose as part of my wardrobe. First of all, the gown had to be taken off completely to allow access to the support straps over my shoulders. I threaded my way out of the sleeves and frantically groped at the top band of the formerly slack waist area. For some reason it was now snug and required much maneuvering to wriggle it down over my hips. I had to clutch at the top of the material at the thighs to prevent the whole suit from snapping right to the ankles. Sweating with exertion and exasperation, I waddled my way to the toilet bowl to take up the required stance.

The time and energy required to redress and struggle back the few steps to my bed rocked me from my confidence of some ten minutes earlier when I had set off on what I anticipated to be a 30-second excursion. I collapsed, exhausted and demoralized, and began to wonder about the future.

My premonitions of worse yet to come were well founded and can only be written about some considerable time later, when the Jobst is safely tucked away in a cupboard as a thing of the past. Only the clear proof now of its huge contribution to the great success of my recovery, lessens the memory of the anguish the Jobst experience caused then.

My hands were still in a bandaged state and had not yet been readied for tolerance for the unquestionable benefits of Jobst gloves. However, I was ready for the skull cover garment. The majority of the grafting had been performed on my nose, forehead, and top and back of the scalp.

Measuring the various diameters and dimensions of the skull was a long and tedious experience. Having by then accepted that the panty hose were, in fact, just right, although still a bit snug, I knew that all the meticulous measurements were worthwhile. Even in that lengthy tabulation of statistics, there had been lots of humour produced by the staff as they determined the widths and thicknesses of my lips in a smile, leer, or kiss position. Did it really matter, I'd asked, if my nostrils were flared or puckered up for a sneeze, and who cared that my right ear was now half an inch shorter than the left.

The great day arrived! "We've got your mask." I'd seen Bill Quilley struggle into his mask a week earlier. I mentally assured myself that it would be less work than putting on my panty hose, and faced the first fitting with undeserved calm. I should have wondered why I was taken to the private fitting room in occupational therapy. Although it was not completely soundproof, its thick walls and door certainly lessened the impact of my dissent. Despite my earlier experiences with the minuscule panty hose, I was shocked and totally unprepared for the brevity of my new mask. I swallowed hard and took a big breath, although exhaling might have been more appropriate. With skill, experience, and appropriate briskness, Delilah stretched the contraption and its key chin attachment over and around obstacles like ears and nose, and gently molded it over my tender skull. Delicately pressing the velcro closure strap, she succeeded in clamping on the imprisoning device.

I couldn't believe it could be so tight. I hadn't even had bandaging on my skull for the past few weeks except for a small patch of gauze taped at the back open area. The sudden pressure appalled me, but the pressure wasn't everywhere. My ears were protruding painfully and I was aware of the edges cutting in around the lips. It wrenched up the lower lip, scrunching the face into the contorted appearance of a two-year-old who has just bitten into a soap bar.

I was far from impressed. It was so bad I was speechless. Delilah anticipated the eventual explosion and hastened to assure me that masks always felt a little bit uncomfortable for a period.

"Uncomfortable!" I tried to screech.

The restraining chin band wouldn't allow sufficient opening of my mouth to let me vent my full description of my feelings. Being partially gagged was the ultimate indignity and my muted reactions were as unintelligible as they were unprintable. Even worse than the onslaught of physical pain was the horrid vision glaring back at me from the mirror. The few visible edges of skin were crimson with fury as I viewed the puckered, unrecognizable distortion of my features. Without a word of thanks for her patience and gentleness I stomped off, agreeing to wear it as long as I could. Within a few minutes my tolerance was exhausted. I kept my hand on the bedside emergency buzzer until the insistent beeping brought her running.

"Get this damn thing off," I wept.

With gentleness and urgency she removed the offending garment. She recognized the multiple components contributing to my pain; she knew the right words to bring solace. Her experience informed her not only of my discomfort from the physical pressure of the mask, but also the much greater psychological trauma of first seeing myself in the mask I'd have to wear, night and day, for the next two years. Kindly, she tucked me into bed. I glanced at my watch through tear-filled eyes. I'd worn the mask such a terribly short time.

"Only twelve minutes and 27 seconds," I whimpered to her.

She slipped away quickly so that I wouldn't see her tears. She, too, suffered with me at Jobst Time.

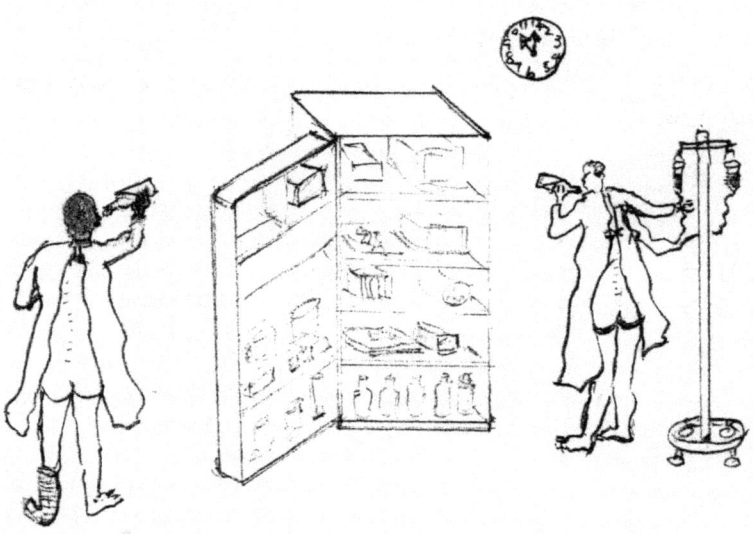

CHAPTER 23
40 Pounds in 20 Days

"When was the last time you had something to eat?" Dr. David Lenz asked shortly after my arrival into the Emergency Department at Cranbrook Hospital, Saturday, October 1st, 1983. His inquiry was made so that he could ascertain if recent food intake would preclude sending me to the operating room for immediate surgery.

Anxious to get to the 8 a.m. start of the Search and Rescue training program, I had only managed a quick cup of coffee at seven in the morning and then in my excitement at the training program during the day, had indulged in only a sandwich and a glass of orange juice for lunch. That had hardly been adequate to nourish me through the 20 days of my fast before I started taking in any food by mouth.

During that entire time, but more especially in the early days, there had been a serious loss of calories through the open areas of the burns, and the energy sapping attempts of my body to heal the wounds and fight off infection.

In addition to the early need to provide adequate fluid in my circulatory system and body tissue, one of the earliest treatment regimes was to pour in electrolyte fluids through intravenous transfusion.

Very early in my stay in the Trauma Unit, energy replacement by food intake was provided by means of a constant slow drip-feed via a nasogastric tube. In my delirium, I had done my best to tear the offending tube from my nose. If I had seen the murky brown colour of that highly nutritious fluid in its see-through plastic container, I would have been even more eager to dispose of the whole apparatus.

From past experience with other burn patients, the staff were well aware that rapid weight loss occurred in cases such as mine. It wasn't until a week or so after my arrival on the Burn Unit that I was finally perched on a chair-type weight scale and some approximation of my true weight loss was established. I had plummeted almost 40 pounds from my original lean build.

As I became moderately cooperative, I tolerated only small amounts of pureed foods. This was a far cry from my tastes and eating habits of former times. I had always had that enviable ability to eat mounds of food, especially desserts, and never had my weight vary more than a pound or so from the 175 I'd been since I was 20.

The nursing staff did a great job of coaxing me; "Just one more little spoonful."

To try to assess my actual intake, calorie estimates had to be recorded after each meal. "Quarter cup soup, half slice toast, quarter of an egg, two spoonfuls jello." It didn't amount to much at first, but by keeping note of every vital item, those few calories all accumulated, to gain the praise of the dietician watching my progress.

"Two hundred calories yesterday. A great job, you guys. Well done," she had written on my chart by way of encouragement for those spoon-feeding me.

It was a thankless job as I spat out any offending bits. Occasionally, after a laborious effort at feeding me, all would be lost in a moment as I brought it back up. My digestive system, oblivious to the distress it caused the nursing staff, was temperamental.

Gradually, as time went by, I started participating more in the selection of the foods to be prepared for me. Each day, on the breakfast tray, a multiple choice menu had to be filled in for the next day's meals. Pencil in hand, the nurse would conjure up a most appealing description of the listed items, to try to encourage me to order up as much of the high calorie nutriment as I could possibly consume.

I never thought much of it at the time, but it must have been an onerous chore requiring unbelievable patience, to spoon-feed me during those early days. Most of the time it fell to the nurses to perform this task, but occasionally other members of the team would help, and some visitors would offer their assistance if they happened to arrive at feeding time.

Alan Conway would arrive most evenings just before the supper trays were brought in. Very quickly I took it for granted that that was his job. He demonstrated great skill and thoughtfulness and an unlimited supply of patience. Alan was a target for any complaints that I had regarding my care. He would be vigorously informed in graphic detail of any procedures that had been practised on me, and was subjected to embellished accounts of that day's happenings.

One evening, as a special surprise for him, the nurse suggested that I dress up in my own shirt rather than the hospital garment. I was particularly impressed with this new dress code, aware that the shirt had been ironed by some caring person who had invaded my home and done some laundry chores. It was not my custom to perform such housekeeping requirements. Non-iron was a prerequisite of all my clothing.

It was inevitable that, while trying to interject spoonfuls of food into my mouth between my vocal unloading of the day's complaints, Alan inadvertently missed and a spoonful slopped down the front of that immaculate shirt.

With total disregard for all his kindness and effort, I exploded at what I felt was ham-fisted incoordination. He sat silent for a moment, the empty spoon still held aloft as he considered his words. Without a glimmer of a smile, but giving way to a twinkle in his eye, he silenced me with, "It's pretty tough trying to hit a moving target."

I got the message. As a team, we managed to get the remaining food transferred from the tray to my mouth with nary a further complaint.

Gradually, with the help of Occupational Therapy wizardry, I finally started on self-feeding. O.T. gadgetry included thicker handles on the cutlery, friction matting on the tray to stop the plates skidding around, sponge collars on cups to allow better gripping by my cumbersome bandaged hands as well as to insulate me from the heat of the contents.

Self-feeding was a laborious business and still required some assistance from the gang around. At first it was impossible to cut solid objects like bacon and meat, and there were some unexpected messy complications such as when cutting a boiled egg, but with perseverance and a great deal of help, the calorie count skyrocketed.

After a few days of experiencing the exasperation of needing all this help, I started thinking more carefully as I requested certain foods on the menu. Instead of the menu being selected on the merits of palate appeal, my requests were influenced by the simplicity that these items offered my limited self-feeding skills. In a moment of weakness, I happened to mention this jokingly to one of the nurses and I was surprised at the vehemence of her admonishment. Subsequently, I was obliged to overcompensate and select complicated items just to keep the peace.

Perhaps the greatest frustration, one that was practically impossible to overcome, was the difficulty of opening the many wrappings and containers for food condiments. With the hands still hugely wrapped in miles of clean bandage, even before my days in Jobst gloves, opening those small sugar wraps, plastic containers of jam, mayonnaise, cream, salt and pepper, was an unwelcome challenge. It may well have been good therapy for my fingers, but was a source of great annoyance. Even after many long months back in Cranbrook, those frustrations would continue to plague me.

By early November my appetite was responding to my body's needs. The brief note from the dietician, "Don't bother with calorie counts from now on. Thanks," indicated that I was no longer a concern meriting the constant analysis of intake. I had developed a ravenous appetite.

Milk and orange juice were supplied in rather small four-ounce plastic containers, so my increasing thirst provoked a request for the nurse to write in "two, please" beside the little square where one ticked off one's menu selections. Nevertheless, I was surprised when my tray arrived with all the items requested including two of the orange juice. Once I had developed my voracious appetite, I was amazed at the quality and quantity of food I consumed. Consistently, the dietary and kitchen staff provided an appetizing individual tray, punctually, warm, and unfailingly accurate, in answer to my requests on the menu list. It seemed inconceivable that these individualized meals could be provided for the more than one thousand patients in that hospital three times each day. Additionally, thousands of staff and visitors had access to delightful meals in the many canteens and restaurants. It certainly refuted the chronic complaint about institutional food. As with so many other members of the team, those providing the nutrition requirements at Foothills Hospital deserved high praise.

Despite the provision of an abundance of high quality food, extras and tidbits were also welcomed and encouraged. One group of visitors, attending daily to be with their son John in Bed Four, had located a source of luscious milkshakes somewhere on the way to the hospital. At first they brought in a couple of spare small portions of these treats. Having seen the delight with which I polished off that delicacy, sucking noisily on the straw to get the last drop, it soon became their regular contribution and I think they got as much satisfaction watching me consume their gift, as I gained from the joyous taste. It was a sad day for me when John was finally fit enough to go home and his visitors' last gesture of generosity was an unbelievably huge canister of the stuff, which I took as a personal challenge and managed to devour, unassisted.

During the early days when energy deficit was still a concern and the staff encouraged me to take in calories, the rule was, "Give him anything he'll eat or drink." Some visitors, reluctant to come empty-handed to the bedside, took this as an invitation to lavish food and drink, as if there wasn't enough already provided. Baskets of fruit and homemade pastry flooded in and none was wasted. Most of the patients with the voluminous hand wrappings found it very difficult to deal with fruit and were cautious of items that would be likely to stick to the bandages. However, as we were eager to offer back token gestures of our appreciation to the staff, we were delighted when they would help by using up the items brought in for us.

Aware of my enjoyment of the occasional beer, and wishing to bring something special, Evelyne Craig had searched all over Calgary to procure an imported Scottish ale. On her arrival I was not in a sufficiently conscious state to realize the work that had gone into her search for this gift. Days later, during one of Alan's visits, the conversation led to the mention of Evelyne's gift.

"I didn't know about that, " I insisted. "I'll just try one right now."

Even at my best pre-accident imbibing capability, the brown, frothy, evil-looking liquid would have been a challenge. My now sensitive palate did little justice to it, shown by its intolerance to the first over-zealous gulp.

"Where the hell did you find that muck?" I blamed Alan, having already forgotten the detailed explanation of the diligent search for this choice brew. And so the remainder of the untouched six-pack was stored away beside other contributions that had been secreted into the hospital by well-wishing visitors. I finally offered them all as a contribution to the staff's early Christmas party but never did hear whether anyone had managed to survive that noxious Scottish speciality.

As I became more independent, I developed yet another habit in my craving for further sustenance. A late night delight, after the dressing session was completed, was to slip quietly into the kitchenette on the Plastics Unit and brew myself a cup of tea and nibble at a few plain biscuits. I could fill the kettle but was terrified by the steam it produced, and would tiptoe around until I found someone who could help me pour the boiling water into the cup.

That late night routine was an opportunity to meet other insomniacs, and two or three of us would regularly gather and whisper away, during this illicit activity. The staff played along with our little nocturnal tea parties and would finally tiptoe in with a stage whisper admonition that would send us on our separate ways. It never dawned on most of us that our attire was anything but acceptable. With my inability to tie the tapes at the back of my hospital gown, I became inured to staff giggles and gentle joking about my occasional rearward exposure. The necessities of formal dress decorum were not a high priority of that daily windup feed time, and the few extra calories helped regain 20 of the 40 lost pounds, prior to my discharge from hospital.

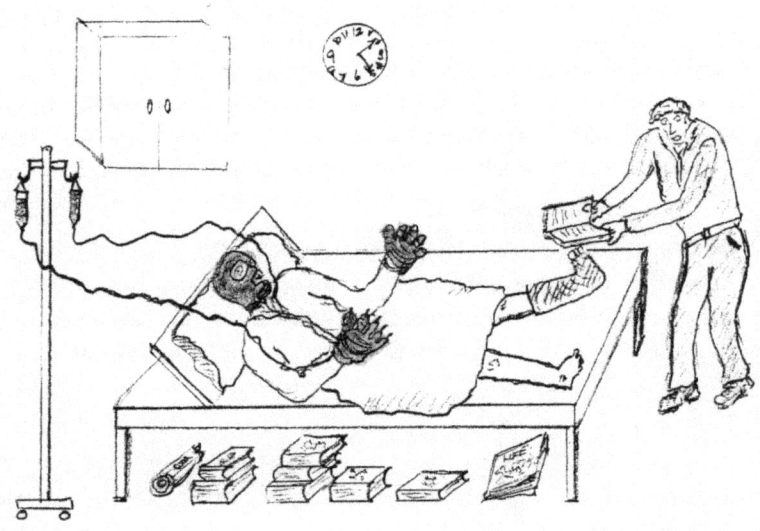

CHAPTER 24
Visiting Time, 2 – 8

The aura of mystery, fear, and restrictions that hangs over hospitals can demolish the self-confidence of even the most well-meaning visitor. Perhaps this is a remnant of the turn-of-the-century days when the incurably sick and dying were placed in infirmaries, where their inevitable demise would occur despite the care and knowledge of that institution's staff.

Despite the evidence offered by the Marcus Welbys and General Hospitals, there is still a dread of visiting the critically ill which deters many friends and family.

Foothills Hospital in Calgary is built on a rise in the western section of the city overlooking the Bow River and can be seen from miles away in most directions. Travelling in from the west along the Trans Canada Highway, this highly regarded medical facility starts its intimidation of the visitor from afar.

That October, many of those travelling from Cranbrook through the early winter rigours of Kootenay National Park and Banff had had five hours' thinking time to aggravate their state of unease into full-blown fear by the time they arrived at the hospital.

Lack of accurate information regarding my state of health was a further source of concern for well-intentioned visitors. The hospital staff had the dual challenge of screening and restricting visitors to ensure my safety and comfort. They had to prevent my exposure to alien harmful germs and viruses that might be brought in by those visitors, and yet try to permit and encourage those who would be of help to them in their search for information about their patient. The staff were cognizant of my need for the reassurance and love of those close to me and the need for my close friends and family to express their love, sadness, and grief about my condition.

Alan, as the first visitor, had established his credibility with evidence of a thorough knowledge of my family situation and history and had proven his awareness of my state of health, fitness, and habits. He had been asked to make a list of my close family and friends which could be used to screen the visitors.

"He is the one in the far bed on the right. His face is still rather swollen and he's a bit bandaged up but he's making excellent progress. He'll be so pleased to see you." With those words of encouragement, the nurses coaxed the hesitant visitor past the point of no return – the door to the Burns Ward. Five minutes earlier the nurse had come in to tell me that Jim would like to visit me. It was still in those early days and as I was spending much time in that twilight zone of semiconsciousness, neither my awareness of surroundings nor ability to recall names and faces was dependable. This dramatically reduced my decision-making abilities. Seeing my hesitation, she patiently tried again with another approach.

"He's a tall blonde young fellow, very pleasant, says he's one of your close friends. He does a lot of skiing and windsurfing with you."

Even this added information failed to pinpoint the identity of the mysterious visitor.

The pain and frustration of my situation brought out an uncharacteristic grumpiness.

"Never heard of him," I insisted, but mellowing I added, "But anyway, send him in."

A tall figure appeared swathed in a nursing gown, the mask perched precariously on the end of a large nose. The reluctant visitor edged through the door and stood momentarily on guard, stopped dead by a grossly alien environment.

As the eyes got even bigger, it was evident that he was dazed by the surroundings. Dressed for the November coldness outside, he hadn't thought to remove his jacket prior to donning the gown.

The purposely high room temperature was the first disconcerting element that struck him.

There were four beds with occupants, none of whom was giving him the welcome he had hoped for, and at a glance each indistinguishable from the other. Their common uniform of miles of bandage, various limbs propped or tied aloft and bloated features defied recognition.

The smell did little to make his progress easy and was the final straw that would have made a lesser man turn on his heel and bolt for the door. It was a distinctive aroma, not very unpleasant, but one which would linger on the visitor's clothing long after his departure. It was a smell peculiar to that environment: a mixture of body odour, antiseptics, medication and an air freshener's feeble effort to cope with an earlier bedpan use.

The noises, too, were threatening to the visitor. A humidifier was hissing away in one corner, and as if caused by his entry, an insistent beeping sound and a warning flashing light started on one of the intravenous drips. All this was superimposed on the regular moaning of an old chap in the corner.

Like a monument and just as immovable, it was doubtful whether he'd have found the strength to take another step but by then I'd surveyed the mystery visitor and recognized him as my old buddy, Willy.

"Hi, Willy. Good to see you," I welcomed him.

At the sound of my recognizable voice, the granite pose melted and he became human again. Lunging forth with newfound energy, he crossed the intervening floor space at speed, only to wrench up with a shuddering halt just inches from the bed. He had suddenly remembered the nurse's admonition not to touch the bed, the patient, or anything.

"What's all this 'Jim' business? I never knew your name was Jim. Everyone calls you Willy," and so the ice was broken. Fortunately, I just kept talking, because Willy was obviously stuck for words.

He had been well-tutored by the nurse on the do's and don'ts of visiting. Do not touch. Do not sit on the bed and, obviously, don't smoke. He had been forewarned that my features were a little changed, but the voice was the old jocular Blair he knew. As with so many visitors, the desire to bring a gift of some sort had provoked a search of the shelves in the Gift Shop in the hospital foyer and produced a selection of paperbacks.

"Good to see you, ol' pal," he said, nervously proffering the books. "I thought you might like something to read."

The books went from his one hand to the other in the dilemma of what to do with them. He had suddenly realized my hands were totally bandaged, so page turning would pose a spot of bother. His fear of doing the wrong things that might harm my fragile state of health made him apprehensive about putting the books on the bed and the side table seemed cluttered with bandages, medications, and a drinking glass with its bent straw. And so he continued his juggling act with the three books.

"Gee, that's great Willy. Wow, that looks like pretty interesting stuff," as I noted a title by one of my favourite authors.

A little light was flashing in the back of my mind. Had I read that one before? It would be weeks later before I became aware that my friends knew me well, and my tastes. The staff would methodically clear away the books and store them for me. At a later time I found I had several copies of some of the books on the current best seller list that were stocked in the book store downstairs. I hadn't the heart to tell him, or the other visitors, generous in their desire to bring a gift, that I had lost my glasses in the crash and couldn't read the print. Nor, for that matter, had I the concentration or energy to stay awake long enough to read a paragraph.

Our conversation turned from the gloom of present circumstance to the glorious past; mile 11 in the Fort Steele half-marathon, the big drop-off on the Stemwinder Run on the Kimberley Ski Hill, and the height of the waves on Moyie Lake in a good southerly blow. With mutual relief, despite our close friendship, Willy took his leave after five minutes. Both of us had gained by the visit. Both of us were exhausted. Willy had had enough for his first visit in this threatening atmosphere and, though I enjoyed his presence, I was already fatigued with the expenditure of energy required to fulfil my obligations as a host. I felt I should try to be pleasant and cheerful, and try to minimize the distress suffered by the visitor.

Even though I felt exhausted, Willy's visit had been a tonic to me. That brief five minutes was hardly his just reward for the five-hour drive from Cranbrook, but as circumstances would have it, that was all I could tolerate and he exemplified the fine art of hospital visiting. His visit had been appropriately short, cheerful, and dwelling on memories of happy times.

Most of my visitors seemed able to judge how long to stay and I was spared the gloom and doom pronouncements that can spring out of the unguarded mouth in moments of desperation for something to say. Even the statements, "I know how you feel" and "It could have been worse" were inadvertently helpful, when the gang of four patients would bandy the phrase around after the visitor left. It allowed us to vent our feelings about the inappropriateness of the phrase without giving direct offence to the original perpetrator.

It was surprising how testy I became about the most innocuous comments, depending on my mood at the time. "You are looking much better," ran the risk of being considered a downright lie if I was low in self-esteem. Conversely, if my mood was receptive to that same phrase, it would just thrill me, affirm my progress and be such a positive influence on my whole day.

The four-bed ward was a mixed blessing for visitor and patient alike. There was little privacy for the sharing of true feelings and that was one of the reasons for my insistence that my sons should not visit me while I was on the Burn Unit.

The crowded feeling also made it rather difficult to confide with my visitors on matters that I would have liked to address.

However, this was balanced by some of the benefits. I particularly enjoyed the sometimes perceptive and entertaining comments that would ensue among the patients in that ward. We were fully agreed that the "Visiting Hours 2 to 8" notice should read "Visiting Minutes 2 to 8."

After a particularly protracted visit by someone who had glaringly overstayed his welcome, the initial comment would be, "Whew – I thought he'd never leave." This was the trigger for a natural sequence of derogatory exchanges. "Thought he'd forgotten where the door was." "I was going to offer him this bed." The benefit gained from all the joking salvaged an otherwise low-key visit into a pleasingly therapeutic experience.

From time to time, some wonderful feelings and perceptions surfaced following a visit.

"You and that old chap didn't have much to say, Joe."

"No wonder," was his instant heated reply, but then he softened a bit, surprised by the quickness of his response. "That old sod hasn't said a civil word to me at work in five years. I just about fell out of bed when he walked in." Grudgingly, but without further prompting, he mellowed even more and said, "I never thought the old fart had a heart in him." Then with a spark of contriteness he whispered, "If it had been the other way round, I'd never have visited him in here. Makes you think, doesn't it?"

In the ensuing silence, spurred on by this observation, we would each reflect on the changes in outlook that were brought on by our common change of circumstances. I was surprised and deeply touched by the presence of some of my many visitors over these months. Busy people would make the time to bend their tight schedules to allow an extra hour to make the return trip from their business appointments downtown.

A very special memory to me is a visit by a friend and colleague who had heard of my accident while he was holidaying in Europe. I was still just struggling up to short time spans of spluttering consciousness and fortunately his visit coincided with one of these spells of recognition. We shared five minutes together in the solarium, I sprawled in the recliner chair and he, ill-advisedly, far too comfortable in a padded armchair. Jet lag took its toll on him. He was exhausted from his transatlantic flight and seven-hour time change.

The nurse curtailed the visit with an astute observation, "We should find a bed for your friend there."

I doubt whether he was sufficiently awake to realize how much that visit had meant to me. I was so buoyed up by the experience that the nurse later commented, "That visitor sure got you smartened up. That's the longest you have been alert since you came to the ward."

Sadly, many visitors didn't get the response from me they deserved. So much of the time I spent dozing, trying to catch up with the restoration of energy, regeneration of damaged tissue and rebuilding of a sound body. Always, the nursing staff made a point of telling me that "so and so" had visited while I was asleep. In the haze of twilight consciousness, I'd struggle to connect names with faces from the past, and while often it was a fruitless search I did, however, gain from the knowledge that someone had cared enough to go far out of his way to make the visit.

The list was endless: friends, associates, former patients, work colleagues. I was moved by the thoughtfulness of some visitors whom I had never even met, who came because they had heard of the accident and wished to show their caring. A Calgary couple had met me only once in the ski lodge in Kimberley the previous winter and were kind enough to make the trip up to the hospital. Ambulance staff and nurses bringing new patients from Cranbrook to Calgary were regular drop-ins, as well as Search and Rescue team members, flyers, and Toastmasters.

A soccer player from a team from Fernie that I'd played against once, three years earlier, introduced himself. The protracted explanation of where our paths had crossed took up the majority of his short visit.

"Did our team beat you?" I asked. "Yah, you did that time, but next time we'll get you." As his German accent came through I recalled the isolated meeting in an invitational soccer old-timers contest. His visit was doubly rewarding as I cherished the memory of bygone happy days and his assurance, presumptuous perhaps, that we would have more exciting clashes chasing a soccer ball in the future.

All of the visitors gave of themselves unstintingly and brought on an afterglow of gratefulness in me long after their departure. Ironically, close friends sometimes did not enjoy the same credit for their constant generosity as the unexpected visitor who provoked disproportionate feelings of gratitude.

It was the influence of those many visitors that sparked in me an increased concern for others. This would later cause a change in my way of life and allow me to reap the rewards of involvement in church visiting and the Hospice organization. The example shown by others, and their kindnesses to me when I so desperately needed their support, brought a new understanding and meaning of visiting time 2 to 8.

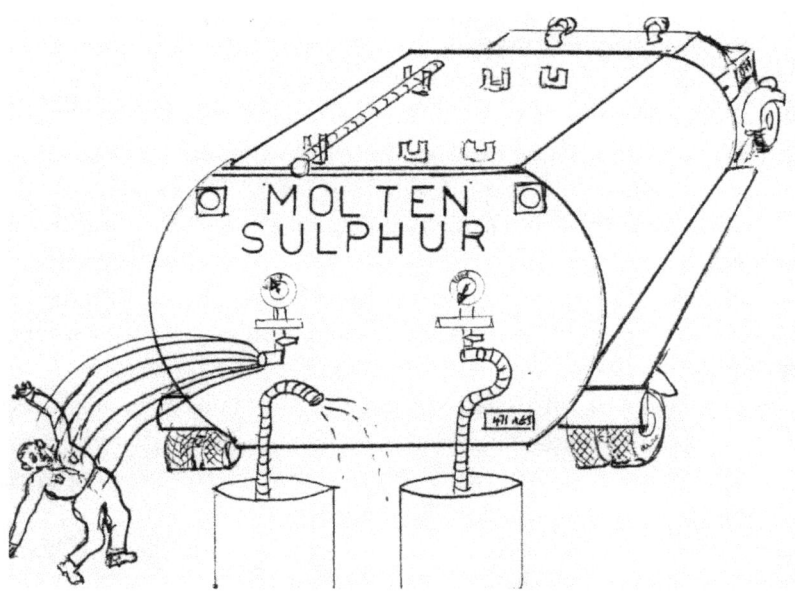

CHAPTER 25
Storytime 1001 Ways

Patients told many and varied stories describing the accident which had caused their burns and led to their subsequent transfer into the Burn Unit.

While many local hospitals have staff competent to deal with less seriously burned patients, the Foothills Hospital Burn Unit is renowned for its successes with extensive area burns and for the advanced support services of other specialty sections in that hospital. Children with burns are usually directed to the Alberta Children's Hospital in Calgary.

It is common that in air crash accidents the resultant escape of gasoline is likely to produce large area skin loss and inhalation burns. However, in many of the cases in the hospital during my stay, a common thread among the causes was carelessness, or the sheer folly or lack of recognition of danger in the misuse of volatile materials.

In my own case, it was the drenching with high octane aircraft fuel following the rupture of lines, and the almost predictable spark produced, as metal and electrical lines were torn, that caused the inevitable conflagration. Some of the causes in my fellow patients' cases were blatantly avoidable.

The monotony of routine was the cause of Tony's mishap. Transporting molten sulphur in a specially designed hopper truck, Tony was nearing the end of a 12-hour shift when fatigue and repetition took the edge off his usual safety routine. The double-lock safety mechanism for securing the discharge hoses that drained the molten sulphur was just at shoulder height as he filled his last load of the day. He had performed thousands of previous fillings in a safe manner, until that one time. Failure to lock the extra switch was his downfall.

As the lethal molten sulphur spewed out, Tony jackknifed backwards, but even his fast reactions were not quick enough to spare him a liberal spraying of the bubbling material.

The resultant extensive burns caused prolonged agony as tiny fragments of the corrosive material, too numerous and small to isolate and remove, kept eating away at his flesh.

Tom's was a similar case of dulled vigilance to the dangers of his work brought on by years of repeated daily exposure to their presence. As a foreman in a bottle cleaning factory, he was used to working around and stepping over the numerous steam hoses so prevalent in that work area.

Straightening a kink in the safety snap-and-lock joint on the heavy rubber hoses, Tom inadvertently touched the coupling with his foot, causing the hose to break loose and fire a jet of high pressure steam onto his leg. A second in that consuming flow caused a month's hospitalization, three episodes of surgery, and required two years' wearing of Jobst stockings on his legs.

During my stay, there were only two of the twenty new patients whose burns were the result of automobile crashes. Considering that there were more than 1,000 vehicle collisions in those three months, the fear of being unable to escape in case of fire is an insufficient reason for avoiding the use of seat belts. Statistics have confirmed burn injuries in auto crashes are infrequent. It is well documented that the likelihood of skeletal damage or unconsciousness are more probable factors limiting a passenger's exit from a crashed vehicle, and chances of survival are greatly improved by wearing a seatbelt.

Bert's saga with flame came about in the most innocuous fashion. The old settler, with a penchant for tidiness, was occupied with fall cleanup on the bank of the driveway to his farm. Armed with a shovel to douse patches that might get out of hand, he was carefully setting light to tufts of dried-up grass. Further back along the bank, he noticed a patch had again sprung into life. Throwing on a few shovelfuls of loose soil, he stamped vigorously at the remaining few flickers to snuff them out. Some persistent tongues kept flaring up, and as he tarried longer than he should have, the flame came into contact with the loose folds of his overalls, still saturated with oil and grease from his work on the tractor earlier in the day. A month in hospital was a heavy price to pay for his overconfidence.

Old Johnny's story was a sad reflection of society's blind eye to the elderly and less fortunate. Few were the luxuries that he enjoyed beyond the stark necessities covered by his paltry pension. He did enjoy his Saturday afternoon two beers and the joy of a bath. His dwelling place was a cramped one-room unit in a downtown back street. From his own shabby room, armed with his small threadbare towel and bar of soap, he meandered his way along the corridor to the only bath shared by the 20 rooms.

"I like it steamin' hot," he would say. "The more steam the better."

Turning the hot tap fully on, he locked the door, sat and ruminated for a few minutes while the bath filled.

Mellowed from his modest imbibing, he dozed briefly, then chilled by the draft from the small cracked windowpane, he quickly dragged off his clothing, dumping them where they fell on the floor, and lunged into the scalding water without testing its temperature. The searing heat numbed his body to immobility. He had neither the strength nor self-control to leap out of the cauldron. He screamed and screamed and eventually this was answered by pounding on the door, but it took minutes before the gathering throng managed to break the lock and finally turn off the still gushing hot tap and haul him out of the water.

Although at the time he was lapsing in and out of consciousness, he would often recall the horror of the ambulance personnel's difficulty in maneuvering his stretcher down the three flights of zigzag stairway.

Saddest of all was Ted's story. Shifty and secretive, even when pressed for information, Ted's stories varied from time to time. The only common element was that his clothes had caught alight. Deciding to take his own life, he poured gasoline over his clothes and then lit a match. Neighbours managed to douse the flames, but not before they had devoured much of his body. His prolonged stay in hospital and multiple sessions in the operating theatre were a desolate reversal of his search for peace. In addition to his physical suffering, he had to endure his own self-recrimination. Despite their best intentions, it was difficult for some of the staff, aware of the cause of his injury, to be as sympathetic to his suffering as they might. For other staff, the cause of his injuries provoked even deeper sympathy and the desire to provide extra special supportive care.

Events leading to burns were myriad in their diversity: battery explosions caused by a spark from jump cables, military accidents, high voltage electricity incidents, children playing with firecrackers, sparks igniting cleanup rags, tuning chainsaws in the basement, explosions of sawdust and other dust particles in basement cleanup, gas furnace explosion due to improper relighting procedures, and squirting more fire starter gas onto charcoal barbeques. A common simple cause of severe burns in households is water from boiling pots and kettles.

One story involved a lovely lady's disfigurement due to burns while cooking fish and chips. She removed the fish from the boiling fat and tipped frozen chips into the bubbling cooking oil while the pot was still on the stove. The sputtering of the icy chips caused the fat to boil over onto the red-hot stove, bringing the whole pot and stove top to a flaming mass. Instinctively trying to save further household damage, she grabbed the burning pot and as she rushed to the door she deluged another family member with the scalding fluid.

Ignition of flimsy night clothes, especially in children, is a source of tragedy as those tots teeter near a flaming hearth. The dreadful potential of candles on birthday cakes or Christmas decorations continues to threaten the joy of those occasions.

Firefighters around the world are not immune to the ravages of flame, but their practised skills and safety equipment help to lessen the frequency of their injuries by fire. Seeing the results of fire tragedies, they are consistent supporters of fund raising activities to help equip burn unit facilities and to better inform the public of the inherent dangers in everyday activities. Ardent supporters of the Foothills Burn Unit, the Calgary Firefighters Association has been generous in its provision of time and money to assist those sufferers.

Many other organizations, notably Kinsmen clubs in Canada, are well-known for their provision of help for those disabled through burns. Another major international society, widely recognized for its support of burn victims is the Shriner organization. Its contributions have assisted in financing Shriners Burn Units in several American states where expertise is extended to those needing specialist care and financial assistance.

Just as there are so many careless ways of exposing oneself to injury by burns, with a little more thought there are also 1,001 ways of preventing many avoidable catastrophes.

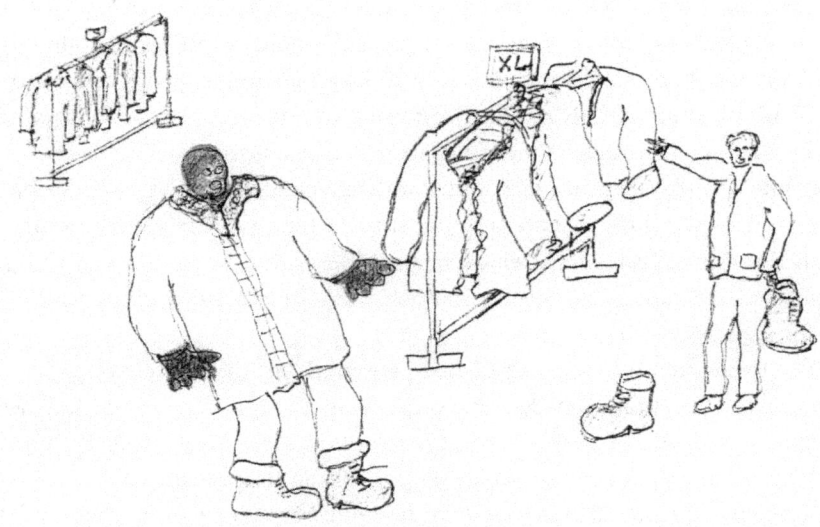

CHAPTER 26
The Big Shopping Trip

After two months of hospitalization, I developed a misguided sense of self-confidence in my mobility and independence. Able to carry out much of my self-care, I overlooked or judged as unnecessary some of the features of life which I'd previously felt were important. My inability to grasp the laces of my shoes developed the appalling habit of leaving the laces undone. Occasionally, when I observed this, I self-consciously looked around to see if anyone had noticed my sloppy habit. Remembering my previous paranoia about untied shoes, I was glad Ian and Craig couldn't see me now.

In the comfortable warmth of the hospital the gown and pajamas made up the standard uniform of the mobile patients. The lightness, comfort, and practicality of this outfit set the stage for a series of surprises in my preparation for my first half-day pass into the great outdoors.

With the exciting prospect of leaving the hospital in a few weeks, Alan and I had started realistic planning of my needs when I would return to Cranbrook. We decided that a shopping trip was needed which would not only allow me to stock up on some items of clothing, but also give me my first practice session in the big wide world.

The preparation for this outing proved to be a mixed blessing for anyone in the ward who had the misfortune to be involved in my care.

I was awake even before the staff moved in with the morning wake-up routine. It was like Christmas and my first Sunday School outing all rolled into one. The nurse had hardly closed the ward door before I was badgering her to take the night splints off my hands. Boisterous and oblivious of my roommates' wishes for those last precious moments of peace, it was my day for action.

My state of hyper-excitability was instantly checked when the nurse stopped me dead in my tracks with an appalling threat. Tiring of my speedy shuffling around the ward disturbing everyone, she ordered me to sit down until I got my temperature, pulse, and respiration recorded. That routine chore was mere trivia for us healthy up-patients.

"And if your temperature or pulse are elevated, your pass is cancelled."

That got my attention. I sat there quiet as a mouse but trembling with excitement, willing my rapid heart rate to slow down and unobtrusively slipping off my hospital gown to ensure that I'd cool enough to pass the test.

As I gazed at the clock, the second hand seemed to crawl around the required two minutes for the thermometer to have warmed up enough. I had never seen a nurse take so long to measure and document three patients. Eventually the nurse returned to check my pulse while I tried to stop my heart. She gave me a frightening look. The second the thermometer was out of my mouth, I started jabbering again, complaining of the terrible delays on this, the busiest day since I'd arrived in Calgary. She shook the mercury down with nary a glance at the reading. I could see this wasn't an auspicious start to my great day. Undeterred, I proceeded with my morning routine at breakneck shuffle speed.

No patient had ever voluntarily arrived for hydrotherapy ten minutes before his scheduled bath time, and there I was, pacing up and down the Rehab corridor as Abby arrived. She was muffled up in a down jacket, scarf, ski warmup pants, huge fur-lined boots, and a toque. Her cheeks and nose were bright red. Before she even had time to get her gloves off, I explained the cause of my excitement was that I was going out on a half-day pass.

Unenthused, she informed me it was 35 degrees below zero. Warmed up as I was by the excitement of my plans for the day, I was unimpressed.

The morning dragged drearily on and I could hardly do justice to my lovely high calorie lunch. Alan was scheduled to arrive at one o'clock but I found assistance to button up my shirt and tie my shoelaces long before his arrival.

Although he was six minutes late, in my gratitude for all his help I purposely avoided mentioning his tardiness. Perceptively gauging my excitement, he took no umbrage at my glance at the clock.

"It's pretty cool out there," he informed me as he started bundling me into outdoor garb.

As I stood there, heavy with the unaccustomed weight of normal clothes, I began to have some apprehension about the travels ahead. Jobst panty hose, stockings for the cold, denim rugby trousers, a shirt, and a track suit top, completed the list of the indoor extras. The Jobst gloves and Jobst mask meant that only lips, ears, and eyes were going to be exposed to the fearsome cold.

"I'll carry these other outdoor things down to the main door," Alan advised, and with a cheery farewell we set off.

By the time we reached the elevators a mere 30 yards from the ward, I was feeling uncomfortably warm.

"We'd better get you started doing some of the jobs, " Alan suggested. "So press the button for the elevator."

I pressed the down button and stepped back, wondering which of the six elevator doors would open. As luck would have it, it was the one furthest away and as I shuffled at my top speed across to the open door my anxiety at all this rush started to bother me. To my surprise I made the distance to the door before the doors slid closed, but I stopped short, realizing there were six people in that elevator. Observing my hesitation, they discreetly stepped back, making a small space, and Alan coaxed me inside what I'd judged to be an already full compartment.

Although I'd done a dry-run to the main door a few days earlier, now encumbered by the heavier clothing and threatened by the crowds, I was ill at ease as the doors closed. Avoiding their eyes, I glanced around. Seeing the "Capacity 15 Persons" notice, I couldn't comprehend how closed in that might feel, as I was already claustrophobic, one of only eight in that cramped elevator.

Although the ride down was smooth, I was apprehensive, awaiting the jarring stop as we plummeted the two floors to the foyer. The passenger next to me, working on a crossword puzzle, seemed unconcerned about the prospect of the landing but I had my knees bent, ready for the crunch that never came.

With a quiet hiss, the doors opened before I realized we had arrived at the main floor.

My eyes opened wide. I was appalled at the seething mass in front of me. I would be killed out there. Only the urgent shuffling behind me forced me to step out into that awful throng. Conditioned to hold my hands up and uncertain in my step, I moved out, trying to keep close to Alan and frantic at the commotion around me.

Everybody was in a hurry. Visitors were pouring in, armed with injurious weapons – bunches of flowers, baskets of fruit. It was devastating. Surprisingly, we made it to a quieter area near the door where Alan cajoled me into having a seat. I was already exhausted by the nervous and physical energy of that short trip.

After a short rest, Alan bundled me up into a voluminous parka that he had brought in, a toque, and a huge pair of woollen mitts. Zipping up the parka for me, he said he'd just be a minute or two while he brought the truck right to the door. For a moment I stood looking out the windows. Then, realizing I was sweating profusely in my Arctic outfit, I shuffled out through the first of the double doors that formed a barrier against the fierce cold outside. Even getting out through the first automatic door held its terror; I quickly passed through lest it slide shut and guillotine me. I was shell-shocked by all this speed and action.

In the pleasant coolness of the space between the inner and outer doors, I stood and relished the first icy blasts. Nearby, another pedestrian stood waiting for his transportation.

Suddenly, a spine-chilling horror hit me. I was struck immobile, although all my senses told me to leap. My nostrils sensed it before I saw the smoke, and my adrenaline pumped, ready to give me the needed lunge of speed. A movement to my left caught my eye as the man standing nearby lowered his hand from his mouth, a cigarette glowing in the cold. It took me ages to calm down from the shock that this proximity to smoke had caused me. I was glad to see Alan drive up in his truck at that moment and was relieved to be able to leave that environment and sample the crisp clear air. I reached the passenger door before Alan did and was again halted by the sudden awareness of my inability to perform the simplest and most natural tasks. I just could not press the knob on the door strongly enough to open the catch. Without a word, Alan opened the door and stood aside to let me enter the cab. I'd never realized what a big step up it was to get into a half-ton truck. Bundled up as I was and unable to hang onto anything, I suffered the humiliation of requiring a shove from the rear to get inside. As I lurched in, my unwieldy body made me inaccurate in my judging of distance and height, with the result that I lightly touched my scalp against the inside roof of the truck. I howled more with fear than pain, anxious in case I had ripped off the entire scalp.

With due forewarning, I leaned well away to the left while Alan gave the door a solid shove to make sure it was firmly closed. While he made his way around to the driver's door, I started making efforts to locate the seatbelt. It didn't take long before I realized this was another of life's simple little chores that I'd need assistance with. Despite his own heavy clothing, Alan swung into the driver's seat with enviable ease. With a croak in my voice, I asked him if he would be good enough to do up my seatbelt. The buckle end was lodged between the edge of the seat and the door and it required his moving round to reopen the passenger door to belt me in, reclose the door and walk around to his side again.

In his thoughtful way, Alan had had the heater going full blast to make sure I wouldn't suffer cold and by the time he was in, belted up, and ready to move, my exasperation boiled over.

"Turn that damn heater off, will you," I shouted.

I was sweating profusely and could feel it trickle down under the bundle of clothing. As we eased out, Alan drove carefully down to the main exit. It was all so different. Already I was beginning to realize that leaving my hospital home wasn't going to be all that easy. Lost in my thoughts, I didn't notice that we had travelled the 200 yards up to the intersection of 16th Avenue North. Not just another road, this was a six-lane busy thoroughfare. I was fully alert, readying myself should my navigator-copilot assistance be required. As the lights changed, Alan deftly swung right and accelerated, moving up through the gears as I strained over to watch fearfully as the speedometer needle swung to 50 km per hour. I was horrified at the speed with which street lamps and bushes shot past just a few feet from the side of the truck. This was a far cry from my accustomed wheelchair or stretcher trolley pace.

As we caught up with the lines of vehicles stopped at the next set of traffic lights, I couldn't believe my eyes at the number of vehicles.

"Where did all this lot come from?" I half shouted at Alan.

"Well, this is the Trans-Canada Highway and we are at the Sears turnoff on a Saturday afternoon," was Alan's quiet explanation.

We turned south onto one of the expressways. Moving into the middle lane brought new horrors. We became sandwiched between a bus and multi-wheel truck, both plowing forth at breakneck speed, converging on an unbelievably narrow underpass. I lambasted Alan with some of my best backseat driving, all to no avail, and as the bridge approached the noise was deafening. I shocked myself with wishing I was back in the cocoon safety of the Burn Unit.

Observing my terror, Alan thoughtfully got off that expressway and onto less-travelled streets, slowing down his speed. Finally we arrived downtown, which surprisingly was much less crowded. The ride up the spiralling entry of a parkade was another fearful experience as the right wing of the truck passed only a few inches from the ever encroaching concrete wall. Very relieved when we finally parked, I willingly tolerated the inconvenience of having to be unbelted and helped out of the truck.

"I hope I don't have to give you a tip each time you open the door for me," I jibed, but was grateful for the assistance.

We walked the 50 yards or so to the entrance to the downtown shopping complex, and once inside I was struck with the oppressive heat caused by my over-clothed state. There was a bench just inside the door and Alan suggested that I have a seat while he took my parka and heavy outer garments back to the truck.

"I don't need a seat," I said stubbornly, but by his return two minutes later, I had relented and was glad of the resting spot.

Moving on into the shopping area, I was devastated by the narrowness of the corridors between the merchandise and the uncaring haste of the pre-Christmas shoppers.

Our journey to the menswear section involved descending an escalator and I was ill at ease as I approached that first step. Unable to grasp firmly on the moving handrail, my first lunge onto the step was frightening. All the way down I worried about getting off at the bottom and finally did a half-jog for several steps before I fully regained my balance. I turned and looked at the familiar apparatus, exasperated that such an everyday, simple task had caused me so much concern.

Our shopping spree involved getting me fitted with winter boots two sizes bigger than my usual requirement, to accommodate my swollen left ankle. The biggest mitts we could find in the store were tight as we tried to get them on over the Jobst gloves and some residual bandaging. An easy zipping, large anorak took some searching because of our requirement of wide sleeves and easy zip closure.

Exhaustion and frustration soon took their toll, and with poor Alan loaded with my bundles we made our way to a cafeteria. Knowing my sweet tooth, Alan brought back a tray with a pot of tea and a chocolate eclair for me.

In my fatigued state I thought this would be just right to pick up my energy. Alan poured the tea. My independent streak prompted me to try to open the paper-wrapped sugar pack, but it tore and spilled all over the tray. That warned me not to attempt to pull the tab off the plastic milk container.

I couldn't get chocolate on my gloves so Alan had to cut the eclair into pieces, and using the teaspoon to lift the portions I realized the advantage of the padded handled spoon that had supplied for me back at the hospital. Normally I took my mask off to eat but it was such a labour getting it off and on that I decided to try eating with it in place. Stretching my mouth open enough to get the pieces of chocolate eclair into my mouth was just too complicated and to my consternation I had to leave that delicacy untouched. Disregarding his diet, Alan polished off his own and then, bit by glorious bit, consumed the cut-up portions of mine. I enviously watched each morsel disappear.

Exhausted, I viewed with trepidation the return to the hospital. The traffic still had its horrors but I was surprisingly anxious to get back to the fold. As I waited inside the main foyer of the hospital while Alan parked the truck, I was oblivious of crowds or the oppressive heat in my desperation to get back to the safety of the ward.

It was a strange reversal when I entered the ward. As Alan helped me off with my extra clothes, I wanted only peace and quiet, while the other three envious roommates, confined as they had been to this room, demanded to hear of my adventures outside.

"It was all right. No problems at all," I grumped and felt embarrassed that I hadn't shown more gratitude for Alan's efforts and kindnesses.

Back in the safety and comfort of my lightweight gown and pajamas, I lounged delightedly on top of the bed. I felt a mixture of pleasure and fatigue following the exertions of the day, but was bothered by the memory of the unexpected threats of so many common-place activities. I lay ruminating, building up dread for what lay ahead. The urgent desire to get out of hospital had been lessened by the awesome experiences of the big shopping trip.

I had survived only three hours outside my sheltered environment.

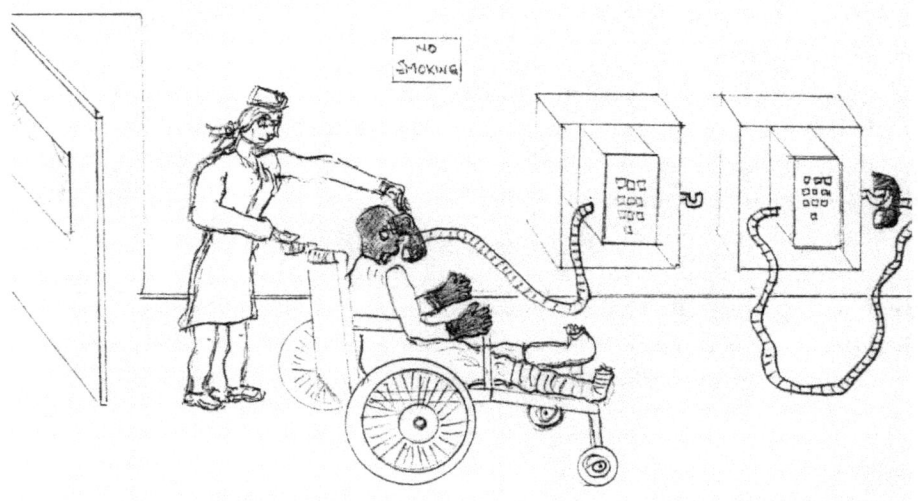

CHAPTER 27
Phone Time

Throughout my stay in the Foothills Hospital, the telephone played a vital part in keeping open the link with the outside world.

Initially it was a rather one-way conduit, and the hospital, understandably, provided very guarded information. Until more firm lists were drawn up naming my immediate family and close friends, it was stringent hospital policy that no information be given out.

When Bill Gordon deemed it imperative that my mother be informed, overruling my credo to the contrary, his call to Scotland was the start of a regular flow of transatlantic communication.

The incoming call from Paisley, Scotland, gained magical priority in reaching the Burn Unit. My cousin Nielson's distinctive Scots accent got instant action and response, and an honest, yet reassuring, relay of my status and progress.

The communication was not always factual. On one occasion when I had begun to show some self-control, the Scottish callers were shocked with joy and disbelief at the sound of my own voice. Using the 20-foot extension line from the nursing unit phone, the self-recoiling capability of the wire long since exhausted to a bedraggled kinky string, I had my chance to pass on my personal message of how well I was.

Remembering my mother's increasing hearing deficit, I bellowed into the phone all the pertinent information I felt they should know. The phone was held close to my scabby face by a nurse who was becoming increasingly anxious about the impropriety of this communication. I was exhorting the listeners in Scotland, in the Burn Unit, and down the hall to the whole Plastics Unit, about how unnecessary my transfer had been and how short my stay was expected to be. I'd be in hospital a few days, at most!

The nurse cringed with indecision, caught in the dilemma of the worthwhileness of letting those overseas hear my voice and the deceptiveness of the lies that I was dispatching across the waves.

The quandary in Paisley was equally perplexing. As the glaring mistruths in my outlandish remarks struck home, the phone receiver was hurriedly passed from one to another with equal shocking effect. My mother, cousin, and uncle struggled to interject a question, while I continued my unstoppable soliloquy.

I have absolutely no recollection of this call, which was so memorable to others. I am told I slipped back into my semiconscious state with a look of joyous satisfaction, not knowing or apparently caring about the consternation my wild tales had caused in Scotland.

For some time thereafter, great care was taken to keep me clear of the phone, and the staff reverted to dependable and more objective relaying of news. At some later stage when I was mobile in my wheelchair, I again had the opportunity to answer one of the incoming foreign calls, but with the nonexistent privacy of the nursing unit desk on the main floor of the Plastics Unit, and with an audience of a dozen or so busy staff, it was not the most satisfying conversation. Unawareness of the circumstances of my immediate surroundings made it difficult for the listeners near Glasgow to understand the uncharacteristic brevity of my responses.

Bill Gordon was the reliable personal link. Following each of his weekly trips to Calgary he would phone Scotland and give my family the news and the opportunity to ask their anxious questions from the confines of his home.

My progress to the independent mobile state of heel-dragging myself around in a wheelchair, allowed me to make regular evening calls to my sons. There was a bank of phones in the main corridor and I'd wait anxiously for the prescheduled 7 p.m. time to make my call. A nurse helped me make that first call to Ian and Craig, as I still had difficulty lifting the phone off the hook and dialling. When she had finally placed the call, she cradled the phone against my shoulder and discreetly stepped back. I fought that emotional battle of saying my first words to my sons, and the heartrending joy of hearing their young voices. I had insisted that they must not be brought to the hospital to see me in my bedraggled state. Whether or not that was the best decision, those first few words after four weeks were the toughest of my life. Terrified in case I should choke up or cry, I sweated my way through trivial chatter, not daring till the last few moments to say how much I missed them and how very much I loved them.

The nurse had waited just out of sight yet providentially near, and choosing her time with perceptive skill, gently took the phone from my shoulder and hung up. Although I usually liked to show my independence and ability at propelling myself along in the chair, on that particular night I was glad to be wheeled back. The grief of missing the boys, mixed with the joy of having spoken with them, overflowed in great sobs of self-pity. The soothing hand that gently clasped my shoulder did more than any words could have, to lessen my turmoil. It told me that that patient nurse had previously witnessed and consoled the anguish of others, at telephone time.

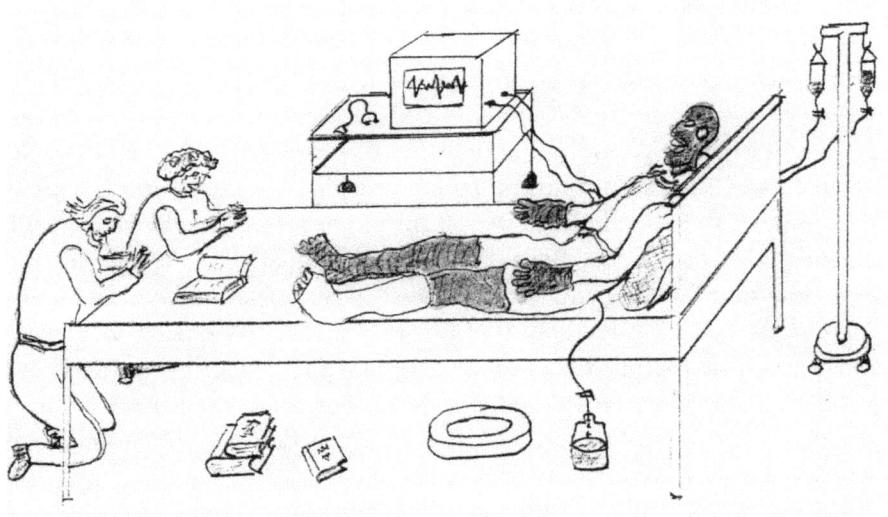

CHAPTER 28
Prayer Time

Just as my running career had had its cyclical ups and downs, so too my involvement in religious matters had had a very mixed history.

As a child and youth, family example and encouragement had channelled me into regular, albeit passive involvement in a branch of the Church of Scotland, "The Wee Free." This was followed by a nine-year wandering in something akin to the biblical wilderness, while I prioritized sports, travel, and the fun and frolic of military life as a substitute for any recognized religious needs.

My wedding in the Anglican Church in Brighton, England, was the start of very sporadic attendance. As my two children went through Sunday School age, I felt obliged to make token appearances in church to keep the peace.

The breakup of my marriage sent me scampering to the consolation of church where I received undeserved supportive counselling and unexpected friendship. However, having survived the first year of divorce, my urgent needs seemed lessened and attendance in church again became infrequent.

It was that sad state of noninvolvement that left me poorly prepared for the travails that beset me October 1st, 1983.

During what seemed an interminable wait at the crash site, it didn't occur to me that prayer might be appropriate. Perhaps it was just my having failed to practise the power of prayer in the preceding quarter century and consequently I lost the habit. I just never considered prayer as a way of getting a search plane to pass over that tiny gap in the trees in that desolate 50 square mile landscape.

Fortunately, many others thought differently, and belatedly, I now believe that their prayers made the difference.

That three-month period in Foothills Hospital provided many memorable insights for me, showing the strong faith and actions of others to have great impact. My lack of belief in the power of prayer was severely challenged.

By the third day in the Burn Unit, I was gradually coming out of my unconscious state just long enough to spit and swear at all around me. Suddenly, at the end of the bed there appeared two very frightened-looking teenagers. How they had managed to make their way past the numerous hurdles that kept visitors from my bed I could not guess, but there they were. Dressed in the visiting gown and masks, their eyes as big as saucers, they stood there speechless, taking in all the horrors of that Unit.

Focusing on them in my exhausted disoriented state, I was of no help in calming their fears. Their very presence intrigued me enough to keep me concentrating on their frightened faces. I was not aware that they had been brought in or introduced to me by a nurse. I do hope I didn't ask them, "Who the hell are you and what do you want?"

After an endless wait they finally stuttered out some semblance of self-introduction. Their aunt in Cranbrook, a former patient of mine, had phoned to their home in Calgary and asked, or ordered, them to visit me.

With my first attempt at acceptable social behaviour, I managed to mutter a brief thank you, but tiring fast, with my patience and skimpy self-restraint receding, I half-hoped they would take their leave as briskly as they had arrived.

I might have known that the courage that brought them there would give them the persistence to stay their allotted time. After another interminable silence and mutual observation – they staring, I glaring – their faith helped them to pronounce the reason for their visit.

In a barely audible whisper, because by this time, the two other patients in the room were all ears, those two brave 15 or 16 year old girls asked, "Do you mind if we pray for you?"

I was stunned. Lost for words, I remained silent. I ran a few practice responses through my mind, "Sure, why not," or "Be my guest," or "If you must," but providentially rejected these. With a huge lump in my throat and a tear in my eye, I croaked out, "I'd be pleased if you would."

It was my first experience of thinking of others, and it left a wonderfully pleasing sense of well-being.

While they took turns to say their few kind words, the whole world of noise and pain and anguish receded. They were aware of my unspoken thanks as they quietly left. I sank back into fatigue-induced semi-consciousness a little more at peace with the world, thanks to their courageous heartfelt action.

The next day saw the arrival of a lady who had travelled from a distant city, her journey dictated by her strong religious beliefs. Our meeting through Toastmasters a year earlier had brought about a lasting friendship. On hearing of my accident and the critical state of my health, she took the time to travel many hundreds of miles to spend two days at my bedside. Her radiant smile and the totally unexpected decision to make her visit were simple manifestations of her deep religious faith. After her departure, a card arrived to inform me that her priest would say a rosary on my behalf the following Sunday.

Another visiting couple whose many kindnesses also helped in my recovery, told me they had asked their close friends in a Transcendental Meditation group to join with them in considering my needs in their individual meditation sessions. I was moved deeply that their concern for me would be expressed in such a manner.

The awareness of the power of prayer and the recognition of those offering that gift was not always as clear-cut as in those examples. Among all the heavily disguised, be-gowned and masked visitors, a pleasant young chap appeared from time-to-time out of the haze of my stupor. No doubt he was on the receiving end of my anguish-induced obscenities in early days, as anything that moved was fair game.

Eventually, in a moment of more lucid observation, I got straight to the point and asked with all the appropriateness accorded to such occasions, "What the hell is your job here anyway?"

With no hint of resentment and no doubt assessing my gruff question as mild compared to earlier communications, he diffidently replied that he was the Anglican chaplain.

Generally, my visitors made only passing mention that their prayers were with me, many being aware of my past sparse involvement in religious matters. In hundreds of cards and letters that I received, well wishers were much more ready to express in writing their true feelings and convey prayers for my recovery. Many took the time to write full prayers and lines of poetry to wish me well.

Even the serious business of prayer was not devoid of entertainment value in the Burn Unit. Sid, in Bed Four, was a happy-go-lucky comic, the last person on earth you'd have matched up with his quiet, pretty, and unbelievably kind wife. It seemed their religious affiliations were also at odds. She was a devout church-goer and my guess would have been that Sid hadn't darkened the door of the establishment since they had stood briefly at the altar some 20 years earlier.

In deference to her, her preacher made one, no doubt memorable, visit to Sid.

The lack of mutual recognition between the two told its story, but unperturbed, the man of the cloth opened the conversation with the pleasantries of the day, an attempted anecdote, and finally the offer of prayer for Sid's recovery.

Becoming more relaxed with confidence and comfort in his avocation, the preacher's voice took on a deep catchy resonance that got even Sid's undivided attention.

Tom, in the adjacent bed, was a sports nut and his escape from pain was the Saturday afternoon football game. The shared television mounted near the ceiling and facing their two beds was controlled by a remote switch with a special huge dial which Tom could manipulate with his elbow instead of his bandaged hands. Tom did not tolerate interference with his football game, and his vote was for the sports commentator rather than the prayerful preacher. With a radical elbow adjustment on the dial, Sid's visitor's words were drowned out. Rising to the challenge, the clergyman dug deep and with practiced projection got his message across.

Tom, recognizing his indiscretion, suddenly overcorrected, and as th now mute TV personality continued his silent facial gyrations, the entire ward boomed with the threatening decibels of prayer.

The request for divine help quickly subsided as the pastor cut short his visit. It was later agreed that only prayer could muffle a strident TV sportscaster.

Even years later, meeting new patients in my clinic, I am inspired by their mention that, even though the patients had not met me before, they knew of me because they remembered their church had prayed for me all those years ago.

The examples of others in those earlier days and the recurrent kindnesses of the many church families in Cranbrook and elsewhere have moved me to a deeply satisfying and rewarding closer association and participation in church life.

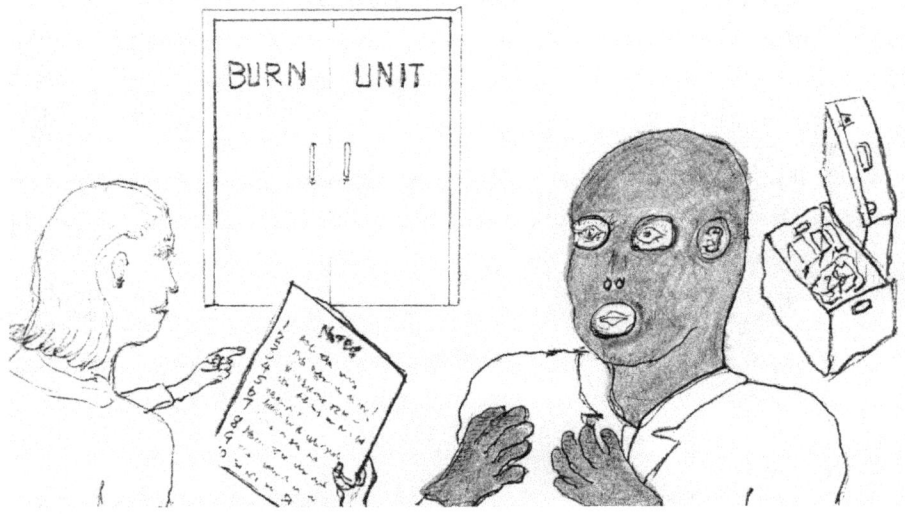

CHAPTER 29
Departure

Two days before my scheduled departure on December 9th, a sudden influx of three new serious burn cases necessitated yet another round of bed hopping as some of us more independent types, capable of most of our self-care, were moved into adjoining rooms on the Plastics Unit.

In a way, this was a token weaning and helped to prepare us, at least psychologically, for the independence of returning to our homes. It felt strange being out of the Unit that had been my home for ten weeks and I found the night silence quite threatening, missing the habitual noises and disturbances of the Burn Unit.

I felt isolated, collecting my own meal tray, taking it to my room, and eating in solitude. To everyone's surprise, I spent almost the whole day in Physio or O.T. rather than face the loneliness of that room.

The last morning at the Foothills Hospital was a solemn ritual of performing the last of each of the daily activities.

Having graduated to the use of the smaller whirlpool bath for my immersions, I went through the routine of careful soaking and removal of the cling bandages covering the few remaining stubborn open patches, and then proceeded with the scrubbing and cleansing of those wounds. The time spent in the pleasantly warm water was mostly used for exercise and stretching of the stiff joints. The final triumphant parade back to the ward in the distinctive garb of the newly-cleansed was a bit of a ceremony. With the customary hospital gown on back to front to provide some modest covering, and draped with one pre-warmed flannel sheet over my head and shoulders, I appeared more Middle Eastern than Scots. I made my way back along those now familiar corridors, past the Burn Unit, to the isolation of my own room.

It took me half an hour to perform my skin care, putting on the special ointment, Dermabase cream on the healed patches, Flamazine on the residual open areas, and antiseptic cream on my ears. The required bandages were all held in place with the Jobst panty hose, gloves, and the inevitable face mask.

Normally, I would gorge myself on my late breakfast after my dressing procedure, but that final morning I just picked at the customarily tasty enticement on the food tray in a detached, uninterested way.

I had written out a firm morning schedule, so that I would not fail to attend to each detail.

My 9:30 a.m. visit to the business office on the main floor was a novel experience. I had to retrieve my wallet from storage. Its full contents had been carefully listed by the staff when I was admitted.

"Could you please check that each item listed is in your wallet and that the cash recorded is accurate."

As the staff member spread the wallet's contents and the $62 across the little shelf in that cubbyhole window, I felt a strange and almost numbing sensation. Seeing my driver's licence, credit card, a few blank cheques, and cash that I had apparently had on my arrival that fateful night, the thought ran through my mind that I hadn't spent a penny in ten weeks. What a way to save money!

As if she had been reading my mind, the young lady presenting my documents, announced, "There are no charges as your account has been fully covered by your insurance."

I was to learn much later that the account was over $40,000 and I was duly thankful that other agencies were picking up the tab. On future occasions I used this horrendous figure as a scare tactic when I encountered patients in my clinic who had allowed their insurance coverage to lapse, heedless of the potentially ruinous consequences of such oversights.

I was mesmerized by the long list of items stored in my wallet, so the staff member patiently identified and ticked them off on my behalf. It felt ridiculous that I'd now need 17 items in my wallet when I had managed well without them for all these preceding weeks. As a gesture of finality, she proffered a pen so that I could sign the clearance confirming the transfer of these precious goods. The writing instrument must have been her personal possession. It was a slim-lined high quality ballpoint. In any other circumstance I would have admired and relished the opportunity to use such a fine instrument. However, its shiny frictionless surface played havoc with the Jobst gloves. My stiff awkward grasp at the pen made the effort of scrawling my signature a disproportionately difficult task. I was glad finally to get some mark on the paper and hurriedly tried to scrape together the money, cards, and papers.

Seeing my dilemma, she gently took over for me and placed all the items neatly in their individual pockets and spaces in the wallet. She folded it closed and handed it to me, smiling, and with an unrushed closing communication, added that she hoped I had been well looked after during my stay.

"You have all done a great job," I said, with heartfelt sincerity, anxious to include this final previously unseen member of staff and her department to the long list. They had also contributed in the total team, but were often unrecognized and unthanked for their work.

As I automatically swung my hand behind my back to put the wallet in my hip pocket I became suddenly aware of yet a new difficulty. I couldn't feel for the edge of the pocket because of the loss of sensation in my gloved fingers. I had to grope around in a contortion of a two-handed search to find the lip of the pocket and finally managed to wedge the wallet inside. I wasn't the least bit confident that it was safely tucked inside and constantly kept testing to be reassured of its presence.

An important scheduled event on that final morning was the Discharge Conference. This was a meeting attended by the head nurse from the Burn Unit, a physiotherapist, and an occupational therapist to provide last-minute details, and the repetition of instructions for my ongoing self-care and independence when I left the hospital. The Nursing Department's review included: the importance of healthy nutrition, a review of the prescriptions needed, and provision of small quantities of required drugs to tide me over the few days until I could obtain replacement supplies. These included sleeping pills, pain pills, and various creams and lotions. Judy stressed the importance of getting enough rest and particularly urged me to adopt sensible sleeping/waking time schedules to avoid slipping into the late-night/late-morning reversals that can so easily trap those unaware of the dangers involved in those antisocial timetables.

Occupational Therapist Delilah reviewed Jobst care, washing and drying routine, the fitting and proper insertion of cleft space pads and wedges for my fingers, my nose contour plate, and my assortment of night splints and stretch string splints to straighten out the contractures already starting in the small fingers.

In her capacity of farewell agent from the Physiotherapy Department, Abby brought expected levity to an otherwise serious meeting.

"You know that we know that you know all you've got to do," she started off. This was followed by detailed but quick recitation of all the strengthening, stretching, mobilizing exercises I should do and all the things I should avoid. "Now remember, you won't be fit to drive for a few weeks. And don't imagine you'll run for a while…"

"Yeah, yeah, yeah," I cut her off, knowing she would not be offended. After all, I had just completed a three-month's postgraduate immersion in my training as a physiotherapist and felt reasonably confident about the routine. During the subsequent months and years, I would fervently wish that I had listened a little more attentively to the guidance of those caring and experienced individuals. There were still some glaring gaps in my knowledge.

My final packing was far less onerous than it might otherwise have been. During the preceding three or four days Alan had been gradually taking out boxes and bundles of the huge accumulation of clothing, dozens of books, and other gifts brought to me by many kind visitors, including a tape recorder, cassette player, Scrabble, and four hundred well-wishing cards. He had expressed concern that he would be stopped and searched at the main exit, but all his good help in removing these items made my packing of just one small suitcase a simple matter. I paid a token visit to O.T. and Physio once more to say my goodbyes to the staff who by this time had become very much a part of my close circle of friends. It was a day of mixed sadness and rejoicing, a parting of the ways and the final recognition of how important so many people had been in providing my care.

There was also the sadness of leaving other patients in the Rehab Unit who would have to stay on longer. Witnessing their envy at my departure was a touching experience. Emotions mounted, and finally I had to make a quick exit and head back to the ward. Lunch arrived, another high quality, beautifully prepared rendition. I had been fed like a king and had already regained more than half of my lost 40 pounds, thanks to the careful analysis of my nutrition needs and the painstaking thought and care in preparing and presenting the food. But on that day I felt like the prisoner awaiting the executioner's footsteps. It was the last meal. I had no taste for the offering, and hoped no offence would be taken at my declining to eat.

I couldn't face the loneliness of the empty room and wandered around the solarium. In exasperation, I went back into the Burn Unit in search of the security it had held. There had been complete change in its clientele in the 48 hours since my move to the semiprivate room down the corridor. Although the familiar faces of the nurses and other Unit staff gave me the welcome I had hoped for, the three new patients that I had not met made me feel somewhat alien. I quickly left, not bothering to introduce myself, and felt a deep sadness that I was now an outsider in what had been my own domain.

The euphoria of a few days earlier when I had been given the news that I could leave that Friday was gone, and now I ambled aimlessly, watching the clock, anxious lest I overstay my welcome.

Right on schedule at one o'clock Alan appeared, reliable as ever. He picked up the suitcase, but I insisted on carrying my coat, gloves, and toque, eager to prove some independence. Putting on a rather more jaunty step than I felt, I exchanged a fleeting farewell with those on staff. I knew the road ahead was not going to be easy, but felt an exhilaration derived from having overcome those earlier tough times.

Surprisingly, the moment I left the ward I had a much more self-confident and positive attitude. I knew I was no longer an inpatient, and the descent in the elevator held none of the terror it had on the previous outing. I swung through the foyer, almost leading Alan with my forthright pace and newfound surge of self-esteem.

I declined his suggestion that I wait inside until he brought the truck to the door and strode forth into that chilling grey December day. I left Foothills Hospital without a backward glance.

We descended down the ramp, into the underground parking area and Alan unlocked the passenger side of his truck. Gauging my mood of determination, he stepped aside to let me clamber laboriously onto the seat. To set the tone I ordered, "Hang on a minute with that door until I get this seatbelt fastened." It took me ages to complete, but Alan, in his perceptive way, refrained from comment as he eventually closed the door. As we drew level with the time keeper at the exit, Alan struck up a short conversation with the elderly uniformed watchman. From his previous 70 visits, Alan was now well recognized by the staff on the gate.

"You didn't stay long this time, mate," the old chap said, observing that only 15 minutes had elapsed since Alan had parked the old blue Ford.

"No, this should be my last trip, I hope," he said, as he introduced me. "This is my friend that I've been visiting all these times."

The old gent ducked his head down to look in through the open window, and as Alan offered him the coins for his parking time, a smile and chuckle accompanied Foothills' farewell gift to me. "It's time we gave you a freebee," he said, declining Alan's proffered payment.

And so, this tiny gesture triggered my awareness of another yet previously unrecognized member of the team.

As we drove away, Alan's quick humour surfaced, "It seems you need a Scotsman in the truck to get anything for free."

It felt wonderful to be out in the wide world. The pain was already forgotten, but gratitude remained along with the euphoria.

As we drove to the airport I hardly noticed the traffic. We passed a jogger, sweat-suited and well-muffled in a toque and gloves, each expelled breath instantly visible in the frigid air. His steady pace and even stride caught my eye.

"Eight-minute mile, I'd guess," I murmured.

The transition was complete. I was well again. I was ready for my re-entry into a competitive world-departure time was here.

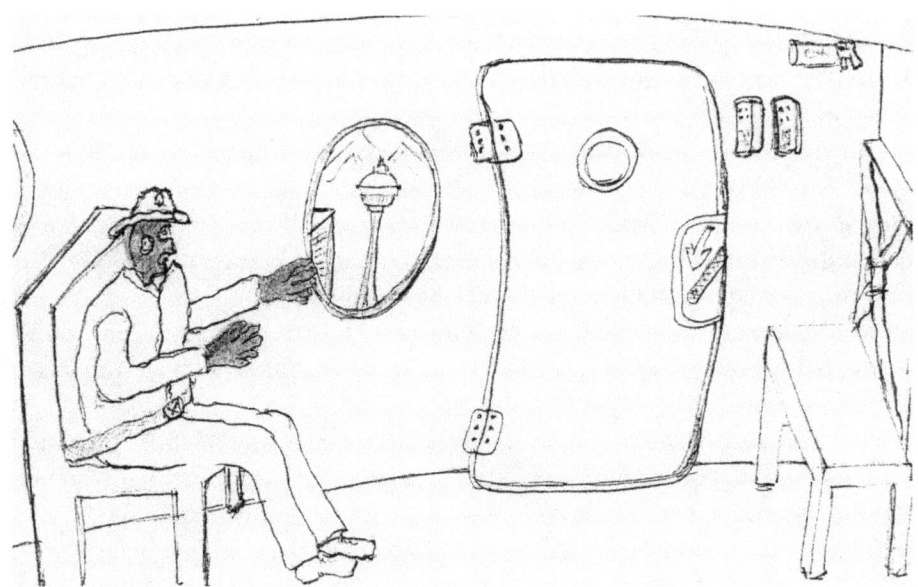

CHAPTER 30
The Homecoming

The journey from the hospital to the airport held more nightmares than my earlier trip just days before. Alan took the quiet route up through the University grounds and onto the main highway towards Edmonton. It was early afternoon and the traffic was blissfully light as we made our way north, parallel to the main runway.

Up ahead, crossing at 500 feet above the road, a 737 jet glided majestically across our path to settle with just a wisp of smoke as the tires touched the concrete.

"He'll be going in on Runway one zero," Alan announced. A satisfying sequence of thoughts brought me the conclusion that the head wind from the east was responsible for the bitter cold blowing across the prairies. Alan and I had a couple of hours together and enjoyed sharing what had for so long been a common interest – plane spotting. It seemed so natural that we'd discuss the various merits of the wide range of craft visible from the glass viewing windows. Engrossed in this delightful pursuit, I was oblivious of the stares of other passengers. My full attention was given to the unbelievable dimensions and weight factors of the 747 compared to the amazing lift capabilities of the Dash Seven with its short takeoff and landing potentials. The smaller planes were gathered mainly at the southern end of that airport complex, in what had been the main airport prior to its massive expansion some ten years earlier. The sight of a Cardinal might well have changed the mood and levity of our time together.

No visit to the airport was complete for me without browsing in the book store. Assuming I'd have some time on my hands in the months ahead, I picked up a couple of new editions of my favourite authors. I'd been unable to concentrate sufficiently to read while in hospital. I was certain that I'd succeed now that I would again be in my home environment.

Ready to move into the departure lounge at 4:30, I quipped, "Alan, you're going to be home early for once. You won't know what to do with all your spare time."

"Well, there are a few things to catch up on," Alan answered, and I gratefully remembered his regular after-work arrivals at the ward for the past many weeks. Punctual to the minute, each evening he had arrived ready to help feed me in those early days, read my mail, and help in so many ways by just being there. He had gone from being just a superb reliable friend to being as close as any brother. I stepped away quickly lest the emotion of the moment expose the depths of the debt that I felt for all his kindness.

With a last wave to him, I approached the security clearance and the Pacific Western boarding-waiting area. My brisk pace forwards startled the two security personnel. I had forgotten I was wearing my Jobst mask. Carefully I slowed my approach as I observed the consternation in their faces. It was my first lesson in public reaction to the mask.

"Is this the way for the Cranbrook flight?" I asked, certain that I was in the right exit, but anxious to let them hear the commonplace intent of my travels.

The two young staff answered simultaneously, both self-consciously wanting to cover up for their momentary alarm, having undoubtedly mistaken me for a high-jacker or robber with my mask and ski toque. There was a Pacific Western attendant at the gateway, and although the flight was not yet due for boarding for another 20 minutes, I purposely strolled towards him so that he would not go through the same alarm at first seeing me. To confirm that I was clearly a recent hospital patient, I asked that I might be preboarded, although I didn't feel any need for this special attention.

I made a point of sitting in the centre of the waiting area where other passengers would see me from a distance. Although I was a little distressed at this first exposure to the gawking public, I felt an inner satisfaction that I was in command of the situation and able to take some measures that would minimize the likelihood of untoward reaction.

My strategy in keeping control of this new environment was to look as if I was reading one of my new books, but really I was keeping my gaze riveted on the page to avoid eye contact with other individuals. I recognized a couple of Cranbrook residents among the passengers, but steadfastly eyeballed the page, fearful that they would not recognize me if I approached them.

I was relieved at last to hear the preboarding announcement and was the only person to move at this call. I felt every eye follow me as I went forward to the agent. I presented my boarding ticket and made my way down the short inclined corridor to the plane. Turning left for the final four steps, I suddenly panicked and my legs became leaden. All our flippant discussion of planes, lift and flight characteristics, just an hour earlier, was gone. This was the real thing. I remembered another aperture in the side of a plane, a vision, the other side of a wall of flame. I remembered a door that would not open.

A welcoming voice beckoned me in. I hadn't realized that I had come to a full stop just short of the entrance. Wary, but a little embarrassed, I stumbled forward and the smiling hostess took charge and guided me to my window seat in the front row of the plane.

"Would you like to take your coat off?" she asked. "I'll put it up in the rack."

"No, thanks," I mumbled, anxious that I have lots of protective clothing on in case... my mind went back to another awful time.

"Would you like your hat off? It's pretty warm in here."

"No, thanks."

I felt very self-conscious and hoped the toque would cover the mask. I busied myself trying to get the seatbelt around me but she was there instantly, ready to assist. Although I felt anxious to assert my independence, it seemed the lesser of two evils to let her fix the belt; then, I hoped, she'd leave.

"There you are. How does that feel?" she persisted.

"Just right," I assured her, trying not to be too abrupt, but hoping she'd get the message and leave me alone. Perceptively, she stepped back and I concentrated fiercely on the blank wall just inches outside the window. There was nothing on it, but I scrutinized it for several minutes, sweating from the discomfort of my heavy clothing and from the alarming situation in which I found myself.

Stealthily, I stole a look and to my relief found that the hostess was busily engaged in some of her preflight tidying up. I had to check the belt. I tried to do it quietly so that she wouldn't hear. I lifted up the release clasp and the other end shot out, clanking against the arm rest. I grabbed at it quickly to try to reinsert it before the young lady turned around at the sound. The slim metal insert had jammed between the seats and I couldn't dislodge it. Furious, I saw the pretty ankles approach, but I couldn't look up.

"Oh, it must have slipped out," she said in a pleasant voice.

"Let me help you." She again reattached the belt and discreetly stepped away, sensing my exasperation.

I swooped into feelings of self-pity and fear. This isn't going to be easy, I thought, but at that moment the remaining passengers started trooping onto the plane. I returned to my scrutiny of the blank wall beyond the double glazed window. In the reflection, I could see the feet move past the end of that front row as they made their way further down the plane. I had never seen so many people get on a plane. Another pair of slim ankles came into the peripheral vision of my averted face. They stopped, turned, and with a gentle bump, I had company. I glanced up to my right and saw an attractive young woman with long blonde hair and a pretty face. She could not disguise the shock of being on the receiving end of both barrels of a Jobst mask at 12 inches. Her reaction was instantaneous. The surge of adrenalin shot to her tongue.

"Hi. I'm going to Cranbrook. I live in Calgary but I'm visiting good friends in Cranbrook. I go there to ski quite a lot."

It was quickly obvious that she was going to talk her way out of needing to see whether or not the Jobst had a voice. That was fine with me. A monologue was preferable to having to exchange pleasantries. I had some heavy thinking to do. As she babbled on, I checked my wall again. I quaked as I saw it move; we were easing back from the confines of that loading bay. Suddenly in the darkness, the snow-spattered concrete was visible 15 feet below. An attendant was dragging away the wheel chocks. The insistent chatter went on as my neighbour kept up her dissertation. During a momentary pause, I interjected a mumbled "yes" in the half-hope that it would discourage further communication. On the contrary, it was taken as an invitation to press on with greater diligence. Her prattling became muted by the sounds of the jets as they built up to their preflight test revolutions. I gripped the seat handles tightly as we started to taxi. I wanted to snug the belt more securely around my hips, but daren't touch it in case I inadvertently opened the buckle again and incurred the scorn of the flight attendant.

As we turned onto the threshold of the runway, I got an unobstructed view of the dazzling blue lights diminishing to vanishing point on the horizon. At least it was clear at the moment. The plane paused, restrained for a brief moment to allow the buildup of revs, then with a surge, we were off down the runway. I sat there, helpless, horrified when the vibration ceased, knowing I was again airborne, hypnotized by the fast-receding ground and increasing height as airport buildings and then high-rise apartments swept past.

Somewhere over central Calgary I realized my neighbour's chatter had ceased, snubbed, no doubt, by my lack of response. I dared not look to see if she had left, in case it started up again. As the plane turned and crossed west across the city past the Calgary Tower, I had a momentary clear view of the Foothills Hospital standing on the hill. I thought of those still there in the Burn Unit, and of the staff and for 15 minutes reminisced gratefully, oblivious of our closeness to the snow-capped peaks below.

A deep bass voice announced, "We are just over Skookumchuk, turning south for a straight run into the Cranbrook airport. We'll be there in eight minutes. It's snowing in Cranbrook and the cloud ceiling's quite low so we won't see anything until we're just about to land."

I was brought rapidly back from my escape into memory lane to the terror of the present. This was not the homecoming I'd have chosen. Low ceiling. Blinding snow. Why didn't I drive home? I peered into the black void that was the window, then turned back in fear. As I gripped the seat, my movement activated the voice again. Uninvited, she started recounting what she'd read of the horror of the Cranbrook air crash some seven years earlier in a similar snowstorm. She itemized the sequence of unforgettable coincidences that lead to that tragedy.

I heard the pitch of the engines change and guessed that the captain was in the final approach, in a state of readiness to abort the landing should that prove necessary. The landing lights were on, battling into the impenetrable cloud and flying snow. We were sinking lower and lower, when suddenly we were flashing past tree tops just a few hundred feet below. I glared into that window, teeth clenched as we kept dropping. My knotted innards recalled other trees as close as these, which had brought death.

Suddenly, the first landing light flashed past. A bump, airborne again, then we were down, the retro-thrusters screaming, and as I lunged forward the belt held. Still moving forward at a fearful speed, the pilot swung sharply to the right into the leadoff to the terminal. The voice next to me had stopped. Still pent up with the tension, but with the mingling of remorse for my lack of communication, I made my belated offering, "Nice flight."

The stoney silence told me, "Too little, too late." As we glided up to the terminal, I was exhilarated to be home. My enthusiasm negated my customary caution and chivalry. My belt was off, and I was up and gone before we finally stopped. I didn't really want to have to face my neighbouring passenger in view of our strained, one-sided relationship during the 25-minute flight.

Noticeably bored with cautioning passengers to wait till the airplane had come to a full stop, the attendant gave me only a mild reproach.

"You're in a bit of a hurry, I see," but understanding was evident in her sympathetic look.

"Glad to be home," I answered. My smile was visible only in the eyes, but fighting through the restraint of the mask. I was first down the steps and with only a catch of a limp, I put my best bounce into my step and led the disembarking passengers to the door of the terminal. I had a moment's dread at the thought of having to struggle with the door. I'd never get it open with my cumbersome gloves. The door swung open as I approached and there was Bill Gordon with a smile nearly as wide as mine.

"Welcome home, Blair."

"It's good to be back," I responded and we hugged with a public show of affection uncharacteristic for Scots. As we waited to get my suitcase off the carousel, several other friends and associates came over to welcome me home, but I felt a little barrier in each well-meaning greeting. Bill had been exposed to the mask and had helped me suffer through those early times with it, but it was new to most of the others there, and I quickly realized that this would be a challenge which I must face and work hard to help others to overcome.

It was all arranged that I was to stay with Bill and Maureen Gordon for a couple of weeks, until I was capable of moving back into my own house. Arriving at their home, I was made to feel welcome and shown to the bedroom designated for my stay. One of Bill's two sons had been kind enough to move to a basement room to allow me to have the convenience of the main floor location close to the family room and bathing amenities. It epitomized this family's thoughtfulness.

Half an hour later, as I sucked on a large mug of Maureen's specially brewed tea, my sons came over to visit me. Aware of their imminent arrival, I had removed my Jobst mask for my initial contact with them. It was a tearful reunion. They had both grown so much in the three months. I knew they had suffered with me.

To prove my physical well-being I squeezed their hand to show my strength and performed some knee, if not toe, touches to prove the integrity of my spine. As I stomped my foot firmly on the ground to show that my ankle was sound, I had to hide my anguish as my over-enthusiasm caused some stabbing pain. Having warned them a bit about the Jobst, I finally got the mask back on with Bill's help, and in next to no time the boys were accepting its garish appearance without evident concern.

Overcoming that hurdle was the last of my major fears and brought special gratitude and joy into that final homecoming time.

CHAPTER 31
In Four-Wheel Drive

The energy expenditure of that memorable first day of freedom had gone unrecognized, hidden by the excitement. Farewells from Foothills, the flight home, the wonderful welcome, and the emotional reunion with my sons took a heavy toll. Although I was excited and very anxious to spend time with my hosts, Bill and Maureen, by 10 p.m. my head was drooping and I was packed off to bed. I was amazed at the unbelievable silence as they tiptoed around, anxious to avoid disturbing me.

I had been fretful in case I would sleep poorly and possibly disturb them with my need to get up in the night or that my tossing and turning might keep them awake. My concerns were totally unfounded. I slept soundly throughout the night, waking almost 12 hours later, having had the best sleep since my accident.

I awoke unusually refreshed and was bathed, breakfasted, and ready for action by midmorning. I knew I'd meet with resistance as I outlined my plans for the day, but Bill's cautionary disapproval was only token as he knew me too well to think that I'd sit around all day. He had even anticipated my plans and had my little Subaru ready in four-wheel drive mode, parked in his carport. Such was his thoughtfulness that his own two cars were out on the street blanketed with a three-inch overnight snowfall.

He had even cajoled his sons into shovelling the snow from the driveway, in expectation of my insistence to get on the road again.

Bundled up against the cold, I waddled out and did a cursory walk-around, inspecting the little car. It was just as beautiful as I remembered. New just a month before my accident, it still had less than 2,000 km registering on the odometer.

Abby's words still rang in my ears. "Now, remember, you won't be able to drive for a few weeks, until your hands are stronger and your reflexes better adapted to traffic."

I sat in the driver's seat and did my preflight check. It was great to be back in control! The huge boots I was wearing, two sizes larger than I normally wore, accommodated my still swollen left ankle but were very cumbersome as I tentatively tried the clutch, brake, and accelerator pedals. The compact size of the car with all its instrumentation within hand reach, automatically started me thinking of the little Cessna trainer. Checking my grasp on the steering wheel with my rather unwieldy fingers that couldn't quite encircle the rim, I did a trial turning of the steering wheel. I automatically looked left and right to check the appropriate response of the imaginary ailerons. To get a bit more room to move around in the car, I moved the tilt steering wheel lever and dreamed of the tail wing elevator response.

Despite this meticulous care with prescribed safety checks, the forewarning of those who knew better were instantly validated as I lurched into reverse and leaped down the steep driveway, backwards.

I came to a scraping, sliding halt, shocked at my gross incompetence and incoordination. I sat and sweated in exasperation and fear, the engine revving furiously. My feet were jammed desperately against the clutch and brake pedals, the huge boots overlapping onto the accelerator, racing the motor. Gingerly I maneuvered the clumsy foot, inclining the pedals back as I dared myself to proceed slowly down the remaining few yards of the driveway.

Judging my moment to swing around to back down the street a little, I bumped over the foot-high mound of snow that had recently been packed across the driveway by the snowplow. The car zigzagged down the road while I tried to regain control. Fortunately, the street was deserted. Putting the car out of gear, I got the brake on and sat and thought about those last 20 seconds. Abby's words again crossed my mind. I was uncomfortable with the heat of the cumbersome clothing and sweating with fear. This was less than my great expectations for the start of the day.

I swallowed hard and decided to persevere. Creeping forward up to the stop sign at the end of the street, I took an inordinate time to perform the required hill start and right angle turn onto the avenue leading away from the familiar territory. It was like learning to drive all over again. I took the next left and proceeded up into a quiet backwater of streets. There I spent ten minutes practising hill stops and starts, right and left turns, backing up, and all the driving skills I would need in the days ahead.

Reaching a quiet section of the road, I finally stopped and went for a 50-yard hike.

My pace was unbelievably slow. Swaddled in all the heavy clothing, my feet dragging with the unaccustomed size of the boots, I struggled through those few inches of new snow. That walk was the heaviest work I'd done in months.

I stopped for a minute to drink in the splendour of the scenery. The town below was blanketed in a new coat of snow. The smoke from the chimneys was rising straight up in the frigid, still air, and the majestic peaks of the Rockies were a brilliant white, cutting into the clear blue sky.

All my enthusiasm returned as the beauty before me removed all thought of my own discomforts. Even the Jobst mask failed to curb an irrepressible smile of victory. I felt a sense of freedom, and was exhilarated by the success of overcoming the obstacles that had blocked my path.

I returned to the car not noticing the distance, but with a lightness of step, quite unlike the outward journey only minutes earlier.

With renewed purpose, I continued with my planned journey, demonstrating driving ability commensurate with my newfound self-confidence.

I had planned this moment for a long time and drove with joyful heart to the door of the veterinary clinic to retrieve my old dog, Yogi. She had been put into the kennels the day after my accident, but she became very frail, dejected, and looked on the verge of death. Finally she had to be removed from the kennels to the veterinary clinic where she was nursed along on a day-to-day basis, all tests failing to point to a specific malady. As each week dragged by, her veterinarian, in consultation with Bill Gordon, postponed again and again, the inevitable need to put the poor old dog out of her misery. Finally, a week before my release from hospital, it was diagnosed that she was simply pining away, quite heartbroken about my disappearance.

Bill had warned me that the dog was not in good shape, but as I clambered up the five front steps into the clinic I had great hope for her recovery. Even before she saw me, the sound of my voice got her shakily onto her feet in that wire cage.

"She hasn't got up by herself for a week," the vet assured me, quite astonished at the sight.

I leaned right down to pat her and she gave the Jobst mask a lick. It was the ultimate proof of acceptance. She saw only the person behind the mask.

In all the excitement, I forgot to pay the account for her stay and care, but excitedly we moved off, a right unsteady pair. Those few steps back down to ground level were a great challenge. I rocked and swayed and couldn't get a proper grip on the stair rail, and Yogi, too, was wary of the precipitous six-inch drop to each successive step.

Getting her into the front passenger seat involved teamwork. She would normally have leapt in nimbly, but now I had to get the front feet in and then lift the rear legs up and gently ease her onto the seat before I carefully closed the door. I then staggered around to the driver's side, exhausted but delighted with our progress. It took me an age to get settled in, started up, and seat belted. As I looked across at Yogi she was sitting up looking out the window as if the intervening three months had not occurred. Through the window I saw the vet and his assistant still standing at the top of the steps. They had purposely left me to struggle and overcome those difficulties, recognizing I would have spurned their offer of help. With a cheery wave, I eased away gently with my precious cargo.

The drive through town on that sunny Saturday morning is a glorious memory. Everything was especially bright and shining to welcome the two of us back to life. As I drove north the six miles to my rural home, the countryside had never looked more beautiful. I could see the mountain tops stretch for 50 miles up the valley of the Kootenay River. All was well.

On the little steep side-road into the Six Mile Crossing subdivision the snow was a little deeper but the four-wheel drive seemed to enjoy the challenge of holding safe on the gradient.

As I approached my driveway entrance, I slowed right down to relish the moment of returning home. Even Yogi found the strength to get her paws up on the dash, and with tongue flailing, was full of excitement at the joy of this special moment. I parked on the road, reluctant to drive through the eight or nine inches of snow, unmarked by traffic. As man and dog pushed through that glorious last 50 yards to the house, neither of us felt the pain or weakness of our bodies. I was apprehensive as I fumbled with the key, terrified that I might drop it into the snow, but finally the door was open. Together we stumbled in, dragging mounds of snow across the carpet. I lounged into my favourite lazy boy chair, tilting it fully back. With boots, coat, and hat still on, I drank in the splendid view of the Rockies through my picture window. The sun was streaming through the double glazing and within moments, man and dog were both fast asleep, at peace with the world.

Half an hour slipped by before I stirred. Inactivity and the cold in the house woke me up. In my absence, Bill Gordon had turned the thermostat down to 50 degrees, just enough to ensure that the water pipes would not freeze. Although

I was not going to stay in the house overnight, I turned up the heat for Yogi's comfort. It was a moment of celebration, so I pilfered a blanket from the spare bedroom to lavish extra comfort on my faithful old hound.

The hitherto simple task of feeding the dog was an unexpectedly complicated routine. Trying to fix the dog-food can onto the electric can-opener was an unbelievably difficult exercise. I finally got it wedged so that the cutting wheel was in place on the rim and then depressed the start lever. I was so nervous about injuring my hands that I instinctively jumped back as the whirring mechanism threatened the safety of my treasured fingers. I was shell shocked. The opener tipped over, the can fell to the floor, and I danced back, fearful of all the unaccustomed violence.

I finally got the lid off the can. The frustration continued as I tried to grasp a fork from the cutlery drawer. The slim utensil kept slipping out of my gloved fingers. I missed the sponge-padded handle provided by those caring staff in Occupational Therapy. Defeated, I opted for a steak knife with its wooden handle and managed to get some of the contents out of the can into the dog's dish, spilling most of the food on the floor. Yogi didn't mind this inaccuracy and gobbled up more than she ought to have been offered, as if she hadn't eaten for three months.

Time was rushing past. It was almost one o'clock already and I'd promised to be back for lunch at the Gordons' promptly at 1:30. With Yogi tucked into her new blanket in her favourite basket, I struggled to make up time. The excitement of success lingered on as I puffed and panted back up the driveway to the car.

To save time, I tried a three-point turn in the roadway to get myself facing back towards town. The Jobst gloves and the plastic rim of the steering wheel made a frictionless combination and I suddenly realized there was an extra complication to my driving needs, once again giving credence to the Foothills' caution against driving.

Using extra care, I made it back right on time and with a feeling of huge accomplishment, took on the snowplowed mound and steep driveway without hesitation, stopping exactly on the spot where Bill had parked my car the previous day.

I took great pleasure in making a return trip to Six Mile each day to spend some time with Yogi. Gradually I increased the time away from my adoptive family, preparing myself for the eventual move home.

To my amazement, on the second day when I made the journey home, I found that the driveway had been totally cleared out by some kind soul. It was months before I found out who the Good Samaritan was, who, uninvited and unthanked, kept that driveway clear that winter. It was typical of many acts of kindness that were lavished on me in the days ahead. In this case, a neighbour, several houses down the road, had undertaken this chore.

The cleared driveway allowed me the convenience of four wheel drive access right to my door. That neighbour could not have guessed how much his thoughtful act had contributed to the joy of my homecoming.

I was still incapable of independent living – that time was still ahead.

CHAPTER 32
Happy Christmas

The first three weeks following my discharge from hospital were punctuated by such a sequence of achieved goals that time just flew by. Hosted by the Gordons, I was lavished with encouragement, support, and love. I was anxious not to intrude into their family life, but they made me feel so welcome that I soon felt part of the family. My routine quickly developed into a busy schedule of activity. I would drive out to my house each day and spend some time with the dog, sharing this pleasure with Ian and Craig once they were out of school for the Christmas holidays. It was catch-up time, trying to rebuild the closeness that had been so threatened by the near-tragedy. Although only 11 and 12 years old, the boys were unbelievably thoughtful, supporting me by word and deed. Perceptive to my needs, they'd help me on with my coat unasked, shovel all the snow off the steps at the house, and bring in firewood without my prompting. It was a great learning experience for each of us and brought an understanding that we might never have been gifted with otherwise.

Additionally, I had regular weekly appointments with my family physician. Dr. David Lenz was obviously thrilled to greet me and, much later, when he knew I would be in a better position to cope with the statement, conceded that he had never expected to see me again when I'd left for Calgary that first night.

A time of great excitement was the arrival of my mother from Scotland a week before Christmas. For her it was a stressful moment as, despite Bill Gordon's assurance of my progress, deep down she still suspected the worst. Fatigued by the long anxious flight, and shocked by the minus 35 degree Celsius temperature, she was met by Bill, Ian, and Craig at the airport. She approached the Gordon home leery and suspicious.

I had carefully removed the Jobst mask to minimize the delay in her viewing the full extent of my facial damage. Despite her naturally courageous spirit, she was visibly shocked at the suddenly aged offspring that faced her. Our mutual efforts to minimize the other's anguish seemed to aggravate rather than lessen the concerns we shared, but gradually we settled and she became more accepting of the changes that had occurred. It was a grateful family reunion that rapidly disintegrated into dialects that even my own two sons could not understand.

The joyous mood continued, helping me tolerate the threat of the new stares of the Christmas shoppers as they had their first exposure to my Jobst mask. I gradually became more confident and comfortable in the hubbub of the pre-Christmas crowds. Two days before Christmas I had to make a one-day trip back to Foothills for a review at the Hand Clinic. I had time to think about the flight back over the mountains. By way of preparation I drove up to the airport to visit Horizon Air Flying School, steeling myself to make the contact again. Kelly, my flight instructor, was visibly touched by my visit. It helped me greatly just to be there and chat, as only flying enthusiasts can, about the exciting, positive things that are a part of that environment. The whole gang was delighted with my progress and most supportive in their praise and encouragement.

The midmorning 25-minute flight in the PWA 737 was smooth and surprisingly enjoyable. I had a moment of apprehension during the climb up the stairs into the aircraft, but felt good about the daylight takeoff procedure, being able to see the mountains and feeling greater control as we swept past each familiar thousand foot mark on the runway.

The combination of a glorious flight over the snowcapped mountains and a whisper landing in Calgary did much to rebuild my comfort and faith in air travel.

I was excited as I travelled by taxi from the airport, anticipating a pleasurable visit with some of the wonderful staff whom I now held as close friends.

It was like returning home. It was hard to believe that I would have missed the place so much. There was a joyous reunion in Physio and O.T. My visit to the Burn Unit was very special. I felt I'd been away a long time but some of the same patients were still there, with little change evident. A little cloud of sadness overshadowed my excitement, but I was pleased to see them and anxious to encourage them and report with sensitivity the pleasures that lay ahead for them on their discharge from hospital. Abby and Delilah both gave encouraging remarks about the progress of my range of movement and strength in the hands. As if orchestrated, they simultaneously admonished me for having dry skin, indicative of the neglect in my required use of the lotions for my grafted areas. Next was the visit to the Hand Clinic, where reviews by Dr. Lindsay, Dr. Hamilton, and Dr. Davidson encouraged me with their positive observations on my progress.

An added bonus was Alan and Jan's appearance at 4 p.m. to pick me up to take me back to the airport. They, too, were very encouraging and I took a special pride in being able to fasten the seatbelt by myself when I got into their car.

It had been such a busy and exciting day that I didn't have time to worry about the flight before I boarded the jet in the early darkening winter evening. It was the same flight crew that had been on the plane on my morning flight from Cranbrook, so their recognition of me and my mask made for lighthearted conversation. The contrast to that wretched first flight home only two weeks earlier was unbelievable.

Christmas Eve was disturbed by an emergency visit to the dentist. The pressure of the mask clenching my teeth so solidly together on a 24-hour per day basis had been too much for the temporomandibular joint of my jaw. Kindly fitting me in by reshuffling his day's appointments, my dentist managed to provide a temporary night splint to gap my teeth from their over-closure position and give some relief to my aching jaw.

Christmas Day started off leisurely with attendance to my bathing, wound dressing, and exercise activities. After a short visit with Ian and Craig to the house and dog, we returned to the Gordons' to enjoy a memorable pleasure-filled exchange of gifts, love, and gratitude. The joy of being with those near and dear, sharing our closeness, was very special proof that I'd overcome the worst of my trials.

Later, my hosts demonstrated their combined culinary expertise by laying on a feast fit for a king. Bill, Maureen, their two sons, Andrew and Ian, my mother, Craig and Ian, and I shared that lavish table. It was a Christmas dinner to remember forever.

The emotion culminated as we held hands and Bill led us in thanksgiving for the food, especially giving thanks for my recovery and the pleasure of that expanded family togetherness, closing the grace in his traditional manner, "and keep us ever mindful of the needs of others." I was grateful for the hubbub ensuing as they started dishing out enormous helpings of that abundant fare. I quickly took my leave, cloistered myself in the bedroom, and sobbed uncontrollably, so aware of the good fortune of my survival and recovery. I was suddenly desperately aware that there was, in contrast, deep sadness in two other families who had suffered painful loss in the same accident. My heartfelt thoughts and prayers went out to them, and with somewhat restored composure I returned to that Christmas feast. It was a time I'll never forget.

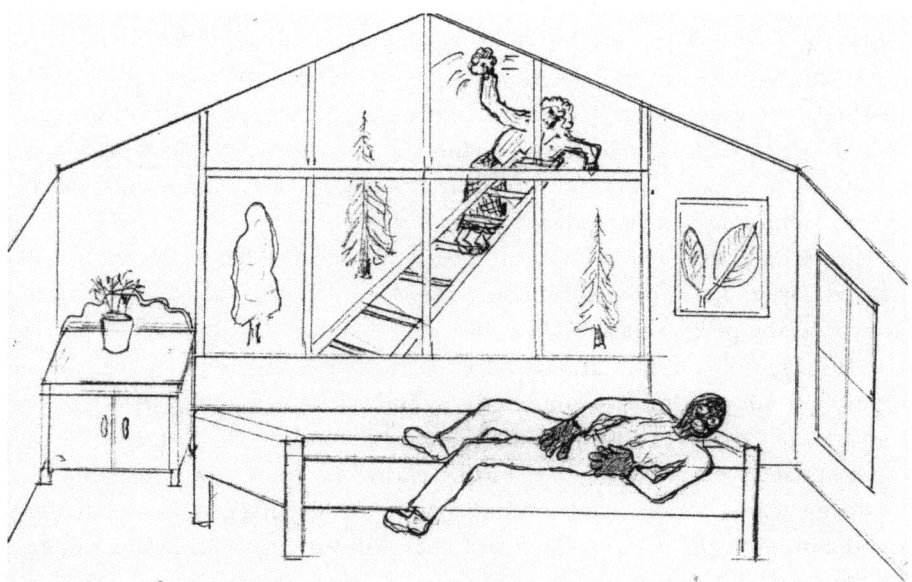

CHAPTER 33
The Impatient Outpatient

New Year's Eve, 1984, had special significance for me as I spent much time thinking about the year ahead.

That Hogmanay, celebrated with more than usual gratitude at the Gordon's home, was something of a farewell party. My mother and I had been blessed with generous hospitality in that family home but despite Bill and Maureen's insistence that we stay longer, I had firmly fixed January 1st as the day to move back into my own home, and start off my new life.

Consequently, 1983's closing was observed by a gathering of friends and neighbours who celebrated the New Year in fitting style.

As it was traditionally one of the times for wearing a kilt, I felt that getting back to normality and starting the New Year off right dictated the need for sporting the tartan.

While historically the Scots have been reluctant to divulge the secret of whether or not there are any items of attire worn beneath the kilt, there was little to disguise the discordant Jobst suit worn under the kilt on that occasion. In a crazy sort of way it gave me some perverse pleasure to don the two ill-matching outfits. It proclaimed my defiant spirit and desire to overcome every setback.

Instead of the customary tardiness and protracted suffering of a New Year's morning, I was up early and full of energy. There was much to be done.

As the household slowly emerged, I was ready to make my move. I hadn't realized just how much I had accumulated in personal possessions, and box after box had to be loaded into the car. Eventually, by late morning, we expressed our deep thanks to our hosts, and Mother and I took leave to start the next phase of less dependant living.

There had been a small snowfall overnight and the beauty and quietness was exhilarating. Traffic was virtually nonexistent and the six mile drive to the house was the perfect start to a new life.

This tranquility lasted until the moment we got to the house, at which time we started our inevitable wrangling. Our individual viewpoints were each so indisputably correct. My mother was doing what mothers do best. Her instinct was to protect her offspring. Nurturing, caring for me in every possible way, guarding against the chance of my injuring myself, she grasped the opportunity to be mother again. This was at direct odds with my desire for independence. I looked upon this moment as an opportunity to rebuild my shattered ego and a chance to prove to myself that I was again able to face the challenges of that threatening outside world.

Before I could even lumber my way out of the car with my still unaccustomed over-clothed and under-coordinated new style, mother was out on the front veranda and busily sweeping away the two-inch snowfall.

While I tried to inflict my chauvinistic rights and send her packing to the kitchen, it became clear from the resulting standoff that there had been a perfect genetic transfer of stubbornness.

It grieved me greatly that she wanted to carry out this snow clearing chore and although I knew she was doing the job more capably and speedily than I could have, it reaffirmed my relative helplessness. It seemed to emphasize most exasperatingly, her spritely energy, disproportionate to her 70-plus years. Together we huffed and puffed, she with the exertion and I with petulant poor sportsmanship. This was just the forerunner of many heated clashes which, over the next six weeks of Mother's stay, brought me belatedly to an even greater admiration of her patience and forbearance. While consistently unlikely to back down once she had made her mind up about a course of action, she was, however, blithely forgiving of each of my tantrums.

Finally, a truce was called in the guise of my desperately needing a cup of tea, and with no dispute in her superior skill at that task, she proceeded to perform her magic, simultaneously turning a blind eye to my bringing the boxes in from the car.

Unloading the car, stumbling in an ungainly fashion up the few steps into the house, and tripping over my huge boots, I was inordinately proud when I managed to dump the ten or so boxes just inside the front door.

As I managed to get the cumbersome outdoor clothing removed, I suddenly realized that my stubbornness had been a costly indulgence. I was bathed in sweat and exhausted from the effort needed to do this simple job.

With some hint of remorse, I realized that the Jobst outfit was saturated with sweat, clammy, and uncomfortable.

Armed with a huge mug of steaming tea, I took the line of least resistance and retreated to the comfort of a hot bath. The blissful joy of that hot soak, combined with my state of exhaustion, created the perfect environment for a midday snooze.

Ages later, fearing my drowning, mother pounded on the bathroom door to wake me. The water had cooled but I was refreshed and reluctant to leave. Finally, I emerged, spending the next half hour on my required skin care and getting back into a new outfit of Jobst. By the time I had completed my ablutions and dressing, the boxes were all empty and their contents put away in their appropriate places.

The acorn fireplace was lit in the sitting room, and with the additional warmth of the sun's rays, I offered little resistance to the invitation to sit in my lazy boy chair and allow myself to be pampered with yet another cup of tea and a sandwich. We chatted for a while; my most energetic contribution was to stroke the dog with my slippered foot.

Predictably, the comforts and mollycoddling sent me off again to the land of nod, and thus started a habit of day-night reversal that was to plague me for weeks.

I slumbered away another hour while mother toiled at the stove, preparing supper. Ian and Craig were coming over to spend the evening with us, and that first meal in our home was celebrated with our favourite traditional Scottish fare of mashed potatoes, mince, cabbage, and turnip prepared as only a Scots mother can.

The boys always took great delight in Granny's cooking, and my Jobst gloved hands coping well with that particular food which required no cutting, I gorged myself with the satisfying simplicity of this special meal.

The feeling of normalcy was shattered soon after. The pack of cards was dealt for an after-supper game of Canasta before I suddenly realized the impossibility of my picking up the cards and sorting them in my hand. Again I was jolted by the feeling of helplessness at being unable to participate in such a simple activity.

Rather than spoil their fun, I took on the task of scorekeeping, and while the three of them played I scrawled the figures, labouring over holding the pencil in my gloved hand. Craig innocently struck a nerve by his perceptive observation of my scribbles.

"Gee, Dad, your writing's almost as bad as mine," he chided.

They laughed at his youthful honesty. As happens with the lure of a pack of cards, time flew past and it was 1 a.m. before we finally scooted the boys off to bed.

Mother and I had the inevitable final nightcap cup of tea and, wide awake, got into some serious conversation. Before we knew it, it was 4 a.m. Even at that, on retiring to bed, I needed another hour to finally drop off to sleep. Not surprisingly, although mother was up an hour or two before me, I finally struggled out of bed at 11:30 a.m. After their late night, the boys, too, were still abed, and bath and brunch carried the day through to one o'clock.

It was another beautiful sunny but cold winter day. We bundled up and took the short drive up to Kimberley to the ski hill. Although I didn't do more than clamber ten feet or so onto the flat area near the T-Bar, there was a very special excitement at being on the slopes again. Standing there, watching the speed of the skiers as they swooped down to the T-Bar lineup, got me thinking of the day when I'd again be on the boards.

By the time we had driven back into town, dropped the boys off for their planned supper with their mother and stepfather, and paid a short courtesy visit to the Gordons to show that we were alive and well, I finally had to drag back home, overcome with fatigue. Although I'd already recognized its onset, and was distressed by my daytime slumbering, my resolve weakened and I partook of a quick hour's snooze before supper.

After supper I became fully awake again and busied myself with a few little jobs tidying up my office. By happenstance, I came across a huge box of well-wishing cards and letters that I had received in hospital. As mother and I got engrossed in sharing the thoughts of all those kind folks, the hours slipped past as we worked our way through the four hundred cards that had been sent during my early days in hospital. We were amazed by some from overseas addressed simply "Blair Farish, Calgary Burn Hospital, Canada." It was a credit to the imaginative dedication of the Canadian Post Office and the Foothills Hospital's reputation as a Burn Unit that some of these pieces of mail were successfully delivered.

Despite my resolve to get to bed early, the late-night/late-morning regime quickly became entrenched. Breaking the habit and reverting back to a more socially acceptable time pattern was a difficult project and contributed much to the frustration of those early days. Trying to establish a routine became a goal in itself. Despite the use of pain drugs and sleeping pills, I was still sleeping poorly. My disturbed sleeping pattern made my attempts at early morning activities meet with poor success.

I set up 9:30 a.m. appointments at the hospital Physiotherapy Department and, despite my good intentions, just could not get there punctually. The staff were very tolerant of my tardiness, and although it tied up the whirlpool room and a treatment cubicle, they were only gently reproachful over my recurrent lateness. The visits were a mutually dissatisfying arrangement, as I resisted their well-meaning efforts to encourage my exercise activities. They, in turn, were not entirely at ease trying to provide treatment for a fellow physiotherapist and their former department head. Despite my lack of cooperation, gradual progress was made in stretching the stiff joints and strengthening weak muscles.

I certainly did enjoy, and gained from the camaraderie of meeting and briefly chatting with so many of my former fellow workers. With a bit of dawdling over trivial shopping assignments, it was usually almost noon by the time I returned home. I tried to conjure up specific missions for the afternoon to resist the attraction of an afternoon sleep. Unable to concentrate, sitting down with a book was guaranteed to induce sleep within minutes.

One of the very positive things that came out of those early days was the joy of visiting school and watching my boys play basketball. This was a special pleasure from which I had been excluded during my busy working days.

At first, every eye was on me as I sat at the edge of the school gymnasium, but soon the students became accustomed to the mask and my hidden features and they would crowd past me with hardly a glance.

Mother was unbelievably tolerant of my raging impatience. She quietly busied herself with all the jobs that I couldn't attend to. Some of her activities, however, added to my suffering as her endeavours encroached on areas that were clearly my domain.

It was heartrending to watch her struggle with the wheelbarrow, bringing logs from the carport, wobbling her way across the snow-covered lawn.

On another occasion, my afternoon nap on the sofa in the warmth of the sunlight was disturbed by a fleeting shadow. In that twilight area between dream and wakefulness, a rhythmical movement recurrently blocked the sun's rays, throwing a disturbing flicker over my face. It was caused by the moving arm of my 70-year-old mother, cleaning the outside panes of window. She was perched high up on a ladder to reach the 12-foot peak on the end of the house. Not content with the danger of this high altitude window washing, her choice of day with a minus 20 degree temperature drew my full wrath and highlighted my exasperation at my disability.

To punctuate those distressing days with positive experiences, I tried many varying activities. Each had its own innate setback. Walking in those intensely cold days proved a discouraging activity. I had to be bundled up so heavily to cope with the extreme cold that anything more than a hundred yards caused me to perspire profusely, forcing my hasty return home, and obliging me to go through the whole bath and change routine.

I joined a pleasant group of adults in the time slot set aside for disabled swimmers at the local swimming pool and found that an enjoyable distraction and worthwhile exercise regime. Disappointingly, two sessions of this caused a painful skin reaction, possibly brought on by the chlorine in the water, so this routine had to be discontinued.

All told, the euphoria of my homecoming and independence quickly vanished. It was a trying time as an impatient outpatient.

CHAPTER 34
Goal Setting Time

Although my frustrations with my disability and the restrictions it imposed upon me did little for my mood, the battles with Mother were usually over silly little things. Despite these many mini-altercations, her presence was a Godsend, and it was one of the hidden benefits of the whole tragedy that I was able to spend a bonus six weeks with her before her return to Scotland. Her tolerance of my idiosyncrasies brought a new realization of the distance we'd grown apart in the quarter century since I had left home. She had had her three-score-and-ten-years of life to gain great experience in dealing with the ravages of war and family suffering. This equipped her well to deal with my churlishness.

To combat some of this strife, I set aside an hour or so each day to get away by myself. No doubt my absence from the house for that time was equally peaceful and acceptable to her.

This became a treasured time for me and I would drive to some quiet spot by the frozen river or up to the lookout tower behind the house, where I could sit and survey the city. It was a wonderful time for thinking.

It gave me time to argue with myself about the pros and cons of various short and long-term goals.

As each day passed, there was a paradoxical mix of confidence gained by seeing little improvements and achievements, and devastation at the distressing evidence of inability and failure. Gradually the balance of logic and reality started pointing to a realistic hope for return to work one day.

I spent many quiet hours in my physiotherapy clinic trying to analyze what I could or could not do. It was hard to dream that I would ever be able to perform the wide ranging requirements of my profession, as my style had always been one of dynamic energy, and I tired at the very thought of it.

On those visits I would do a mock trial run with a hypothetical new patient. Instantly, unanswerable questions bombarded me. How would the patient accept the Jobst masked professional? How could I walk into the waiting room and face four or five new patients? With my slow scrawl how could I write notes about the patient? How would they feel about being touched by the Jobst gloves? How could I wash my hands after treating each patient? How could I demonstrate the exercises that I recommended to patients? Above all, with my main interest and specialization in the care of sports and spinal conditions, how could I carry out the demanding yet sensitive work of spinal manipulation with my gloved, stiff, and uncoordinated hands?

It all seemed an overwhelming impossibility. With some difficulty, I leafed through the pages of my appointment sheets for the last few days of that September prior to my accident. As I browsed through the names of patients, I was greatly reassured by being able to remember who they were and link conditions to names. The list grew: a sprained ankle, a wry neck, a lumbar disk, sciatica, knee cartilage, a hockey player with a shoulder separation. It was all coming back. There was something very positive and reassuring in the knowledge that I automatically knew what treatment would be required. I returned home bounding with enthusiasm, but afraid to even mention the thoughts in case the ensuing discussion might reveal new realities that I had overlooked.

One of the achievable short-term goals that became a vital stopgap in the passage of time was my regular return to Calgary to the Hand Clinic. By the time I made that late January visit, I had set the first week of April as my projected date for return to work. The more I thought about it the more I convinced myself that this was a realistic aim. I knew I had a long way to go to restore my strength, ability, and stamina, but the pressure was on to return to work. My practice, established over years of hard work, was at risk of disappearing. While I had nurtured a clientele that I could depend on, and gradually obtained encouraging support through the referrals from the majority of the local doctors, my prolonged absence was likely to necessitate my patients and physicians finding other sources of treatment. It was imperative that I get back to work as soon as possible, and six months absence, I estimated, was the maximum they'd tolerate.

Trying to guard my enthusiasm and observe his reaction even before he committed himself verbally, I posed my proposed date for return to Dr. Lindsay. Encouraging and yet cautious, he gave me hope for the feasibility of my goal, curbing my bounding enthusiasm with the admonition that it was not going to be easy. I construed his qualified support as an all-clear to go for that date. From thence forward nothing could alter my time projections, although there were many ups and downs in the interim.

A great concern was the need to be realistic about my practice. Unfortunately, with the doubtful prospects of my return to work in the near or distant future, it had been a painful decision to give notice of dismissal to Diana, my secretary. Bill Gordon had had the unpleasant task of passing on the news. During her visit to see me in hospital a few weeks later, I suffered considerable remorse over this decision. True to form, she tempered my concern with her realistic good-natured acceptance of the decision.

By late January she was still involved in only part-time fill-in positions elsewhere. Although I was very anxious to reengage her as my reliable secretary/ receptionist, I was reluctant to offer her the work in case my own projections of start-up date had been overly optimistic.

Even I could see major progress during each subsequent monthly visit to Calgary through February and March, although there had been harrowing times of indecision and pessimism interspersed between those visits.

During this time, one recurring positive happening was the weekend visits by my sons. We would always do some special things and they were tolerant of the activity restrictions imposed by my physical disabilities. They were tremendously supportive and protective at all times. I'd drive them up to the ski hill where they were quite content with just a few runs while I'd sit in the car or the lodge awaiting their return. It was wonderful to see them swoop down the hill, giving me the joy of seeing their speed and style. It was the reward of years of patient guidance and encouragement both by me and their mother for them to achieve the expertise they now exhibited.

It was clear they sensed my frustrations; they were so willing and eager to help. They'd clamour to see who would cook supper and help in so many ways.

By late February my strength and confidence were greatly improved and an anxious call from Alan Conway informed me of a health concern requiring his hospitalization. That got my mind off my own concerns and gave me the needed incentive to make a trip to Calgary by car. That 250 mile drive further restored my self-confidence and it was a joy to be able to visit Alan and Jan and be of some support to them in their time of distress. Fortunately, Alan's short stay in the Foothills Hospital had beneficial results, with encouraging long-term prospects.

Buoyed-up by my travels, I planned ahead for a mid-March visit to Vancouver to visit with friends, Cliff and Pat Fowler, in Abbotsford.

The prospect of that 550 mile journey was a little intimidating, but its completion was yet another positive experience that greatly helped my recovery.

My stay with my long-term friends that week was a wonderful experience and allowed me the opportunity to wander around and observe in Cliff's busy physiotherapy clinic, without the threat of actually having to treat patients. The ultimate test in reestablishing my self-confidence in my professional skills was my first attempt at spinal manipulation. We had a longstanding rivalry and mutual critical evaluation of our treatment techniques. It was, therefore, a great challenge to perform an adjustment on Cliff's unsuspecting neck. That he could still walk after the maneuver and, furthermore, offer his usual humorous brand of encouragement, was praise in itself.

"That wasn't at all bad. These Jobst gloves really help. You should have used them years ago."

And so the banter went on.

Another positive occurrence was my visit to the Workers' Compensation Board Rehabilitation Centre in Richmond. I had asked for a review by their staff and was invited to visit the clinic and went through their assessment and the start of a treatment regime. Due to the special circumstances of my professional background they accepted my refusal to stay for two weeks of treatment, on the assurance that I would perform all the prescribed exercises diligently on my own.

Not wishing to detract from the professional skills that they offered, I suspect that the best thing that happened to me there was being able to observe the wide range of clientele who were attending the Rehabilitation Centre, either as resident patients or as outpatients. The extent of loss evident in some grossly disabled patients made my meagre limitations seem a paltry affliction. However, my practised eye detected doubtful symptoms in some of those attending for treatment. Each of those observations made me more ready to return to work, confident that I could succeed.

I purposely made the Abbotsford/Cranbrook run in a nonstop 12-hour drive which gave me confidence in my stamina. That whole visit had been a reassuring experience.

On the last Saturday in March, I capped off my six-month absence from work with my first triumphant venture on the ski slope. It was a gloriously sunny day with mild temperatures. My still-swollen left ankle was grateful for the rear-opening Salomon boot's firm support. I had a gentle two-run ski session down the main slope. I was so elated at being back on the boards that the stares provoked by the Jobst mask were of no concern. With Ian and Craig tolerantly skiing at my drastically reduced speed, carving those gentle curves was a fitting finale to my rehabilitation. I had to chuckle that I was out on the slopes while still on Workers' Compensation disability payment, and conjured up all sorts of arguments to use should my ski hill sojourn provoke that bureaucracy's wrath. It would have been ironic had I broken a leg during this misadventure.

Despite the many setbacks and discouragements, I had survived the eternity away from work, thanks in part to the successful completion of a series of short-term goals. It was time to get back to work.

CHAPTER 35
Kicking The Habit

By mid-February a new ogre posed in the way of my total recovery. I was still on analgesics to gain some relief from persistent nagging pain.

The hands gave me greatest cause for concern, as almost every activity which produced the slightest bumps or stretching of the fingers would cause a new bout of suffering. The Jobst gloves, performing their required task of maintaining ongoing, even pressure over the scars, also produced unrelenting discomfort. Even the efforts of trying to get into thick mitts to protect against the cold caused an exacerbation of pain in the digits, and would take hours to settle. Opening the car door or accidentally bumping the gear shift handle, or even the effort required to carry in a small bag of groceries, all had their distressing effects.

Worst of all was the agony caused by wearing the little spring night-splints to try to prevent further contractures in the fingers. To get relief, I was forced to make recurrent use of pain-relieving drugs.

Sleeping pills had also become a set part of my regime. I tried all sorts of techniques to combat the day/night clock reversals and fought a losing battle trying to get to sleep any time before midnight, even by using the sleeping pills.

Although I did not appear to be suffering any specific side effects from the use of these pain and sleeping drugs, I was very anxious about them. I had by then been on steady use of medication for some five months.

I tried gradually cutting down on the dosage of the pain-suppressing medication and although I became cantankerous, I persisted. Mother had by then gone back to Scotland so I had only myself to be angry with.

I made trial runs on half dosage of the sleeping pill but all this seemed to do was aggravate my need for sleep during the day and make for some horrendous sleepless nights.

Falling into the trap of getting advice from several sources, I was assured that the sleeping pill use was nothing to be concerned about, but my deep fear of becoming addicted drove me to find a way to get off the drugs.

In desperation, I reverted to the disastrous "cold turkey" routine recommended by a friend who had used that system to stop smoking.

That night, I spent a disturbed and sleepless night and was in great ill-humour by morning when I dragged myself out of bed at 7:30. I had been in the habit of having a leisurely morning bath, but knowing I'd be asleep within minutes in the soothing waters, forced myself to take my first shower in five months. That procedure wasn't remotely comforting, but it was just the beginning of a memorably awful day.

I conjured up a busy schedule of visits and activities, packing my timetable for the day so that I'd have no opportunity to sit down and fall asleep.

Somehow I struggled through, staying awake until ten o'clock that evening before finally crashing to bed without even the energy to think of sleeping or pain pills. I slept the sleep of the dead until 1:30 a.m., then watched the clock every hour until daybreak.

Forcing myself up again up at 7:30 a.m., I passed another exhausted day and was in furious fettle by evening.

Hearing of my dilemma, the friend who had recommended this dastardly regime came around to visit later that evening. Compounding his questionable advice, he proposed that a pint of beer at bedtime would do the trick.

The combination of my heavy medication and my doubtful car driving capabilities due to the restrictions of the gloves had dictated I use extreme care in my use of alcohol during the previous months. At my wits end, I grudgingly indulged in his recommended bedtime beverage. My exhaustion, almost 48 hours of sleeplessness, and the lulling effect of the alcohol, presented me with eight hours of wonderful, undisturbed, pain-free sleep.

I woke at 7 a.m. refreshed, encouraged, and ready for the day's activities.

Although I got the usual sleepy afternoon feeling, I tramped around the shopping mall to keep myself awake. Later I busied myself for the evening, readying myself with some gleeful anticipation to my newly-prescribed late evening medication of a pint of beer.

Not only did the late evening imbibing cause sleep but it was also a natural early morning alarm clock as there was no argument at 7 a.m. about my body's urgent needs.

It seemed ironic that my concern about the addictive potential of the drugs for pain and sleep would be combatted by the start of a self-imposed addiction to alcohol. Gradually, as time went by, I found I could exchange the brand of liquid to a more acceptable brew of hot chocolate.

The experience certainly gave me a new awareness and greater respect for those suffering from specific addiction concerns. The battle of kicking the habit of drugs was one which has remained a vivid memory.

That period of near addiction is a time I'd like to forget.

CHAPTER 36
Back in Harness

"Announcing the reopening of Cranbrook Physiotherapy Clinic on Monday, April 2nd, 1984, following a six-month closure due to illness of the proprietor, Blair Farish. Treatment by appointment only."

Taking care to make the announcement discreet and ensuring that it could not conflict with the non advertising ethics of my profession, I informed the public that I was back in business.

Placing that announcement in the local newspaper was my first step in trying to revitalize my practice.

To my great relief, Diana Cavers had accepted my invitation to resume as secretary/receptionist and had returned to the office some two weeks earlier to catch up on mail and generally tidy up the place ready for the big opening day. To make sure that the physicians were aware of my return, I also hand delivered a short note to their offices the Friday afternoon prior to that long-awaited reopening.

That Monday morning, I awoke at 6 a.m. and started my ablution, breakfasting and dressing, and eventually set off in plenty of time to be at the office well before the 8:30 scheduled opening. I was over-awed by what awaited me. Lined up on my desk were three beautiful arrangements of flowers with cards from well-wishers, and the day had not yet started. Throughout the day many more bouquets of flowers and plants arrived, each with a little card. I was touched by the thoughtfulness of those and many other well-wishers, and especially that some came from the most unexpected sources. Throughout the day many former patients, friends, and associates popped their heads in the waiting room door to briefly convey their best wishes and welcome me back.

I was overjoyed to be back in harness and overwhelmed by the emotion of the day and the sincerity and kindness of so many people.

Many supporters phoned in to give me a word of encouragement and many encouraging cards arrived by mail that week.

Although I had been in and out of the office almost daily for the previous few weeks, it seemed strange to be there and to have to spend an entire day in the one building. There was lots to do that first morning just to get into my stride and I really hadn't anticipated seeing many patients on the first day. Newly-referred patients started arriving by midmorning and the trickle of new faces built up to a steady flow by the afternoon.

Although I was buoyed up by the elation of the welcome back, very soon I began to feel the reality of the many concerns that I had anguished over in anticipation of the opening. My major concern was centred around the Jobst garments. I felt reasonably capable of carrying out the required work even if at a slower than normal pace, but there were some distinct drawbacks that surprised me. In anticipation of the patient's shock at seeing me for the first time, I had placed a photograph on the reception desk showing me in my full Jobst mask. I had instructed Diana to make sure that, on each new patient's arrival, she would mention to the patient that I had been in an accident and was obliged to wear the mask. By showing the patients the picture, they were forewarned.

Diana carefully observed the patient's reaction and where it was evident that the patient was particularly aghast, she tried to relieve them with some levity, "It's the same crazy Scotsman inside there that you'll remember from your last visits."

When a patient started lamenting, "Oh, the poor thing. It must be awful," she would mildly rebuke them by saying, "He's not too fussy about getting sympathy and he's still just as mean as ever with his treatments."

Reverting to my regular habit of stepping into the waiting room, picking up the patient's file, and inviting him back into the inner sanctums of the clinic, I quickly found that there was a difference in patient reaction from earlier days. Customarily, my clients would humour their way in with some derisions such as, "Oh, Oh, my turn now," but in this new regime they dutifully followed me, in painful silence. It was all a bit disconcerting for me and no doubt horrifying for them.

Once into the treatment room, the awful proximity to the mask caused consternation in many of the patients. The cubicles themselves measure only eight feet by six feet and with the patient perched on the edge of the treatment couch, there was very little remaining space in which I could distance myself from him to give him a comfort zone. I had always found that the welcoming handshake did much to bridge the gap between patient and professional, but after two or three disastrous reactions as patients leaped back, having felt the clammy unnatural glove in their hand, I quickly discontinued this practice.

It took just the first three patients to teach me that these initial meetings and introductions were going to be tough and would demand a great deal of extra effort on my part to mollify the horror-stricken patient.

Those first few seconds with a new patient, and even with those returning for second or third visits, were diffIcult. In addition to the bank robber appearance of the mask with the large holes for the eyes, the tight oval-shaped aperture which allowed my lips to protrude, tiny holes for the nostrils, and ears sticking out like flattened cauliflowers, the absence of hair and features was what most shocked my clients.

Additionally, due to the restrictive tightness of the elastic structures, I was not able to use my lips and mouth to form sounds in the normal fashion, so my total speech was distorted and unnatural.

Above all, it was the absence of the expected facial expressions that was so disconcerting for the patient. The welcoming smile was gone. The reassuring look of sincerity, sympathy, excitement, humour, or frown had all disappeared. These complementary pictures of body language, which usually helped to portray the meaning of my words, were all lost.

The loss of this visual component of communication caused unintentional errors in the messages patients received.

Trying to elicit a patient's history of injury or disease became a strained procedure. Instead of the flow of information which, once prompted, had previously flooded out came a stilted reluctant proffering of scanty information. All the while their eyes would be huge and full of fear, clearly focussed on the apparition in the mask.

Quickly I adopted a technique of only briefly glancing at the patient and then burying myself into the apparent need to write copious notes.

Another system of avoiding face to face confrontation also proved effective. When assessing spinal disorder, I was quick to get the patient facing away from me, so that I could carry out a prolonged examination of the spine in greater detail than was my custom. The patients would still try to look over their shoulders to see what I was doing behind them. Horrified as they were by the mask, they seemed hypnotized by it.

The distortion of my speech due to my tightly compressed lips and teeth was of great annoyance to me and caused an exaggeration of my existing accent to the extent that many patients had to ask me to repeat my questions.

In addition to these concerns, the patients flinched as they were touched by the Jobst gloves.

The loss of most of the sensory perception in my fingers, made worse by the thickness of Jobst material, finished all hope of using my hands as receptors of extra information and I had instead to rely exclusively on what I saw. I had lost the ability to feel tissue tension of muscle spasm, the softness or puffiness of swelling, or the warmth or moistness of the skin. Gone was the ability to feel for asymmetry indicative of muscle loss. Visually imperceptible deviations in the contour or boney abnormalities could now no longer be sensed by those previously highly sensitive digits.

Trying to write notes about the patient's condition was difficult as the pen constantly slipped from my gloved hand and even when I managed a firm grasp my writing was much worse than usual.

As the days wore on, many more petty inconveniences plagued me. Occasionally, a new patient in his attempt to lessen the gap between us would automatically stick out a hand in greeting. My natural reaction was the reflex proffering of a handshake, at which time the patient's hearty grasp would brutalize my tender fingers and hand.

This would start off a train of abject apology by the patient on seeing me shuddering in pain, and it soon taught me to decline, with the required explanation of my antisocial reluctance to take the hand. One alternative was to make sure my hand was wedged well into theirs to avoid the vice grip phenomenon.

Attempts at testing the patient's muscle strength manually became a nightmare as my weakness limited the counter force that I could provide against his attempts at movement. My previous style of exuberance and energy was replaced by a tired looking, feeble showing. My movements were still a fast shuffle at best and even with my first few days of light patient load, the heat produced by the panty hose, gloves, and mask caused me to sweat profusely.

Demonstrating exercises such as push-ups, pull-ups, or abdominal curls became a thing of the past. I quickly realized that trying to describe an exercise in words was a hard way of getting the message across.

I was particularly horrified at the restrictions brought on by the gloves in my habit of frequent hand washes between patients.

The divergent skin aromas I encountered in a day were wide ranging and distinctive. There was the back country stench of the great unwashed, the unavoidable grease and oil smells of the heavy duty mechanic, or the food odours from the kitchen workers who might slip into the clinic in their work clothes. The opposite extreme was the deliberate overuse of cosmetics and scents. All of these lingered on the Jobst gloves.

Even worse was my attempt to avoid touching the varieties of aromatic feet that presented themselves for treatment of metatarsalgias, heel spurs, bunions, and other foot disorders. I had a trial run at using surgical gloves, but it took time to put them on over the high friction surfaces of the Jobst. The instant increase in heat and sweating in my hands caused severe irritation, so that routine had to be used as infrequently as possible. Furthermore, the insides of most of the surgical gloves had a dusting of powder to try to make them slip on and off more easily. Very quickly the pressure garments became stained with the white powder. It wasn't long before I was going through my full inventory of four pairs of Jobst each day.

In an effort to cope with the loss of sensation and minimize the different aromas permeating into the glove material, I took the urgent step of creating my own open-tip gloves. In my first amateur experimentation in amputation, I snipped off a good half-inch of the material from each finger tip, to be duly horrified when I was reminded that the gloves stretch considerably once they are put on. Instead of having removed a modest half-inch, the gloves slipped right up the fingers, exposing two inches of finger ends. As I cringed at the vision, I anticipated my next visit to Calgary where Delilah could be expected to express great indignation at my botched tip-trimming efforts at tailoring the gloves.

With much greater care, I hesitantly trimmed off a tiny portion of the very end of each finger on the next pair of gloves and was relieved to see that it gave me some restoration of my original palpatory skills. I had been forewarned against this whole experiment and, true to the predictions of the staff at the Foothills, my fingertips were bulbous blobs by the end of each day.

My early attempts at spinal manipulation were exasperating experiences. Normally, I gloried in being able to perform those high velocity short amplitude maneuvers with some dexterity, but with the gloves clouding my perception of what was happening in the joints, I had to use greater than optimum pressure to achieve the desired effect. Gradually those hands began to produce the satisfying pops, and the resultant improvement in range was always satisfying, even if somewhat surprising, to me.

I found it difficult to produce the leverages and strength to perform lumbar manipulations, especially when some of my clientele were gorilla-like loggers and I often came away having merely transferred the pain from their back to my hands.

The ultimate in frustration was trying to tear the hockey tape used for ankle injury immobilization. The tape would stick to the gloves and a full treatment took an inordinate amount of time.

As with so many things, humour saved the day. Within a week, a friend brought in a pen and ink cartoon showing a "before and after" patient. The caption read, "Who was that masked man?" It still hangs in my clinic as a memory of those bygone days.

Children found the mask terrifying. The unease in the waiting room became oppressive as a little child embarked on a screaming session and simply refused to come in for treatment. Some adults, too, would find the pressure of visiting the clinic too much for them, and I was concerned by the number of cancellations and no-shows.

The physical and mental energy required in those early days sent me home exhausted, and for those first few months return to harness was a routine of work and sleep. I had no energy for other diversions and was in bed by 7:30 most evenings. My earlier concern with insomnia was gone, replaced instead by an ongoing exhausting fatigue and a constant fight to stay sufficiently awake to perform the work.

Despite all the frustrations of each day, it was wonderful to be back at work, and the memories of earlier horrors were gradually fading, to be replaced by the joys of each day and the gratitude to those who had helped so much in my recovery.

It was time to enjoy increasing success.

CHAPTER 37
Jobst II

With the passage of time and some great supportive work by hospital staff and friends, the Jobst mask gradually became more acceptable to me. I started to notice that there was a consistent, bearable, pressure over all the grafted areas of my skull, nose, and face.

An additional feature that was irksome at the time, but contributed greatly to the final result, was a modification required to maintain pressure on the sides of my nose. The tight stretch of the elastic material from the bridge of the nose to the cheekbone lifted the material away from the cleft at the side of the nose. Consequently, a plastic nose shell had to be molded to the contours of my nose and face to fill that gap. This was a tricky operation requiring the preheating of the special lightweight plastic material, molding, and pressuring it to my facial features and simultaneously superimposing the Jobst mask in its proper position over the new nose plate. The combined efforts of several O.T. staff made this delicate procedure tolerable. The shell was visible through the mesh of the mask and was one more unsightly feature in my skull-covering outfit.

I should have been more suspicious of the complexities ahead when I was issued my identity card, signifying that I was required to wear the Jobst mask for medical reasons. At the time of receiving the card at my discharge meeting, I hadn't given much thought to its value, but my experiences over the next few months gave me a clear indication that it might well be needed.

I had also been advised to ensure that I phoned ahead when I first went to my bank to forewarn them of my imminent arrival dressed in a rather threatening headgear. In a town the size of Cranbrook, and being reasonably well-known at the bank, this did not pose a significant problem, although the staff subsequently expressed their gratitude that I had bothered to call ahead, as there was little to show the true identity of the Jobst mask wearer. After a couple of visits, I became as recognizable as I had been prior to my injury.

Likewise, I called ahead before visiting the RCMP detachment. My approach to the front desk dictated the need for my best fast explanation of who I was, in a purposely loud but friendly voice. I had no concerns with the young police officer sitting at the desk, but I knew that large one-way mirror behind him allowed several other officers to observe me from their hidden location, and I wanted to make sure that they could hear me before they made any precipitous misjudgments of the situation. As the majority of the staff were out on other duties or off duty, I left a mug-shot photo, with my name and a brief outline of the reasons for my wearing the Jobst mask. As I presented it to the duty officer, I got a reassuring grin as I gave my parting shot, "I'd prefer you didn't write 'Wanted' over the top of it."

"We'll try not to," he assured me as he studied the photo with interest.

As I gradually gained experience in dealing with the public and their reactions, I became more aware of predictable responses, and took appropriate action to try to mitigate their initial reactions.

At times I felt I needed a forerunner to warn people of my approach, but eventually found that there were some things that should be avoided. After the first few episodes of jumpy reactions of a store clerk, I found it important to get her attention while I was still at some distance, by a little cough, or to delay until her eye caught me while I was still at some safe distance. Then I'd approach and start my spiel before I got to her counter.

After a couple of scary episodes, I avoided late evening or night visits to all-night corner stores. One night clerk, a huge young lad, jumped, and his startled reaction terrified me and I nearly turned on my heel and bolted. I didn't dare imagine what that might have precipitated. Instead, I just stood stock-still and sweated in an adrenaline-induced fear. No quart of milk was ever worth all that anxiety.

My natural good neighbourly habit nearly got me into trouble late one night as I drove home. Well out in the country in the pitch black night I saw ahead the emergency warning lights of a parked vehicle on the roadside. With never a second thought, I pulled up a few yards behind it, dipped my headlights, unbuckled my seatbelt, and had the door half opened before I realized the potential confrontation likely to ensue. As the horror of this possibility invaded my mind, I shot the car into gear, leaped forward onto the highway, and bolted like a scared rabbit, hoping all the time that the occupant of the car didn't see me, or recognize my vehicle. Further along, around a couple of sheltering corners, I drew up on the roadside to get control of myself, trying to slow down my frantic pulse.

Even walking through large department stores posed moments of uneasiness. I was very anxious to protect Ian and Craig from the pain that could happen in routine meetings with others. We talked about why people were shocked and surprised at seeing the mask, and I tried to make light of the varied reactions.

Walking through the stores with the boys, we'd play a guessing game of predicting reactions of passersby, and scoring them on our coded scale, designated 0, 1, 2, and 3. Seeing someone approach 15 or 20 yards away, Craig would glance up at me and whisper "2." The categories were defined thus. Zero was a firm no-looker. The passerby would steadfastly avoid eye contact with me by either turning his head vigorously to look to the other side of the passageway and somehow manage to walk past us in the military "eyes right" position, or, conversely, look straight through me as if I didn't exist.

A "1" category was an insidious hypnotized stare of disbelief until such time as the observer would realize he was staring. At that time he'd jerk his head violently away from his earlier focus and keep the eyes studiously averted to prevent further contact with the masked man.

The "2" designated a double look. A first automatic eye swivel was attracted by the unusual sight, but they would avert the eyes quickly, and then again look back in disbelief to check that they had really seen what they thought, before quickly looking away again.

The "3" was the ultimate entertainment and the boys became adept at checking this out. A "3" was really a regular "2" and then after having passed me the observer would turn around and watch my receding steps. The boys became skillful at simply looking sideways and out of the corner of their eyes managed to see whether the passerby had given that extra stare from the safety of my back view. With a typical 12 year old's pleasure in being right, they'd comment, "Yeah, Dad. Told you. A '3'." Sometimes this was said in a not-too-quiet voice.

As in all tough situations, there were some joyous moments. Craig and Ian were just the tonic I needed on occasion. They seemed to take particular pleasure in grasping my gloved hand protectively, and proudly stood buoyed up to their full four feet height daring anyone to threaten me in any way. One day while I was paying for some purchase, Ian had moved a few paces away. A school chum came along and in a sincere stage whisper inquiry asked, "Is that your Dad there?" Responding in an unbelievably mature manner, my 12-year-old took the situation in his stride explaining that I was improving as well as could be expected and affirming that I would be completely better one day.

Caught off guard, I turned my back to him to cover up my mixed emotions. I fumbled with my change as my eyes misted

over and a huge lump stuck in my throat. As an uncontrolled tear dripped down the mask leaving a huge dark stain, he was perceptive enough to see it, but astute enough to avoid mentioning it. He just took my hand and gave it a gentle little squeeze and we went on, silenced by our pride in each other.

There were days when I was glad the boys weren't around. Infrequent as those occasions were, they remained as knives in the back and were not negated by the many wonderful, thoughtful gestures of consideration and human sympathy by others. One such occasion occurred as I was passing by a handsome hunk of a teenager. His arm was dragged down by a fawning, giggling girl, who was drinking up his every word. They weren't three feet past me when his intentionally loud stabbing remark sent his young admirer into paroxysms of hysterical giggles.

"How'd you like to bed that?" he asked her.

I faltered in my stumbling stride as the impact of his remark struck home.

I struggled on, almost blinded with fury at the poignancy of those few words. I promptly left the store and drove home, driving purposely slowly, as I knew that my natural instinct was to let my anger dictate a breakneck speed. I had calmed down somewhat when I got home, but stomped around in the cold and dark in the driveway, angry at myself for having allowed myself to be so disproportionately bothered by the remarks of some absolute jerk. Fortunately, a few nights later everything fell into perspective.

I had built up my courage to go to the local cinema to see a movie that appealed to me. In the crowded foyer, I was confronted by a young man whom I recognized. I knew him to be a developmentally delayed person who with his mournful, contorted features was a well-recognized personality in the community. Startled by my mask, he elbowed his friend to get his attention. In the loudest of stage whispers he proclaimed for all to hear, "Isn't he ugly?" Every eye swivelled around to see the confrontation and silence instantly descended on the place. Even the popcorn popper fell mute. In the embarrassed silence, feet shuffled, and a titter of a giggles escaped further back in the crowd.

Oblivious of the tension he had caused and demanding reaffirmation from his friend, he tried again, "Isn't he ugly?"

The silence dragged on, each second a lifetime.

Things were going from bad to worse. From somewhere deep inside me an instinct prodded me.

"Hi, young fellow, how're you doing," I said, looking straight at him and using my friendliest tone. As the place erupted in nervous cover-up conversation, he recognized my voice. I moved slowly away through the crowd as a precaution against further aggravation, as he proclaimed to his friend, "Oh, he's okay. It's that nice man from therapy."

I hardly needed to attend the show, as I had just experienced, in that instant, a mixture of irony, horror, and sadness. Despite it all I felt good about myself, knowing that there had been a happy ending to such a potentially calamitous moment.

Once I was inside the theatre, I was glad when the lights went down and the show started. It was to be a night to be remembered. My interest and love of the wild had drawn me to Farley Mowat's "Never Cry Wolf," in which the early scenes depict some death-defying flying. A rickety old aircraft splutters over the desolate northern Rockies, at treetop height, and swoops down into almost certain death over precipitous mountain sides and lakes.

If ever I was going to have nightmares about the air crash I'd been involved in, it had to be that night. It was a rugged way to exorcise both memories and fears. Waking up the next morning and realizing I had survived the night unscathed, I knew I was cured.

A recurrent dilemma that I never did solve was a particularly bothersome one. Walking through the shopping mall, I'd see a friend or associate approaching, and as the gap closed between us there came a point of no return at which I knew he had decided against acknowledging my presence. I knew with certainty that he had recognized me, as the town was abuzz with the news of my return, and I was "the one in that awful mask." However, there were occasions when, for whatever reason, former friends and associates declined coming forward to speak with me. Perhaps it was their fear of saying the wrong thing or simply not knowing what to say. They could hardly say I was looking well, when they could only see my eyeballs! I respected their reason and avoided pursuing these threatening encounters. I felt it would be bringing greater misery to the moment, to approach them and introduce myself. I had done this on a couple of earlier occasions and had caused devastating embarrassment for the individual. It clearly showed that they had known who I was and they had wanted to avoid the confrontation. It became a rather sad "I know that he knows that I know that he knows" situation.

On one memorable occasion, I did lose my self-control and was fortunate to avoid a perhaps deserved explosive reaction from the recipient of my anger.

While having my car filled up at a full service aisle in a gas station, I observed a young fellow standing and smoking close to his friend who was pouring gasoline into his car at the self-serve aisle. Without thought, my paranoia giving me the uncharacteristic courage, I stomped over to him with all the tact of a raging bull.

"Keep that bloody cigarette out of there, you fool," I shouted.

Providentially, I had stopped a few yards away from him. He paused mid-drag, and eyed me up. He spat out an obscenity, but he did condescend to flip the glowing cigarette away over the car into the street.

As my wrath fizzled, I mumbled that it was actions like his that could cause the sort of mess I was in. As a final gesture, he spat into the intervening few feet of concrete between us, turned on his heel, slammed the door, turned up the stereo, and revved the still-running motor, while his friend continued to pour in gas. I quickly retreated to my car, rolling up the window for token protection against the threatened inferno.

The Jobst gloves also were a source of trial. Making a credit purchase in any store where I was not instantly recognized was an opportunity to check on the diligence of the operator. Some wouldn't even bother to check the signature against that on the back of the card, and some made a token glance but made no comment about the incompatibility of the "new" and "old" writing styles. It was to be a couple of years before my signature would revert to some semblance of my original scrawl. I was always quite reassured that someone would ask me to explain the difference in signature.

Paying for items and trying to extract individual notes from my wallet was a frustrating maneuver. It was very difficult to gain some friction on the slippery notes and the lack of sensation made it hard to have any discriminatory feeling for the paper's thickness, and thus made it difficult for me to ensure that I wasn't giving double payment. My Scots blood would have boiled at such an error.

One infuriating habit that many sales clerks would perpetrate when giving back change following a purchase, was to place a few notes into my gloved hand, then balance the additional coins on top of the paper money. Inevitably, the whole lot would slide off and the coins would roll into slots on the countertop.

A further exasperation was when they would set the coins onto the counter, expecting me to pick them up. If there was any sort of ledge or edge on the counter it was hopeless, but on flat surfaced countertops I'd slide the money off, hoping to catch it as it toppled off the edge. Even after I had the coins safely directed into my palm, my inability to fully close my hand made inserting the money into my pocket difficult. Once the coins were in the pocket, however, it was a guaranteed safe depository, as unapproachable as a Scottish savings bank. Getting the gloved hand into the depths of that recess to regain the coins was impossible.

The last item of my Jobst outfit was seldom publicly seen. The panty hose provided the required consistent counter-pressure on my swollen ankle and over the scarred areas of my legs and donor sites.

The greatest drawback posed by these extra garments was the encumbrance and complexity of the hitherto routine visit to the washroom. The straightforward simplicity of stepping forward to the urinal stall became a mammoth unclothing venture, made no easier by the insensitivity of the gloved hands. After invoking some curious stares, I soon made it my habit to enter the closed sanctums of the toilet stall, but occasionally would be thwarted disastrously in locations where this necessitated the insertion of a dime into that impossible little slot in the door.

For every serious action there is the potential for humour. On one occasion, after the time-consuming mind-boggling readjustment of layers of garments, and having taken an inordinate amount of time to look for and grasp the little toggle on my trouser zip, I put an extra bit of energy into the up-zipping procedure, and managed somehow to catch the end of my glove thumb in the zip teeth.

I toyed with the idea of removing my hand and just leaving the glove dangling there, but the thought of arrest for unusual obscenity made me work at the trapped digit until it finally escaped.

All told, Jobst Phase II was far from dull, but it would take two years before I'd look in the mirror and see the evidence that made me accord the mask the gratitude and praise that it deserved. It was time for thankfulness.

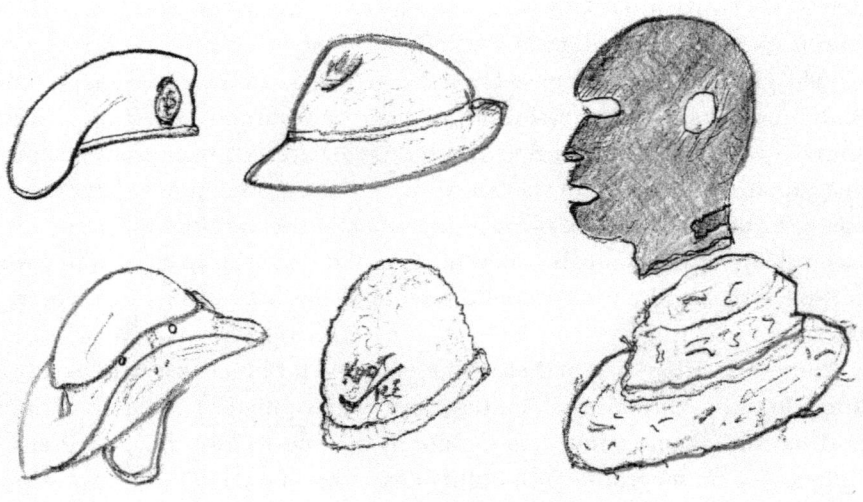

CHAPTER 38
The Year of the Hat

Nine years in the British Royal Army Medical Corps had provided me with more than a lifetime's opportunity to wear a hat. It had developed in me an aversion to the wearing of headgear in all but the most inclement conditions, to the extent that by habit I had been one of those hardy (or crazy) individuals who would ski bareheaded even at 20 below. In consequence, I would regularly sport an enviable bronzed mid-winter tanned face.

All this changed radically for a two-year period. The wearing of the Jobst mask and my fragile pate dictated a reversal in my bareheaded habit. My need of warmth, shade, and camouflage brought forth an entirely changed wardrobe of headdress. Amidst the myriad of items that had been stressed at that memorable discharge meeting at the Foothills Hospital, so many of which had already been proven to be prudent pieces of advice, the care of my newly bald dome was particularly emphasized.

The majority of my scalp had received grafted skin from areas of thigh and leg donor sites. This new tissue, lacking sensation, could not tolerate either the potentially harmful rays or heat of the sun, or the extremes of cold. In consequence, it required careful protection from the elements. It had been stressed that as wearing the Jobst, with its fine weave, would not in itself block the sun's rays, combating the elements became a vital part of my life.

The ski toque became a versatile item that offered the required warmth and protection against the sun. I soon found, that first winter, that I accumulated numerous colours and styles of ski headwear which provided camouflage, or at least de-emphasized the presence of the Jobst mask.

I had to be particularly careful with the still fragile ears. The right ear, especially, was still sensitive to pressure on its restructured and abbreviated contours, so earflaps were a prerequisite in selection of head covering.

My intolerance to cold and windchill factors made me much more conscious of the need to carry an emergency outfit in the car to cope with any possible delays brought on by vehicle breakdown. In addition to the huge parka, snowmobile boots, warmup pants with zip closure legs, huge heavy mitts, the piece de resistance was my balaclava. The heavy knitted all-encompassing head, face, and neck apparel with its eyeholes and small mouth opening, contended well with arctic conditions and provided perfect concealment of the Jobst mask.

While the balaclava may well have been in vogue in the Crimea during the Charge of the Light Brigade, and was acceptable fashion for skiers, snowmobilers, or Halloween monsters, it was hardly inconspicuous in downtown Cranbrook.

In search of a hat that provided for my needs in winter comfort, I spent much energy, time, and thought in perusing millinery sections of department stores which I'd never realized existed.

By the end of the winter, I felt I had an inventory which would provide a hat for all seasons, but my year had just begun. Although I had accumulated cloth caps, suede hats, felt hats with and without feather, and an Australian slouch hat with optional side-lifting flap as a special feature, the changing elements of spring and summer offered yet new challenges and dictated new requirements. The sunshine and pleasant warmth of April encouraged me to change to a jaunty straw hat that was my acceptable compromise between the Stetson and the truckers' cap. I had failed to develop any affinity to either of those in my 20 years in Canada.

The straw hat seemed to fit the bill ideally, blending almost naturally with the tan/beige colouring of the Jobst mask, although the combination was suspiciously close to a Lone Ranger requiring only a horse for full validation.

The first good blow of the prevailing southerly winds up the Columbia Valley posed a new problem. I had accepted the mask/hat ensemble almost to the extent of being a bit proud of it, but the first unexpected gust took my prize hat scurrying up the street. With the tightness of the mask and the diminished sensory awareness of my scalp, I wasn't fully conscious of the hat's absence for a moment or two, by which time it had a three-second start on me along that windy road.

I was startled when I realized what had happened and instinctively covered my naked masked scalp like someone who had just lost his wig. With my hobbling gait, I limped along at top speed in pursuit of the errant hat. Fifty yards later it came to rest, almost laughing at me. The wayward chapeau was wedged, just beyond arm's length, under a parked vehicle.

The combination of my stiff joints, incoordination, and the inaccessibility of the runaway hat did little for my mood at that moment. I finally had to drag it out with my foot, and the sprawling around on that dusty street, combined with the oil smudges from the car's underparts, finished off any semblance to the well-dressed masked-man.

Belatedly, I recalled seeing chinstraps on cowboy hats and sombreros, and modified my now distinctly well-worn hat with a string retainer strap.

Each activity required specific hats. Later that summer, as I once again attempted sailboarding, the recurrent submersions dictated the need for special headgear. A sun-visored neoprene hat did the job, although in appearance it was rather more appropriate for English-style horse riding. That helmet was prone to fill up with water during my dunkings and the extra half-minute needed to empty it did little to speed up my sail-hoisting restart time.

An alternative to the neoprene helmet was a tight fitting swimming cap. It coped well with frequent submersions and made for smooth head-first entry into the depths. However, the discordant aesthetics of colour of these skull caps conflicting with the mask was just too much for even my residual vanity, and so it was worn only as a last resort in the intimacy of an isolated location.

The spectrum my headgear encompassed was wide ranging, omitting only the Russian fur hat, the kepi, the British Bowler, and the turban, none of which offered the appropriate fit or functional advantage. I became very attached to my favourite straw hat, having forgiven its capricious spring-fever scamper down the street. I felt a sense of sadness and almost bereavement when it came to a tragic end. It happened during a late autumn afternoon as I daringly permitted myself a forbidden snooze in the last safe rays of sunshine on the deck chair in the garden. Misguidedly, I laid the trend-setting headgear on the ground beside me. It had developed a distinctive well-worn identity and a personalized aroma which proved too much for old Yogi's sense of smell. When I awoke, the faithful hound had a satisfied and mischievous look in her eye, as she nestled contentedly in the straw bed she had made from the demolished hat.

That occasion is one of my special memories of our fifteen years together. Man and dog had shared much happiness, fun and frolic, and thousands of running miles as she had paced me step for step. Her faithfulness in all that time deserved nothing less from me than the pain I felt when I had to have her put to sleep later that year, when her suffering in sickness was more than I could bear.

The sadness of her death made me reflect on life's ups and downs and remember more fondly the joys that each day provides.

There had been pain and suffering, but in greater measure there had been fun times too, in the year of the hat.

CHAPTER 39
On the Road Again Over 50

That streak of stubbornness that allowed me to train so hard and finally run my marathon never did leave me completely. Even in those early pain-filled days, I had thought about running. At the crash site, with little realistic hope for rescue, I had still had concerns for the feasibility of cleaning up my favourite running shoes. Although my thoughts on future physical capabilities were still premature and supremely optimistic, there was, nevertheless, an overriding expectation of a positive future.

As time moved on, minute though some of the achievements were, they built up to a list of tiny goals that had been achieved. My first walk along the parallel bars was a memorable milestone, and my half-mile "marathon" on the treadmill was another of the puny successes that punctuated the seemingly endless, uphill road that I had to travel.

As each hurdle was overcome, a new goal would be immediately implanted in my mind. My first full kilometer walk one frigid February morning was another highlight of success that remains vivid in my mind. As with other challenges faced, the cost in pain and sweat was an acceptable trade-off for the achievement of that day.

Some restrictions and obstacles seemed to remain unalterable. The long year and a half of wearing the panty hose did much to hold back my progress in distance walking and attempts at running. Only in retrospect could I forgive the ongoing discomfort of the pressure garments. I eventually recognized that Jobst garments and . speed were not synonymous. Just as the outfit did not facilitate rapid physical activity, neither was haste the trademark of their success as a medical treatment regime.

I finally got the all-clear to leave off the panty hose at the 18-month anniversary of my injuries. It was a great day, and was the start of a new freedom of movement and corresponding increase in the goals that I set for myself. My efforts at running suddenly blossomed with the joy of freedom and fresh air striking my bare skin as I got out in shorts for the first time in a year and a half. I'd also been allowed to leave off the face mask during the day, which made me feel gloriously naked and unprotected as I ran.

I should have known that all this exotic sensation and liberty was going to have its cost. Three kilometers from the start of that first run, I got my initial inkling of a discouraging setback. My enlarged and stiff left ankle was throwing a disproportionate stress on the forepart of the foot, and this change in the biomechanics of the foot brought on an inevitable trauma. Adrenaline and euphoria carried me on beyond logic and discretion. By the time I had pushed myself to finish the five kilometers, my foot and ankle were so painful that I could hardly walk the last 100 meters. The foot stayed miserably sore for three weeks and brought a new reality into my future plans and expectations. Gradually over that second summer, I resumed a consistent gentle three-kilometer morning run as my wakening-up, thinking-time routine.

Later that summer, I finally struggled around a 10K circuit. It was only 20 months since the accident and although my run/trot speed required 50 minutes to finish the circuit, it was yet another occasion where a great step in progress had been achieved.

As I battled through the ups and downs of pushing myself beyond the limits, pushing through pain, the third anniversary of the accident was to be the ultimate challenge. I dared myself to enter the Fort Steele Trek. That annual half-marathon, an uphill battle, has become a classic in the Kootenays. There was more than simply the distance involved in this run. Somehow I knew that I would have to stop chasing rainbows and accept this as the final distance limit.

The welcome I got from fellow runners in the local club at that pre-race gathering was touching indeed. Many of those members of the East Kootenay Big Foot Club had gone on to distinguished successes in other races during my three-year absence from competition. My old marathon mentor, Bruce Williams, now a Boston veteran, was again there with words of encouragement and sincere joy at seeing me back in the running crowd.

The pre-race tension built up to the starting gun at high noon, Mountain Standard Time. A field of 100 set off in that blissfully cool, late September day. One circuit took us around the historic Fort Steele Park; then we were out onto the open road. Pushing for a course record in the low 70 minute range, the fast runners spread out like diminishing dots on that seemingly endless uphill climb beyond the Kootenay River.

Near the summit of that hill, forcing my complaining body to run faster than it had for three years, I maintained a commendable eight-minute-per-mile pace. There was a moment that I will always remember as I turned momentarily to look back down across that valley to see that there were still 30 or 40 runners behind me. I glanced up at the skyline of the towering Rockies, already tinged with snow on the peaks, and saw Mount Fisher standing there in all its majesty. Even then, with success in that day's challenge still doubtful, I set my next goal for a climb of Fisher the following summer.

My pace slowed, exhaustion and pain started eroding my willpower, and as my mind fuzzed over and lost its ability to calculate rate and finish time projections, only the desire to prove that I could complete the distance became the dominant feeling. As I got onto the more level terrain past the halfway mark, my pace picked up again and I was pleasantly surprised, despite that pain-filled haze, to find that I had reached the lO-mile mark in 80 minutes. I pushed on, fuelled only on desire. I felt little concern as a steady stream of runners started passing me. Time became of less consequence. The whole goal became finishing, at any cost. On the last push up Victoria hill, half a mile from the finishing line, my pace dragged down to a mere stumble and could hardly have been defined as running, but I was adamant that I wouldn't break down to a walk. Not even the crowds of cheering supporters and ecstatic welcome by the close friends who knew how important this race was to me, could help me raise more than a laboured zigzag stumble across the line. At that moment, a new maturity came over me, demonstrated by my acceptance of the gratification of finishing, rather than bothering with the usual desperation of beating my previous finishing time.

For me a great feeling of peace occurred that day. It was a feeling that I had tested and found my limit and was at last satisfied with what I had achieved. I knew I would want to continue running but I would be content with less demanding goals in the future.

The dreams and hopes of climbing Mount Fisher that had taken root during the Fort Steele Trek remained with me and came to fruition the following August. In the company of my two sons, it was the climax of achievement. It gave me a time of sharing with them, a grateful joyous confirmation that I was back to as full a physical capability as I could have dared to hope for, and the final proof of my recovery.

As time goes on, my acceptance of the limitations of my body for running becomes less grudging. The urge to feel the wind blow over my now bare scalp still draws me out onto the trails. Having lost time and edge compared to my former running friends, I concede, gracefully I trust, to their greater achievements.

Although there is no rancour in my loss, that irrepressible competitive streak still smoulders within me. A new goal is teasingly appearing. Just days after the fifth anniversary of the accident, I will achieve that fearsome half-century mark and enter the more sedate over-fifty running group, whose time and distance records are just waiting to be broken. Now that's sufficient good reason to get on the road again, as an older but wiser clockwatcher!

CHAPTER 40
Fireweed Time

Five years after that tragic day, the pathway so laboriously hacked out by our rescuers has already become overgrown and is almost indiscernible. That small glade hides, as if ashamed, keeping secret the scarred earth where half a ton of aircraft made its final fiery resting place. There are still remnants of torn wing, wires, and rusted trellis of what were the framework and engine mountings.

The engine had been taken away to be minutely inspected by the Transport Department as part of its investigation. The shock absorbing telescopic front wheel mechanism still lies there, now bearing a multicoloured etching on its once shiny chrome cylinder. Spiral wiring, which had been strengthening bias metallic ribbing in the front tire, is now a rusted naked remnant, the rubber burned off completely. A puff of white fuzz is all that's left of the fire-resistant asbestos in the brake linings.

Thirty yards away, still evident, broken tree limbs and scythed trunks stand stark – a sad monument showing where the plane's trajectory had cleared its own path in that final fatal plunge. A piece of wing remains, FWXH still defiantly showing its name with pride.

The group of trees that formed the final wall to arrest our rearward plunge were engulfed in fire and now stand gaunt. Their surfaces are blue/black carbon cubes where the fiery tongues had penetrated deeply into the outer sap rings, killing all growth. A single bent propeller blade, its former finely engineered cutting edge now a pathetic razed vestige of its precision design, is the last reminder that here rests a once proud flying machine.

In all this bleak ruin a flash of colour has emerged, a pink/purple flicker like the flames that caused the barrenness years ago. Choosing the disturbed soil and ashes as their source of new life, the silky long-haired seeds of the fireweed have parachuted in to that location. The passing of time has brought with it nature's forgiveness. The beauty of the fireweed flower now stands tall, bringing hope and peace to this site of tragedy, just as it did in the bomb sites in Britain and Europe during the war. That slender flower brings proof of rebirth, and renewal of hope for the future.

For me that distinctive flower symbolizes the many unexpected blessings that have come from the tragedy.

I have gained an acceptance of limitations imposed on me. I set each goal with a little more thought to the reality and fragility of life. Still somewhat grudgingly, I cope with the unlikelihood of my being able to run another marathon. Disappointment, rather than malice, marks my feelings of restriction enforced by the cold of winter or blazing sun of summer.

I have a deeper recognition of life's great treasures that I'd previously taken for granted. Being brought closer together and developing a greater understanding of my own family have been the very special joys I've gained through this rugged experience. In fondness I remember how Ian and Craig provided their perceptive sympathies during my suffering. They too, have learned and gained from all of this.

A special gift has been a closing of the wide gap that had grown, due to travel, time, and divergent interests, between my mother and me. Tolerance of the other's point of view has enhanced our love for each other.

There has been a renewal of my appreciation and quiet contentment of being part of a Christian church family. A shining example of that family in his everyday practice of his Christian beliefs, was the kindness and support shown me by Bill Gordon. His untimely death in a car crash just a year after my accident was a sad loss to this world.

The desire to help others in my work has been reinforced by the experience of being on the receiving end of medical ministrations. Being nurtured by those who form the healing team has made me even more anxious to be a part of society's helpers, and to look more fervently for ways to offer help to others.

I have developed a greater respect for the privilege of life and take more seriously the cautions we so often overlook. My flirt with death has left me with a habit of more careful consideration of my actions. Although my 20 hours of flight training remains a joyous memory that offered challenging rewards, that one moment of tragedy has cancelled that earlier goal of learning to fly. The special pleasure of each day makes me doubly cautious to avoid circumstances that might threaten its loss. Each day is already a bonus.

In Kootenay National Park, at the B.C./Alberta border, a sign reads "Continental Divide. From this point all rivers flow west to the Pacific or east to the Atlantic." Nearby, sprouting from the desolation of the immense 1968 forest fire, the indomitable fireweed flourishes, sending seeds of hope across the continent.

Not many miles southwest of those towering peaks, in a quiet glade by Angus Creek, that same flower and a rusting propellor are silent monuments that mark the spot where once time stood still.

Author and sons on Fisher Peak (9,336 feet) overlooking Kootenay River Valley near Cranbrook, B.C. Photograph by Roy Barnett, taken five years after the accident.

CHAPTER 41
Epilogue: Looking Back

Written in 2014-15, the following chapters form the epilogue for the revised edition of The Clockwatcher.

More than 30 years have slipped past since that tragic day when time stood still. The fatal crash of C-FWXH took the lives of two volunteer search and rescue trainee spotters and affected the lives of many others in a diverse range of ways.

What took one second to happen still has repercussions 90 million seconds later. The communities of Cranbrook and Kimberley and further afield have residual connections to that day, some sad and still traumatic, some subtle occurring unexpectedly at the most unlikely moments of the day or night.

The location at Angus Creek is now a designated memorial site and a geocache centre. Second and third generation family members have visited and paid their respects there. Interested members of the public too have made the journey to that spot and have left thoughtful comments in the visitors' book.

The following chapters are intended to offer a retrospective update of the happenings in my life since that awful day. I'd like to think that the reader will gain insight into the many very positive outcomes that I've experienced.

While there were some horrible times and many challenging setbacks, the unrelenting magnificent contribution of the healers and helpers won the battle.

To those facing tragedy, I'd urge them to take hope from my Scottish grandmother's oft-quoted line during the horrors of the second World War: *"Even this will pass."*

CHAPTER 42
Blair's Retreat

Within two months of returning home from the hospital, the challenge of facing the public, in early 1984, in shopping malls or downtown became extremely disheartening in many ways.

The fine line between offering sympathetic words of encouragement and downright hurtful monologues such as, "Oh you poor thing, it must be awful," was a challenge for me, the recipient. No doubt it was equally difficult for the otherwise good intentioned well-wishers.

In February, even before my projected return to work on April 1st, I had to endeavor to escape to a place of peace, tranquility and silence, away from the stares and finger pointing.

I chose as my retreat the hilltop viewpoint at the radio transmission tower near my home six miles north of Cranbrook. The narrow twisting gravel road was travelled most days by the solitary technician who manned that facility and the need for reliable access to the instruments dictated that snowplowing was done when needed.

My glorious little all-wheel-drive Subaru just laughed its way up that tortuous mile and a half, transporting me safely to the top. Accompanied by my now constant companion, Yogi, well recovered from her 3-month stay in the kennels and veterinarian clinic, we made a great team.

Parking carefully on the turn around so as not to block any other road users access, led by my trusty trail blazing collie, I staggered and slipped my way down to a secluded rocky outcrop some 100 yards distant. My chosen spot was not visible from the tower, but gave outlook to the entire magnificent ridge of the Rockies to the east and north to the airport just five miles away. Mount Fisher dominated the skyline at 9300 feet and was the focal point seen from my secret hiding place.

Bundled up in a huge anorak, quilted side zippered snow pants, snow boots, heated oversized ski mitts, ski toque and the omnipresent Jobst mask, I was dressed for a polar expedition.

The chosen site was the ultimate private retreat. As the pioneers did a century earlier, I staked my claim by manhandling a large flat rock to the highest point on that rocky bluff. That was my seat, almost a throne, and consequently I became King of the Hill. Lugging that rock into position made me sweat like a horse but the achievement of what was that first great physical challenge was so very exciting.

I sat there drinking in life in that glorious panorama. I was bursting with pride at what I had accomplished. Despite the mask, gloves, panty hose, grafts, fractures, weight and muscle loss, I had done a significant physical activity that would have challenged a lot of supposedly healthy 45 year olds. Damn, I felt good.

Time was of no consequence. I dallied, unthreatened by the -15° C and slight breeze and leisurely allowed the cooling off of the sweat provoked by the unaccustomed work I'd done.

Logic told me I should make tracks up the narrow path to the comfort of my car but achievement can be an intoxicating matter. I sat pondering the similarity of that isolated spot to a distant memory of Boy Scout adventures on a bleak crag on a Scottish moor. As my mind conjured up that occasion 30 years earlier, I had a sudden vision of a distinct feature in that distant homeland that would fit my circumstances perfectly.

10,000 miles away in the land of kilt and heather the lonely Scottish shepherd and his faithful collie dogs gather their flock into a rock walled enclosure called a keep. There they'd be sheltered from the elements and he could count them and check for injury or disease.

Those stone walls, five foot high, called "stane dikes" encircle the 40-foot diameter enclosure. The sole entryway, just three feet wide might seem a narrow doorway for 50-60 sheep to enter, but those two border collie dogs can herd that entire flock through that narrow gap and then lay silently guarding the opening.

Sitting on my stone throne I pondered the feasibility of building a mini "keep"; a place of refuge, seclusion and shelter. As the cold crept into my bones, I surveyed the surrounding area and was delighted to see an abundance of broken rock ideal for my purpose. Of course, I was pleased that this entire project would be at no financial cost.

It didn't take more than five minutes before I was soaked in sweat as I heaved, rolled and dragged 30-pound rocks to form the foundation of the eight foot wide keep. As the plan was to only build walls three foot high, the structure didn't need a gateway.

I had to giggle at the thought of what Abby McLeod, the burn unit physiotherapist, might think of this wild activity. She had berated me with a huge list of do's and don'ts as we parted, but there had been no specific mention regarding rock wall building. Delilah Bailey, the occupational therapist, would also be horrified seeing this abuse of her major contribution to my care. She had spent an inordinate amount of time, patiently doing meticulous measurements of every tiny variation in circumference of each finger to ensure that the Jobst elastic gloves would fit perfectly. They were never intended for wrestling with razor-edged chunks of granite.

All the unaccustomed physical violence took its toll but my excitement at the progress buoyed me up. I struggled up the short climb to the car, and then swept down the track, the little Subaru uncomplaining about the outrageous speeding commensurate with the euphoria of the driver, as I mumbled an almost recognizable version of, "A Scottish Soldier".

That night, after a scorching long soak in the bath and a wee dram to celebrate the day's progress, I had a better night sleep than any in the previous five months.

Next morning at the crack of dawn I was ecstatic about the day's planned continuation of the dike building. Yogi cast a skeptical eye at my off key rendering of "On the Road Again", showing that being out and about doing crazy things was better than being housebound.

It was still -15C when we reached the construction zone, and the attack on row two got underway. I had planned ahead and brought a 2 x 6 plank to enable me to slide some of the heavier rocks up onto succeeding heights. I got the wall up to two feet high before exhaustion and sweat overtook me and I had to call it a day.

Man and dog set off at 8:15 am the next morning with determination to finish the job. A fierce wind had cleared off all the snow and exposed a huge variety of rocks. With the extensive experience gained on the two previous days, each stone seemed to fit into place with geometric precision, seating snugly against its neighbour.

Before I knew it, the wall was three feet high and while not windproof, it did offer some shelter. I anticipated completion that day and had come with a miniature bottle of Drambuie to celebrate and toast the new structure. I named it 'Blair's Retreat" and sat on that throne rock and meditated deeply, with the full realization of how very fortunate I had been to survive that awful day five months earlier.

As I sat there, my dog lying contentedly at my feet, I took stock of the many individuals who had contributed in making me whole again.

As if to signal that all was well, an aircraft took off on Runway 16, proceeded south towards me, then changed course to fly west to Vancouver. It was the moment when I knew all would be well in the days ahead.

30 years later, I still visit Blair's Retreat quite regularly. On occasion, I have escorted my family there to share the healing of the wounds that they too have suffered through it all.

The grandchildren each add a small stone to the keep, contributing in a meaningful way in maintaining that special place with all its therapeutic value.

Most recently, Blair's Retreat has been established as a geocache site. A booklet nearby directs visitors to look northwest to where another geocache site at Angus Creek commemorates those who died in the wreckage of Cardinal C-FWXH. That site is named "The Bent Propeller", and my visits there each October 1st are healing occasions and a time of prayerful gratitude.

CHAPTER 43
Boy Meets Girl

Subsequent to divorce, many individuals are in a mixed-up state of mind. Depending on each unique situation, their psychological health zones can run the gamut from depression to euphoria or worse.

I suspect that some who find themselves in this interlude just muddle through the often-radical life style changes, accepting or at least tolerating the inevitable financial and accommodation changes.

Behavioral reactions by divorcees, as viewed by friends and onlookers, can be seen as bizarre, pathetic, unimaginable or justified as deserved, but not necessarily logical or sensible. Perhaps I fell into the last two categories when I chose to take flying lessons.

"Expense be damned!" must have been my excuse because my precarious financial situation didn't budget for that selfish over-indulgence.

After 20 glorious, exciting, and sometimes terrifying lessons, my pursuit to earn a pilot's license met with an unexpected glitch. During a routine eye test, a pre-requisite for further escapades in the bright blue yonder, the words, "No way," occurred. An elderly physician, entrusted by the flight safety testing bureaucracy, looked half asleep as I flipped through the almost unfathomable colour vision test numbers. I already suspected that my ability to discriminate colours was marginal, so I took a risk and did some crafty guesswork. "Seven, four, eight, three, two." I quoted glibly. "Oh that last one is a bit difficult," I admitted.

"So were the previous half dozen," he said, straight-faced. "You're almost colour blind."

Damn, I thought he was snoozing. And so, my personal advancement to instrument flying was shut down.

The attraction and involvement in search and rescue seemed to further opportunity to be airborne. Sadly, as the previous chapters have shown, that flight path lasted 20 minutes.

The combination of these disappointments and the consequential hospitalization and wearing the Jobst mask for two years left me pathetically insecure on the romance front.

My childhood and early teenage shyness resurrected itself, so the arena of, "boy meets girl," was problematic. My self-esteem had taken a bad thrashing.

During the latter stages of wearing the mask, I dared myself to take a course at the local college, as a way to get out of the loneliness and isolation of my country home. I'd taken and forgotten high school French a million years earlier so I joined a dozen or so other mature students. I slunk into class uncomfortable with the mask, and sat as far back as the three rows of four permitted.

It was conversational French, and with the encouragement and entertaining style of the superb instructor I settled in better than I had hoped. I knew I was in the right group when he promised that we'd have an après class gathering at the local pub.

One lesson and a pint later, my shyness lessened and I found myself in almost comfortable discussion, en francais, would you believe, with a very attractive lady some 12 years younger than me. Maureen seemed to see the "real me" that existed beyond the mask and she made me feel interesting and attractive once again.

As we talked in French class, she shared with me her frustration with chronic knee pain that she was experiencing from running. Her doctor had suggested that she might need to give up running altogether. I told her to come to see me with her medical card. She took me up on this offer and over a number of visits; I helped her to get back to her passion for running and other sport endeavors.

Our friendship deepened during the French classes and we shared many enjoyable times together. When the classes ended we continued to see each other in passing in town and took a few moments each time to catch up on the news but it wasn't until her marriage ended 10 years later that we were able to connect again.

We met socially one evening, accidently, at the home of a mutual friend who was hosting a "Guy Fawkes" bonfire evening, but that night I lacked the courage to pursue matters further. The evening ended and I kicked myself for not being a bit more macho in my non-existent advances.

A few weeks later, on Christmas Eve 1995, I dragged myself reluctantly to the late night service at the church I'd been attending for several years. I was not enthused about the visit. Earlier that night I had driven around town looking at the displays of Christmas lights and chose church as a better alternative to going home to the desolation of my empty house.

My arrival was late and the place of worship was packed, so I tried to sneak into the overflow seats at the back of the tearoom. An usher, who knew me, almost manhandled me into the only empty seat in pew number two.

It seemed every eye in the place was on the latecomer and I was ill at ease with my center stage entry. The Good Lord is credited with many great happenings, and that night he left the only vacant seat for me right next to Maureen. To say that I was a bit flustered would be an understatement, but underneath it all I was overjoyed.

Two readings and three Christmas carols from a shared hymn book later and I was in heaven. Unknown to me, Maureen had planned a gathering of friends in her home a few days later. I subsequently learned that she had casually mentioned to her two teenage children that if she saw me on Christmas Eve, she would ask me to come to the party. She was as shocked as I was when she looked up to see me being seated right beside her.

At the end of the service, she shyly invited me to the upcoming gathering and I floated out of the building with a dog-eared business card on which she had neatly handwritten her phone number and address. The peace and joy theme continued in that coincidence.

Less than two years later, we married on the lawn of what would become our house in the country. The wedding limousine chosen to take us away on our honeymoon was an ultra posh Vespa Scooter. Perhaps it was my frugal Scots idea. It fitted the old British song that might have been written for just the "boy meets girl" situation such as ours...

It won't be a stylish marriage,
I can't afford a carriage.
But you'll look sweet,
Upon the seat,
Of a bicycle built for two.

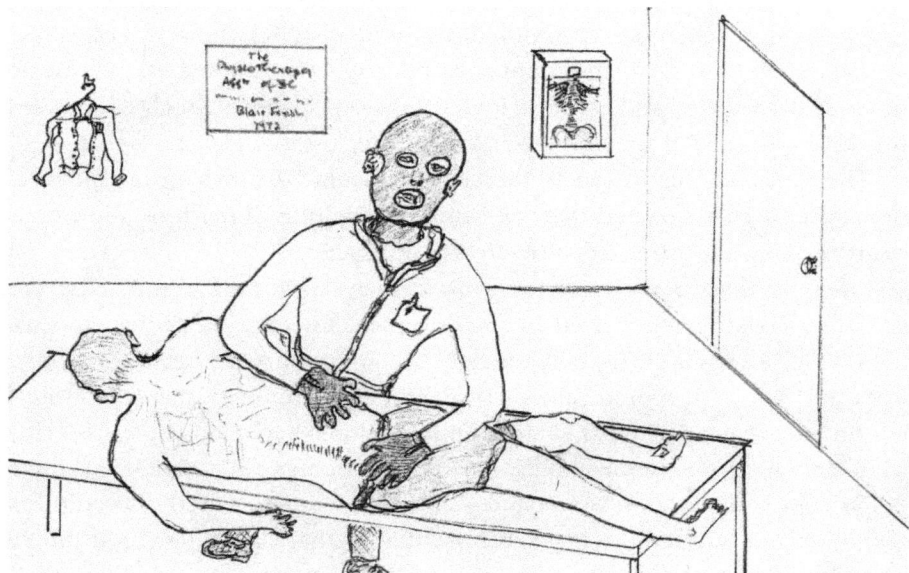

CHAPTER 44
The Practice

Returning to the practice exactly six months from the date of the accident was more than just a challenge, it was a nightmare. Fortunately, my reliable secretary/receptionist, Diana Cavers, played nursemaid and gently bullied me through those awful early days.

Kids ran screaming from the office at the first sight of the monster in the mask, and their parents too were disturbed by the apparition and distressed with their child's reaction.

It soon became evident that I'd lost a significant percentage of my clientele. Additionally, a new phenomenon added salt to the wound, as I experienced a disturbing number of no-shows for scheduled repeat appointments.

There was a real frightening possibility that the standard of provided care didn't meet their expectations. I also suspected that some failed to return because their own symptoms were glaringly less severe than their perception of my evident pain levels and disability.

I recognized that in my absence patients and their referring doctors had been obliged to find alternative sources of treatment and consequently developed allegiances to their new caregivers. Additionally, the physically demanding requirements of certain treatments were both exhausting and a real challenge in my weakened state, which greatly threatened the results.

That spring and summer was a frightening and frustrating time as I struggled to regain my lost clientele. Professionally, I found myself spending outrageously long days trying to build the number of patient visits. It became a real battle to cover overhead costs and I was forced to accept patients much earlier and much later in the day than I'd ever done before, just to make ends meet.

The combination of my shattered self-esteem, the exhausting physical demands on my weakened body and the exasperation of the Jobst gloves was heartbreaking and made those first few months a time I'd like to forget.

Of course I was my own worst enemy in many ways. My eating habits were awful. I was permanently tired so couldn't rouse myself early enough to have breakfast. I'd sip at a coffee between patients, grab a burger from the Deli next door and bite at it sporadically through the conventional lunchtime while I continued to treat patients. (A rather unprofessional habit, looking back on it.)

When I staggered home in the late summer evenings, I'd grab a beer, lounge on a deck chair in the sunshine and wake up at 9 pm, too tired to even think about cooking supper. It was no surprise that by that Christmas, I was still 20 pounds underweight.

By the next spring, gradually but distressingly slowly, the practice rebuilt. I was still in mask and gloves and hadn't had a day off in that full year. Out of the blue, a dynamic young physiotherapist appeared at the door looking for part-time work to build to full-time work hours. She had resumé and references in hand, and a charming personality. Within three minutes, she had accepted my job offer. She turned out to be a splendid clinician and by Christmas the practice was at capacity for the two of us.

Unbelievably, yet another physiotherapist turned up at the door. A phone call to her previous employer confirmed her excellent credentials and work habits and she started later that year. She was a natural at building her own clientele, taking the pressure off my own excessive workload.

At 18 months post air crash, I got the all clear to leave off the mask and gloves during the day. Wow! What a liberation it was! Business continued to leap ahead and that summer I was able to take some time off during my mother's visit from Scotland. Ian and Craig visited many days spending time with their beloved grandmother and me. Those were the happiest moments of time since the accident.

On October 1st, 1985 I celebrated the two-year mark by getting rid of the mask and gloves and panty hose. Jobst was a thing of the past. The results showed they had done a great job. To make it an even greater occasion, I flew to Scotland for a two-week visit to the old family home.

Mother's neighbours and friends had supported her magnificently through all the trauma of my accident. They had received a blow-by-blow account of my misadventures. Consequently, I was the featured exhibit at their generous lunches, teas and suppers. They all seemed to identify me as a miracle survivor, which was, I felt, a true assessment.

By the time I returned to Canada, I'd been fattened up to my pre-accident weight. The time off had been a real tonic and I settled back in to my day-to-day routine. I was happy, refreshed, and approaching my dynamic former self.

Soon the practice had grown to four full-time physiotherapists. That made it possible to accommodate vacation absences without stress. Over the following years, we had the good fortune to find new capable replacements as some of the earlier staff members moved on to new challenges elsewhere.

The arrival of new practitioners bringing diverse skills allowed me to be more selective in restricting my own case load to conditions I felt most comfortable handling. By 1990, I realized that a lot had changed since my graduation thirty years earlier. Although I had been diligent in attending courses and had been a lifelong learner, I was greatly appreciative of the knowledge new arrivals brought to the clinic. It was a joy for me to see the exceptional repartee and sharing among the therapists. Above all, a delightful feeling of teamwork and humour had returned.

One incident brought hilarity to the entire crew, albeit a bit at my expense. An elderly woman of European descent who had been my patient several times over the years was the source of the entertainment. She hadn't seen me since before my accident and was effusive in welcoming me back to full health.

"I prayed for you when you were in hospital," she said in a loud voice, so everyone around heard her words. Pulling down gently on my shoulders, she continued, " I want to kiss you," whereupon she placed a gentle kiss on the top of my now hairless head.

I was taken aback and stuck for words, but mumbled my appreciation. That was one of the most sincere gestures and expressions of caring that had come my way over the years.

After the lovely lady had departed, I took an enormous amount of leg pulling from the entire staff. For days, my entry into the clinic was met with a chorus of, " I want to kiss you," put over in an exaggerated European accent. Of course, even more hilarity ensued when I suggested that the poor lady might have changed her mind if she'd known that the grafted skin had been taken from my rump.

Eventually a talented, young, experienced Australian physiotherapist, Floyde Spencer, bought the practice, adding to the international diversity of Canadian, Scots, Welsh and South Africans on staff. I had worked on those premises for 35 years and felt I was ready for retirement, almost half a century since I entered physiotherapy school in London, England.

Three years later, the new owner was kind enough to offer me a few months of part-time work. I was missing the joy of treating patients.

Having let my license lapse on retirement brought about one last little hiccup in my professional life. My return to part-time practice was met with the profession's bureaucratic requirement that I could only work if supervised by a fully certified physiotherapist.

Everybody in the clinic was entertained that Mark Johnson, a hard working younger physiotherapist, was delegated with the dubious responsibility. Having taken him on as a rookie graduate some ten years earlier, he made the leap from protégé to supervisor with his usual good humour and aplomb.

It was wonderful to re-engage with some of the patients I had treated over the years, and great to see first hand that the clinic was flourishing. I have now fully retired. Looking back, I am very grateful for my long professional career, especially considering that it was almost lost in the tragedy of Angus Creek.

CHAPTER 45
The Sporting Life

Looking back at the three-quarters of a century that I have been blessed with, the clock has been a constant feature that has guided, goaded, prompted and chased me through life.

I'm sure time weighed heavily as my mother awaited the inevitable, impending social dilemma during the nine months before my birth. Being an unmarried mum in the 1930's wouldn't have been much fun in an almost fanatical "Wee Free Kirk" family, amid the non-existent chance of secrecy in a Scottish village.

Oblivious to the tragic upheaval my arrival had caused, my earliest sporting memory is of speeding along on my pedal scooter. One foot propelling, while the other supporting my weight on that mini skateboard apparatus. That speedster was 50 years before its time. Today, silent sleek descendants of that prototype compare disdainfully with the noisy, four-inch metal wheels of yesteryear.

The mechanisms of timekeeping in that era were the grandfather clock or the large pocket watch cross-chained and concealed in the waistcoat pocket. Lacking either at five years of age, I could only guess when successive runs down the twisting road from the village to my home had trimmed a second or two from the previous suicidal jaunt.

Just three years later, promoted to my wee Elswick bicycle and having procured an ancient pocket watch that could time my run, I started the serious business of clockwatching as I plummeted down that slope. Running up the hill to the village school was also a timed affair. No self-respecting kid arrived more than a second before the bell.

Hours and minutes became the calculations as scouting badges were earned in miles per hour over bleak moors to reach some desolate map-referenced crag at the first frigid light of dawn. The ultimate time challenge—"the beautiful game" of soccer—was a joyous 90-minute trial that prepared me for the subsequent physical endeavors I chose to pursue in the years ahead.

Those early days beating the clock, also gave me the lungs, power and stamina to enjoy a wide range of sporting activities and travels through four continents and 20 countries, and continued when I finally found utopia right here in the Rocky Mountains of British Columbia. My background of health-inducing activities set me up to be fit enough to race against "mountain time" in marathon races, windsurfing, downhill skiing, cycling, and soccer.

I now know that my fitness contributed to my survival and consequent recovery following the plane crash. While the first five years were a challenge and frustration, turning 50 seemed to trigger a resurgence of abilities that I'm sure were envied by others my age.

Getting back to windsurfing at that mature age was a glorious reward for the fight I'd put into a half-decade of rehabilitation. I had slowed down from my previously reckless skiing style, and a new reluctance to face the moguls on the Easter run at Kimberley's ski hill spawned a new delight as I took up snowboarding in a sedate manner at my half-century mark.

Joining the over-fifty soccer league maintained the memory of more youthful days. Summiting Mount Fisher in five hours, accompanied by my teenage sons, was the ultimate reward and proof that I was again able to beat the clock.

My need for speed has diminished as I now enjoy the pleasure of sedate cycling on the Rails to Trails, a 30 km world-class paved pathway that runs from Cranbrook to Kimberley. Leaving the chronometer at home, kayaking leisurely on the numerous local lakes, is the pace I now enjoy. Even closer to home the wonderful walking trails in our very own Community Forest gives us moments when time stands still as we inhale the beauty that surrounds us.

I am grateful for my total recovery and the joy and love of my extended family around me. Each day stretches timelessly as I reminisce over my bygone sporting days. I watch the children and grandchildren in our wonderful blended family and get great pleasure observing them in their teams and sports. I'm thankful that they too find happiness and healthfulness in their opportunity to race against the clock.

CHAPTER 46
The Blended Family

Arriving at the decision to create a blended family is often faced with some trepidation. Memories of past relationships can be still raw. A suspicion of the new venture's apparent idyllic status can cause alarm right up to the "I do" moment for both participants.

I was still on the mend from the long healing process of my divorce 15 years earlier, and continued to carry feelings of self doubt from the plane crash's mental and physical trauma.

Added to this, for me, was a nagging question in my mind, "Why would a beautiful school principal in her mid-forties marry a nearly 60 year old, worn out and fragile Scotsman?"

My gain in this radical change in circumstances was the addition of a superb and caring extended family that has been instrumental in bringing happiness and the continuation of my healing over the last 16 years.

I couldn't have asked for a more diverse collection of wonderful people to add to my family circle. I just wish my mother had lived long enough to meet them. I know she would have been delighted, and would have described Maureen as "a bonnie lass".

In our blended family we have nurses, a social worker, teachers, an accountant, a graphic designer, musicians, a computer-expert, photographers, a floral designer, a nurse practitioner, a minister, college instructors, a preschool administrator and an outdoor education instructor.

The intermingling of my sons Ian and Craig with Maureen's children, Ryan and Jen, was the start of the full family interconnection and ongoing friendships that have thrived over the past two decades.

As if our example set the bar for future matrimonial celebrations, the wedding march has drawn this assembly together for joyous occasions in Kingston, Cranbrook, Calgary and Tofino.

For Maureen and me, there has been unimaginable happiness and contentment brought about by our marriage. Our blended family, now with 10 grandchildren, is guaranteed to keep us young at heart in the days and years ahead.

CHAPTER 47
Reigning Cats and Dogs

Some readers may be less enthused about relationships with domesticated animals and consequently might wonder about the inclusion of my portrayal of the canine and feline species' contribution to the health and happiness of my family.

Read on, I urge you. It might engender a new awareness that could change your perception and offer unimaginable enjoyment in your life.

Settling in the comfort of my lazy boy chair as I write these final pages, our two cats are nestled on my knee. Max, the king of the house at age 18, and Zoe, the heir apparent at 12 years old, exemplify comradeship and coziness. They are part of the family.

Presently there is a dearth of their canine cousins as the last of our wonderful dogs, Ripley, passed away recently. Each has given their share of affection and allegiance in their time with our family. All are remembered fondly as loving creatures. Their individual uniqueness recalled as they brought laughter and healing or the occasional eye rolling, where their behavioral idiosyncrasies had been a challenge on that day.

As early as I can remember, and reinforced by an extremely faded photograph from that time, Billy was "my" dog. He was a lovable, slavering, hair shedding Springer Spaniel. He was the creature of comfort in my blissful childhood days, both of us oblivious to the all-pervading horror of wartime Scotland.

The huge aromatic armchair in the corner of the kitchen was "Billy's chair". Due to its distinctiveness family members never sat on it, but occasionally visitors occupied that seat, unaware of the pitfalls of such a choice.

Billy helped my healing through measles, whooping cough, and other bed rest enforced childhood ailments, giving extra warmth to my sick bed as he refused to leave my side.

Even in the usually strict confines of military life in Malaya, one aberration in the strict Sergeants' Mess décor and discipline was the presence of a glorious Golden Labrador. He was everybody's friend and he accepted, providentially, silently, the inconvenience of being temporarily hidden in a cupboard during the Commanding Officer's weekly inspection. An unusual human tolerance characteristic occurred in the accompanying and usually dour Sergeant Major, as he skillfully steered the CO briskly past that hiding place.

Two canine family members offered their companionship to the new immigrants in the snowy blasts of North Bay, Ontario. Remembered less cheerfully at the time, was the cat Tiger's Houdini escape from our travel trailer en route to Red Deer, Alberta. That incident caused a middle of the night half naked chase and subsequent capture, somewhere in darkest, most frigid Manitoba.

Yogi, as mentioned in a previous chapter, was my solace and ever-present companion in the abysmally dark and lonely days after my return from Calgary Foothills Hospital. She was the one who licked the Jobst mask on our reuniting, both of us severely traumatized by the prior three month separation. That unparalleled touch of tenderness and love would become a life-long uplifting memory and a moment of great healing for me.

Adopting Max the Doberman was a learning experience. Lovable and entertaining, I knew he'd protect my family even if it cost him his life. Elk chasing, bear treeing and environmentally considerate consuming of their droppings were his errors in judgment. He was also a slow learner. His tangle with a porcupine obviously taught him nothing as he made the same mistake six months later. It was expensive too, at $5 per quill removal.

Tipsy One, my mother's dog in Scotland became part of my inheritance when Ian and Craig's beloved grandmother died at age 80 while driving her car to her curling game. That Border Collie's transatlantic immigration as my flying companion engendered a much appreciated kindness from the flight attendants at London airport. While the dog was carefully installed in the luggage hold, they kindly upgraded my economy ticket to a first class seat. This surely proves that animals can bring you great comfort in life.

Tipsy Two, another pedigree Border collie, was my pace setter for many years on training runs and is remembered fondly for her companionship. She too was a clockwatcher as she listened to the pendulum swings of the grandfather clock in the long lonely sleepless nights of my addiction phase of healing.

The eventual bliss of my marriage to Maureen didn't have the entire blessing of some canine members of the family. Sharing the matrimonial bed had not been on the agenda for Geordie and Toby, Maureen's beloved but feisty Maltese Terriers who considered it their undisturbed place of peace and comfort. Somehow we all survived.

Ripley, the last of the canine monarchy, was our loveable, huggable Shih Tzu. As he aged, he demonstrated with regal composure that arthritis, deafness and poor eyesight are the survivable penalties of the era of maturity that I'm now experiencing. His gentle pace and senior citizen style and patience showed us how to enjoy each minute of each day.

A priceless healing gift was Ripley's visit to an elderly woman in hospital. She hadn't spoken a word for a week but on seeing Ripley, her almost inaudible utterance, "doggie," was the prelude to her miraculous recovery and eventual discharge several weeks later. We felt like calling him Dr. Ripley thereafter.

Max, the king of cats (not to be confused with his Doberman predecessor), never forgave us for moving to a gated community in town. Gone for him was the past life he enjoyed in our previous country acreage. There he performed the "show and tell" drama of snakes, squirrels, birds, frogs, baby rabbits and mice, some still alive and others, thankfully (for us) and disappointingly (for Max), still and dead.

Zoe, our remaining feline companion, provides a residual sparkling of youthfulness in our home. Tolerating her lowly place in the ascension line of feline aristocracy, she is the current clockwatcher who makes sure we are awake by 6 am.

To those of you who have read to this point, doggedly perhaps, I hope you are feline better—I'll be surprised if this passes Maureen's editing.

I cannot refrain from giving immense recognition to the health benefits of having animals in my life. These reigning cats and dogs have been clockwatchers through the many ups and downs that have come my way.

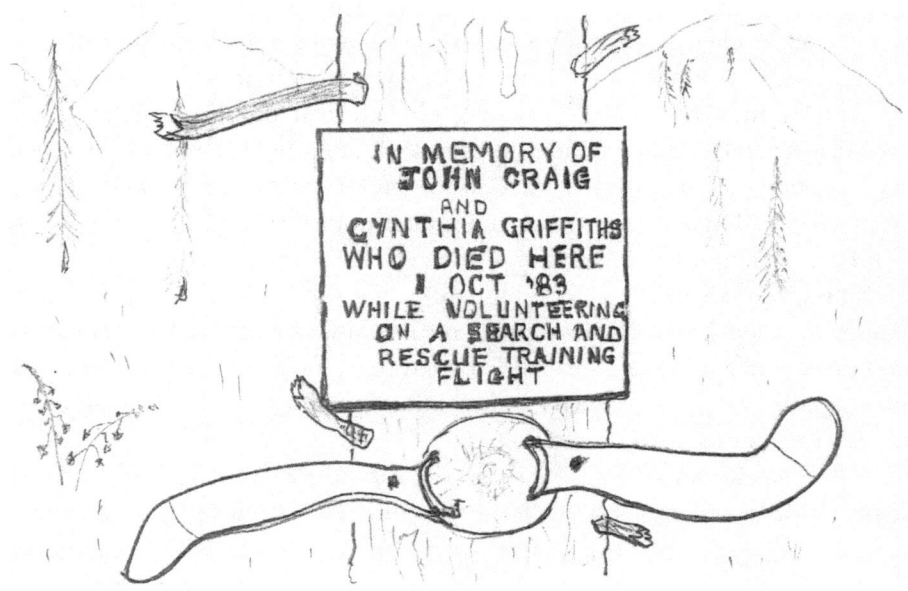

CHAPTER 48
The Bent Propeller

"BRACE, BRACE, BRACE!" That terrifying command bellowed by the flight attendants signaled that potential disaster was imminent. My thoughts and prayers in that moment were, "Oh Lord, not again!"

Maureen and I had just spent the weekend in Vancouver where Maureen was attending a conference. Prior to the scheduled mid-flight stopover in Kamloops, the passengers were suddenly warned that there was a problem with the landing gear. We would be required to adopt the precautionary crash-landing procedure.

The blunt instructions were brutally proclaimed, "Remove glasses, remove shoes, tighten seat belts and lean forward with your hands on the facing seat back and your forehead on your hands when ordered to do so, on the command, BRACE, BRACE, BRACE."

The plane circled over the airport for fifteen minutes while the aircrew jettisoned fuel, and to allow fire and rescue service time to prepare for the worst. Lines of ambulances and fire trucks were stationed parallel to the runway, their flashing lights confirming that they were anticipating disaster.

It was November 1998. We'd just been married over one year. In those final moments we held hands and prayed. A kaleidoscope of horrific memories flashed before me. Although my air crash had faded from my mind after the 15 years, it all came back instantly.

With the anticipated certainty of the impending crash, I also recalled the horrendous pictures of the Lockerbie air disaster when a terrorist bomb blew up an air liner just 20 miles from my old Scottish home. All 300 passengers aboard died. Once on that awful pessimistic line of thought, I relived the pictures of the Cranbrook air crash on the snowy runway in 1978, killing 39 of the 43 passengers and crew.

All was deathly quiet in our stricken plane, except for the soft sounds of a mother singing to calm her crying baby.

Seeing the first fire engine's flashing lights right outside the window implying our last seconds of life, we braced to the ongoing commands and waited for the end. There was a loud bang and a bump, then as if in answer to our prayers, the undercarriage wheels and landing gear held fast. The plane rolled to a stop amid all the encroaching fire trucks with the passengers cheering.

We were unloaded and walked silently to the terminal building while the crew remained onboard for a debriefing. Despite the trauma we had all experienced, sadly, no offer of comfort or counseling was provided for the shocked passengers. The only information that was offered came over the PA system and we were merely more travelers waiting in a busy airport terminal. Our flight was listed as cancelled and we were told that we would have to wait for a replacement plane to arrive before we could complete our flight to Cranbrook.

Maureen's daughter Jen, waiting to pick us up at the Cranbrook airport, was simply told that the flight had been cancelled. She was not provided with a reason for the cancellation or an expected arrival time. Very confused she went home to wait for news from us. Had we crash-landed and died, when would she have learned the truth?

We were grossly unimpressed. Several other Cranbrook passengers who recognized me, aware of my previous traumatic crash history, approached to offer us kind words of support that were much appreciated.

It was with great trepidation that we assembled to enter the arranged flight three hours later. It would have been very easy to vow to never fly again. The horror of that experience has never quite left us, although we have in recent years made several trips to the UK, Europe and Hawaii.

Even today, the most recent tragedy of two hundred lives lost in the disappearance of a Malaysian Airliner that had departed from Kuala Lumpur connects bygone years I'd spent in the military in KL to the reality and the fragility of the present.

I am full of admiration for the crews of two great flight miracles that came to happy endings. Those who were involved in landing "The Gimly Glider", the huge airliner that ran out of fuel at 40,000 feet over Manitoba and was forced to glide onto a small former wartime air force landing strip, with no injuries to the 200 passengers. Accolades must also go to the crew who successfully landed a plane in the Hudson River in New York after losing both engines to bird strikes.

Another hero I admire is Albert Comfort, who volunteered as a spotter on the rescue plane that found us at Angus Creek. Previously he'd had two separate crashes flying his own ultra light planes and suffered broken legs on these occasions.

Overcoming the memory of personal tragedy was also the secret and modest style of Pat Strang. She was the nurse who courageously volunteered to fly with her two burn patients on the night of our search and rescue crash, attending to their needs en route to Calgary. As I visited her several times in hospital and a nursing home just prior to her recent death, she never confided to me that her first husband had died in a plane crash 40 years earlier, leaving her with two small children.

Over the years, my demons are settling. I have been blessed with a great recovery to return to an enjoyable and successful career. I trust I'm even more empathetic now, in my care for others, having been on the receiving end of medical ministrations.

As I visit the "bent propeller" crash location each October 1st, I am pleased it is now a registered memorial site. That it is also a geocache site brings other caring individuals to the Angus Creek location, to add their comments and kind words to the book provided there.

My visits give me occasion to think fondly of those who died on that awful day. They are gone but not forgotten. I take time also to thank the countless numbers who helped in my rescue and subsequent care and recovery.

Above all, I'm so grateful for my good fortune to be restored to full health and to be so blessed with the love of Maureen and my blended family.

CHAPTER 49
The Bucket List

At 75, having already surpassed the allotted three score and ten years of Biblical lifespan prediction, I feel very fortunate to still enjoy good health and am fitter than many who are struggling through their fifties. With genetic connections of numerous relatives who rode off into the sunset in their 80's and 90's, God willing, this community is stuck with me for a while yet.

Consequently, the hope for healthy longevity makes me pause and reflect on the wonderful past and cherish each day, packing in the luxury of family times and friendships in this community that has been my home for nearly half a century.

I like to think I still contribute in meaningful ways to those less fortunate, especially in visiting those in hospital and care homes, but I'm also unashamedly guilty of living life to the full. I treasure each day, enjoying the comforts of home and the delight of family life in this Rocky Mountain paradise.

The memorable movie, "The Bucket List", brilliantly starring Jack Nicholson and Morgan Freeman portrays them grasping a wish list of things they'd like to do in the time they have left. It is a philosophy that we should all pursue in our mature years.

I look back gratefully on a life endowed with millions of happy memories although there were a few bumps on the road that are now fading away.

"The times they are a-changin'," the old song tells us. One of the special features of advancing years is the opportunity to reflect on the many changes over a long life. Maturity, as I like to call old age, lets us compare yesteryears with today, exposing the good, bad and the ugly. If the youth of today bother to read this epistle, they'll no doubt go into eye-rolling mode as I recall my recollections of a past era.

It will seem unimaginable to the cell phone addicted modern youngster, that my forbearers were some of the privileged few in rural Scotland who enjoyed a party-line shared phone.

While we now bemoan the failures and shortcomings of modern medicine in Canada, I remember the stories of amazing improvement in availability and speed of house calls, when the family doctor first visited by car rather than on horseback.

On the brighter side, I'm an example of the miracle of modern day search and rescue and accessibility to modern medical care when I was plucked from the hidden depths of the forest at Angus Creek at the crash site.

Thanks to the many skilled healers and helpers, I enjoy good health and great happiness surrounded by my loving family and friends.

The comfort and excesses that I'm living in now include a move to the security of our home in an urban gated community. Fortunately the wonderful memories of 40 years of nurturing, modernizing and manicuring our previous 6 acre country residence are well preserved and documented in precious photo albums, and more recently, on web sites using what to me is mind boggling technology.

Our recent purchase of a Pleasure Way camper van gives us greater access to our geographically distant families in Calgary and Victoria. Of course, the recent addition of a Vespa scooter on the attached rear-carrier is the icing on the cake.

It's all part of this 76 year old's bucket list. The future looks wonderful with my loving wife Maureen by my side.

www.ingramcontent.com/pod-product-compliance
Lightning Source LLC
Chambersburg PA
CBHW032040150426
43194CB00006B/360